THE BODY IN QUALITATIVE RESEARCH

The Body in Qualitative Research

Edited by
JOHN RICHARDSON
ALISON SHAW

Ashgate

Aldershot • Brookfield USA • Singapore • Sydney

Published by
Ashgate Publishing Ltd
Gower House
Croft Road
Aldershot
Hants GU11 3HR
England

Ashgate Publishing Company
Old Post Road
Brookfield
Vermont 05036
USA

British Library Cataloguing in Publication Data
The body in qualitative research. - (Cardiff papers in qualitative research)
1. Body, Human - Social aspects - Research 2. Sex role - Research
I. Richardson, John T. E. (John Thomas Edwin), 1948 -
II. Shaw, Alison
305.3'072

Library of Congress Catalog Card Number: 98-72621

ISBN 1 84014 500 5

Printed and bound by Athenaeum Press, Ltd., Gateshead, Tyne & Wear.

Contents

Notes on contributors

Angus Bancroft is a graduate of the University of Edinburgh, and formerly a researcher for Save the Children. He is currently studying for a PhD at the University of Wales, Cardiff, researching Gypsies and Travelling People. He teaches Sociology and designs Web pages.

Michael Bloor is Professor of Sociology at University College, Cardiff. He has special interests in the sociology of medicine and has written on issues such as HIV transmission, alcohol and drug use, and health education.

Victoria Butler is currently completing a research degree at the University of Wales, Swansea. Her special interests include embodiment, the negotiation and experience of identity, and the visual communication of adornment.

Sara Delamont is Reader in Sociology at University of Wales College, Cardiff. Her special interests are education, gender and research methods. She has written and edited numerous books, mainly in the field of the sociology of education.

Rebecca E. Dobash is Professor of Social Work at Manchester University. Her special interest is violence against women.

Russell P. Dobash is Professor of Criminology at Manchester University. His special interest is violence against women.

Sally Holland is a Tutorial Fellow in the University of Wales, Cardiff. Previously she was a social worker in South Wales. Her doctoral research is on the assessment of families by social workers.

Duncan Lewis lectures in Human Resource Management at Carmarthenshire College, and in Corporate Strategy at the University of Wales, Lampeter. His doctoral research is on workplace bullying among the lecturing profession in Wales.

Lee Monaghan is a Ph.D student at the University of Wales, Cardiff. His thesis is on bodybuilding subcultures, and he has written on bodybuilding ethnopharmacology, on alleged links between bodybuilding steroids and violence, and on the methodological problems in gaining access to drug-using bodybuilders.

Odette Parry has been an undergraduate, postgraduate and research fellow at University of Wales College, Cardiff. After a spell lecturing at the University of the West Indies in Jamaica, she is currently a post-doctoral researcher in the Medical School at Edinburgh University.

John Richardson is a lecturer in Sociology and Social Policy at the University of Wales College, Cardiff. He is co-author of books on race relations and on introductory sociology, and he has written articles on a wide range of social problems, including alcoholism, juvenile delinquency, and ageing.

Kate Robson is a PhD student at the University of Wales, Cardiff. Her doctoral research is on the employment experiences and workplace relationships of ulcerative colitis and Crohns Disease sufferers, and her other research interests include the use of the internet as a social research tool.

Alison Shaw is currently a doctoral student in the School for Policy Studies at the University of Bristol, where she is carrying out research on consumers' perceptions and management of the risks in food, focusing on the body as a site of risk. Previously she worked for two years as a researcher in social medicine.

Jonathan Scourfield, formerly a probation officer in the South Wales valleys, is now a Tutorial Fellow in the University of Wales, Cardiff. He has research interests in social work and in the sociology of gender.

Trevor Welland lectures in Sociology at Barry College, and is also a lecturer on the PGCE (FE) course in the School of Education at University of Wales, Cardiff. His doctoral research is on the professional socialisation of priests.

Emma Wincup is a lecturer in criminology at University of Wales College, Cardiff. She recently completed a Ph.D on bail hostel provision for women, and is currently conducting research on residential social work with offenders. She is also editing a book in the Cardiff Papers series, entitled 'Qualitative Research in Criminology'.

Introduction

John Richardson and Alison Shaw

This book consists of a collection of papers by sociologists who have used qualitative research methods in order to shed light on 'bodily matters'. Its main purpose is to demonstrate the ways in which qualitative research can further our sociological understanding of the body in contemporary society. There can be little doubt that this collection of empirical studies is timely in the sense that it coincides with an enormous surge of interest in the sociology of the body. One measure of this interest is the decision of the British Sociological Association to devote its 1998 Conference to 'Making Sense of the Body'. Further evidence comes from the popularity and impact of major sociological texts dealing with the body (e.g. Featherstone et al, 1991; Shilling, 1993; Turner, 1992). Of course, it is not just sociologists who have 'discovered' the body in recent years. Indeed, Turner (1996) claims that in the 'somatic society' the body has become the principal field of social, political and cultural activity. Thus, the body is no longer an esoteric specialism but rather a central strand in modern social thought (Scott and Morgan, 1993). Bodily issues now command the attention of sociologists, psychologists, historians, cultural and political theorists, anthropologists, media theorists and health researchers. This common interest has led to a great deal of cross-disciplinary work, much of which has found a platform in major journals such as *Body and Society*.

There are many reasons for the recent explosion of sociological interest in the body (Shilling, 1993). First, the body features prominently in many feminist debates such as those on masculinity and femininity, abortion and reproductive technologies. Particular attention is currently being given to the complex and diverse 'representations' of gendered bodies. Second, the emergence of an affluent postmodern society has created a fresh interest in the sociology of consumption. The body plays a major role in consumption because it is such a visible and effective means of expressing taste, identity and sexuality. Anxious consumers have become key targets for bodily-related products such as diet and fitness programmes, designer brands and cosmetic surgery. Third, the demographic shift towards an older population has triggered greater sociological interest in the process of ageing and in the ways in which the 'decline' of the body can be halted. Finally, some sociologists have proposed the interesting idea that the body increasingly acts as a focus for many contemporary crises and fears such as pollution and disease (e.g. AIDS) or spiritual angst (e.g. what is the difference between a cyborg and a 'real' human?).

As a result of these developments, the body has become a key topic for sociological investigation. Sociologists are abandoning the old dualism in which the body was left to the natural sciences while sociology concentrated on cultural and social matters. Rather, they are now trying to overcome the traditional dichotomies between nature/culture, biology/society and body/mind by recognising the simultaneously biological and social character of bodies. Human beings are 'embodied': our bodies have a material basis which cannot be ignored if we wish to understand what makes us fully human. This recognition of our material nature forces us to address the limitations and opportunities, pleasures and pains associated with embodiment: 'Bodies, in their own right as bodies, do matter. They age, get sick, enjoy, engender, give birth. There is an irreducible bodily dimension in experience and practice...' (Connell, 1997, p.231). However, at the same time our bodies also have a social dimension. Although the body has a material basis it is also socially constructed: social meanings are attached to it, and it is shaped and regulated by social forces. The challenge for sociologists, then, is to understand the particular and changing ways in which human beings are a blend of the material and the social. Some of the insights of this perspective are already being applied to areas such as sexuality, health and illness, and identity politics. Yet many contributions to the literature still have a tentative and pioneering quality, perhaps a fair reflection of the difficulties of finding conceptual bearings in what is still a comparatively 'immature' field of study. So the sociology of the body still has a long research agenda.

It is against this background that the present book was conceived. Although it is only one response to a much wider call for sociological research on the body, it has three distinctive features which should contribute to a broadening of the existing literature.

First, this volume provides useful examples of the ways in which qualitative research methods can be deployed to investigate the relations between the body and society. Until recently there has been comparatively little debate on appropriate methodologies for studying social aspects of the body. The various contributors help to remedy this situation by demonstrating the value of qualitative research in this field. Most of them work in, or are closely connected with, the University of Wales, Cardiff, where there is a long tradition of enquiry using qualitative research techniques. In this selection of studies the researchers draw on techniques such as participant observation, in-depth interviewing and focus groups to explore bodily matters. Some of them pay special attention to the 'reflexive' aspects of the research process. For example, Parry notes that the researcher's own body and the way it is presented to others becomes a major issue when investigating naturism using participant observation.

Second, the contributors provide some much needed empirical evidence on bodily matters. Although the sociology of the body has made impressive advances in recent years, it still seems to be the case that speculative and abstract theories have outstripped empirical research. The body as a topic of inquiry is at the forefront of recent developments within sociological theory, yet there is relatively little empirical research on the relationships between body and society. The research reported here helps to fill this gap. Inevitably, the book deals with only a small selection out of the huge range of topics relevant to the sociology of the body. Nevertheless, the chapters span a reasonably wide spectrum, dealing not only with perhaps familiar issues such as images of male and female bodies (Shaw, Bancroft), but also neglected problems such as workplace bullying (Lewis), unusual settings such as residential institutions for trainee clergy (Welland) and 'exotica' such as fetish practices (Butler). The topics range from the healthy and sporting – bodybuilding (Monaghan) and rugby culture (Holland and Scourfield) – through to the health problems of Crohn's Disease (Robson) and self-harm (Wincup). Also, since the ageing process is a fundamental feature of the human body, it is only appropriate that the book includes chapters on the older generation of 'wrinklies' (Richardson) as well as children of school age (Delamont).

Third, the book contains analyses not only of representations and images of the body, but also of the way these representations affect social interaction and social relationships. Many of the chapters are based on direct observation of bodily interaction in group situations. After all, sociology 'is ultimately not an analysis of representational meanings, but a science or discipline of action and interaction. We need to understand the body in the processes of action and interaction at the level of everyday reciprocities and exchange' (Turner, 1994, pxiii). This book takes important steps in that direction. One interesting example of this is Robson's study, where she describes the continued 'presence' of the body even in social communications on the apparently 'disembodied' internet.

Although the chapters cover a diversity of subject matter, they are accompanied by a common methodological focus, since the authors have a shared interest in applying qualitative research methods to the sociological study of the body. Another organising feature of the book is its thematic coherence. The three main themes are representation (the images and symbols which depict the body), regulation (the social control of bodies) and resistance (the strategies used to avoid or challenge dominant representations and regulations). These three themes are usually closely linked: cultural representations can be drawn upon to regulate bodily behaviour, but this regulation is likely to generate resistance, and these strategies of resistance will eventually feed back to change the cultural representations. These connections mean that every author tends to touch upon all three themes, although the relative emphases vary.

Bodily representations are the main theme of Shaw's chapter, in which she explores media images of women's bodies and uses an interpretive approach (in-depth interviews) to assess their impact on the identities of three distinct groups of women. Her findings lead her to reject notions of homogeneity in favour of an emphasis on the diversity of women's experiences, bodily images and identities. In similar vein, Bancroft challenges the notion that there is a single representation of the male body. From his analysis of men's lifestyle magazines he concludes that 'body culture' has become a key focus for defining contemporary masculinity, but he maintains that this culture is diverse and he argues that this presents a challenge to feminist theories of patriarchal society. The complexity of cultural meanings is illustrated also in Monaghan's study of cultural representations of bodybuilding. His field interviews revealed that muscle had multiple meanings for weight-trainers and bodybuilders, with enhanced sexual attractiveness being only one of the perceived benefits. Turning to another sport, Holland and Scourfield demonstrate that the 'rugby culture' of South Wales communities is a complex mixture of social class, national and ethnic identities, and cultural representations of masculinity and the 'respectable' male body. They suggest that qualitative research techniques are necessary in order to tease out the deeper meanings of male embodiment in this rugby culture.

The theme of regulation runs through Delamont's analysis of an introductory PE lesson for girls in a secondary school. Intrigued by the idea that ethnographic fieldnotes can be re-interpreted, Delamont revisits her original notes on this lesson in order to make links with bodily matters. More specifically, she describes in detail the techniques by which PE teachers produce the 'disciplined body'. Regulation also features as a theme in the chapter by Lewis, who suggests that workplace bullying can be regarded as a strategy to control the body. Bullying is experienced as a direct assault on the body's 'space' and it can result in severe emotional and physical symptoms of distress. A different example of bodily regulation is offered by Welland who considers the 'curriculum of the body' in the residential training of theological students. His ethnographic research reveals how this training acts to regulate and reconceptualise the body in preparation for the critical transition to ordained status. Another example of bodily regulation is found in Wincup's study of bail hostels for women. Many of these women had resorted to substance abuse and self-harm as a way of seeking control over their lives through their bodies. But Wincup exposes the irony by which these 'coping strategies' ultimately increase the power and control of others (welfare service and criminal justice professionals) over the women's bodies and lives.

More effective forms of resistance are identified by Richardson who explores the ways in which older people are challenging social and cultural constructions of the ageing body. Drawing upon qualitative research in a community education project, he shows how the elderly victims of ageism are starting to discard the 'mask of old age'. Rather more 'exotic' examples of resistance are provided by Butler and Parry. Using participant observation in fetish clubs, Butler gathered data on the ways fetishists experience and modify their bodies. She concludes that expressive practices such as body piercing are actually a way of resisting dominant social and cultural norms relating to the body. Parry, too, examines resistance to bodily norms, but in the context of naturist clubs. Her data, derived from participant observation and interviews, relates to the ways in which female naturists reconstruct the naked body as non-sexual, and in doing so legitimate their own participation as 'normal', 'decent' and 'respectable'. Finally, Robson explores the way internet users resist the 'invisibility' of the body in computer internet interactions by introducing signs, codes and expressions which convey 'physical' characteristics. She also shows how sufferers from IBD (inflammatory bowel disease) are free to reinvent their physical selves by carefully selecting the information they convey to others on the internet.

References

Connell, R. (1997), 'Men's Bodies', in K.Woodward (ed.): *Identity and Difference*, Sage, London.

Featherstone, M., Hepworth, M. & Turner, B. (eds) (1991), *The Body, Social Process and Cultural Theory*, Sage, London.

Scott, S. & Morgan, D. (eds) (1993), *Body Matters*, Falmer Press, London.

Shilling, C. (1993), *The Body and Social Theory*, Sage, London.

Turner, B. (1992), *Regulating Bodies*, Routledge, London.
Turner, B. (1994), Preface to P.Falk: *The Consuming Body*, Sage, London.
Turner, B. (1996), *The Body and Society*, Sage, London.

1. Images of the female body: Women's identities and the media

Alison Shaw

Introduction

Debates about the role of the media in shaping women's attitudes towards their bodies have been at the forefront of both popular and medical discourse on eating disorders in recent years. The 'Omega' watch company withdrew its advertisements from 'Vogue' magazine in protest at the use of 'distasteful' pictures of a model of 'anorexic proportions', which could influence its audience of 'young and impressionable females' (*The Times*, 31 May 1996). Following this incident, a psychiatrist working with young women with eating disorders commented:

> I do feel that there is a strong relationship between images portrayed in the media and the onset of eating disorders ... virtually all of our patients report having been influenced by the media in some way (personal correspondence, June 1996).

Similar concerns were echoed in a recent newspaper report on childhood anorexia nervosa, in which a mother expressed her anxiety about her three year old daughter's awareness of her body appearance, saying:

> she already believes thin is good ... Short of isolating my daughter in a plastic bubble, I can't see how I can prevent her being obsessed about her body image ... when the supermodels are promoted as icons of female beauty ... persuading her that you don't have to be slim to be beautiful is an uphill struggle (*The Guardian*, 23 April 1997).

This chapter focuses on a qualitative investigation into the impact of media images of the female body on women's body images, drawing upon this current debate, feminist arguments about the media and women's embodiment, and the growing theoretical debate on the body within sociology. The theoretical work on the body provides a rich base for the empirical study, which serves to enhance a sociological understanding of the relationships between the media, embodiment and self-identity for women in contemporary Western society.

Context

Several social science disciplines, including psychology, feminist theory, cultural studies and sociology, have been concerned with studying female embodiment. A wealth of empirical research on women's 'body image' exists within the psychological literature (e.g. Fallon and Rozin, 1985; Brodie et al, 1994). Some of this research has considered the role of the media, most commonly using quantitative methods such as the experiment in order to examine relationships between media images of the 'ideal' female body and women's perceptions of their own body size (Myers and Biocca, 1992; Hamilton and Waller, 1993).

Feminist writers have provided many critical analyses of media portrayals of women's bodies within patriarchal Western societies (Chapkis, 1986; Ferguson, 1983; Stannard, 1971). A central tenet of feminist arguments is that the media have contributed to the objectification of women's bodies: 'Women's bodies are on show; they are obliged to produce their bodies as adequate and acceptable "spectacles", as objects external to their selves' (MacSween, 1983, p.174). Some have documented a marked shift towards a thinner female body in media images, mirroring a steady decline in biomedical 'ideal' weights for women (Garner et al, 1980; Striegel-Moore et al, 1986). Such 'standards' have been interpreted as reflecting the oppression of women by advocating 'unrealistic cultural images of beauty' (Allan et al, 1993). Further, many feminists have posited a relationship between media images of the slim female body and the onset and development of eating disorders such as anorexia nervosa (Chernin, 1983; Jacobs-Brumberg, 1988; Orbach, 1978; Wolf, 1990).

In recent years the body has emerged at the forefront of theoretical debate within sociology. Reconsidering their traditional acceptance of the Cartesian legacy of a dualism between mind and body, sociologists are beginning to moving beyond a 'disembodied' approach by focusing on embodiment as a key starting point for understanding human social activity and interaction (Turner, 1992). This increased sociological interest in the body has been initiated in part by the rise of 'consumer culture' in the second half of the twentieth century (Shilling, 1993), which has focused on the body as an object of display, a 'surface to be worked on and a volume to be sculpted and moulded, through "beauty" regimes, clothing and lifestyle' (Craik, 1994, p.91). The body has become a site of discipline and labour, a 'project' to be worked at and perfected (Featherstone, 1993). Media images of the 'body beautiful' have a central role in such body projects, particularly for women whose bodies are used symbolically in such images, which act as 'constant reminders of what we are and might with effort yet become' (Featherstone, 1993, p.178). Therefore, the body has become an uncertain entity and a focus of anxiety: 'a changeable form of existence which can be shaped and which is malleable to individual needs and desires' (Turner, 1996, p.5).

Some sociologists have proposed that the increased concern with the body as a site of individual expression reflects a new close relationship between the body and self-identity in late modern social life. Giddens (1991) has considered this by contrasting the sources of identity in traditional and 'late modern' societies. Traditional societies provided relatively stable and clearly defined sources of identity through the collectivity of cultures and 'external reference points' such as religion. In contrast, identity formation in late modern culture has become an 'open', negotiable and uncertain process, mediated by mass communication systems. In the absence of stable external reference points for identity, the late modern individual has to 'turn inwards', and identity formation becomes a 'reflexive project' involving the physical body. Two key aspects of this new relationship between body and self are body appearance: an expression of individuality and personal identity; and body regimes: strategies employed to cultivate, create and control body appearance, such as diet, exercise, dress and cosmetic surgery.

These recent theories of the body and identity within sociology provide a rich base for a sociological investigation of female embodiment. However, grand sociological theories of the body greatly outnumber detailed empirical investigations of people's experiences of embodiment, and relationships between body and society. The research reported in this paper goes some way towards addressing that imbalance by describing a qualitative study of media images of the female body and women's body images which both draws upon and suggests implications for sociological theories of the body in late modern society.

Research questions and methodology

A qualitative approach, namely in-depth interviews, was used to explore the impact of media images of the female body on women's body images. The interviews explored three broad research questions: how women perceive images of the female body in the media, how these media images shape women's perceptions of their own bodies, and what impact they have upon women's body-related behaviour, e.g. dieting and fitness activities.

Previous research on women's body images and the media has utilised quantitative methods such as the experiment in order to demonstrate measurable and quantifiable cause-effect relations between media images of the female body and women's perceptions of their own body size and shape (Myers and Biocca, 1992; Hamilton and Waller, 1993). In these experimental situations, women are exposed to 'ideal-body' images, such as those in magazine or television advertisements. Following exposure, their 'body image' is measured using standardised clinical or research instruments, such as body silhouette scales, which require the individual to rate the body (ranging from very thin to very large) that approximates their current body figure and their ideal body figure. The results of such studies are presented as quantified data, e.g. 'Body Perception Indices' (Myers and Biocca, 1992).

However, the research described in this paper used a qualitative approach in order to obtain a richer, more detailed account of women's experiences of embodiment, as seen through the eyes of women living in an interactive social world. The choice of method was also shaped by feminist approaches to methodology, especially placing women at the centre of the research process, rather than commitment to a single feminist method (Stanley and Wise, 1983). As the research is explicitly concerned with differences between women, it also mirrors developments within feminist theory and research which emphasise the diversity of women's experiences (Harding, 1987; Hill Collins, 1990).

Three groups of women participated: two 'body' groups and one 'non-body' group. These groups consisted of a diet group (members of 'Weight Watchers'); a fitness group (members of a 'Step Aerobics' group); and a 'non-body' or 'alternative identity' group (members of a Christian organisation 'Navigators'). The total number of participants was twelve, four in each group. The selection of women was based on a form of 'theoretical sampling' (Strauss, 1987), guided by the question, 'Where can I find instances of women for whom the body is potentially more or less important to their self-identities?' The women in each group were chosen to exemplify different positions in relation to the body as a 'project'. The diet and fitness groups were chosen as representatives of women for whom the body has perhaps become a 'project', as reflected in their engagement in body regimes. The 'alternative identity' group was chosen to represent women with an 'external reference point' for identity, namely their religious faith. It was not presumed that these women are unconcerned with their bodies, but rather their external identity source might serve to preclude the body as a major source of self-identity. A religious group was chosen because religion has been proposed as a major 'external reference point' for identity in traditional societies (Giddens, 1991). While some theorists argue that its importance has declined in the process of modernisation, many now focus on religion as a key feature of life in late modern society (Mellor and Shilling, 1997).

The interviews were carried out in the home of each participant, and lasted between forty minutes and one hour. The schedule aimed to cover the three main research questions, but interviewees guided the agenda by the extent of their enthusiasm for topics. The interviews were audio-taped and transcribed. Individual transcripts were read several times, and the data organised firstly into three broad areas, according to the three main research questions. Gradually, with repeated readings of the data, particular topics became apparent within each of these areas and these were assigned a code. The transcripts with the coded passages were scrutinised again, and broader themes identified. The coded phrases were placed under each of these themes. The themes and passages were reconsidered in their context within the manuscript, in order to make some interpretation of the individual's perspective concerning each topic. During the analysis process, the women's group 'identity' (diet, fitness or 'alternative identity') and emerging differences between the three groups were particularly considered. Early analysis of the data was fed back to some of the participants for comment, to ensure the trustworthiness and 'validity' of the researcher's interpretations (Bloor, 1983; Altheide and Johnson, 1994).

The data presented below are organised according to the main research questions and emerging themes. While differences between the three groups of women were particularly apparent and are highlighted here, the three 'positions' (diet, fitness and 'alternative identity') are not mutually exclusive, and differences and contradictions were apparent both within the accounts of each individual woman and between women within the same group.

The female body in the media

The first part of the interviews explored the women's perceptions of media images of the female body. Three main themes emerged: the dominant image of the female body portrayed by the media; the media's construction of an 'ideal' female body type; and media images versus the 'reality' of women's bodies.

Dominant image

Firstly, there was consensus among all of the women in each of the three groups, diet, fitness and 'alternative identity', that there is a single recurring image of the female body portrayed in the media - that of the slim, perfectly-proportioned 'supermodel' body, 'very tall, very thin' (Diet, 2). The majority of the women took a negative view of such representations, seeing the female body as a commodity used by advertisers in order to sell products:

> advertising a car they've got ... a gorgeous woman on top of the car, which they're not really selling the car, they're selling the woman aren't they (Fitness, 4).

Constructing an ideal

The second theme to emerge was the media's construction of an 'ideal' female body. The majority of the women in each group perceived the media to be involved in creating such an ideal. The media were seen as prescriptive rather than neutral in their representations of the female body, and were described by some women as 'manipulators' or 'engineers' of an image to which women 'should' conform:

> It is manipulated, the media does manipulate how they think women should be ... they're pushing forward this [supermodel] image ... and it's engineered to be like that' (Diet, 2).

> Any images that you get of women through the media are basically giving you the message that that's what you're supposed to look like (Alternative Identity, 1).

The processes by which the media were perceived to construct this ideal were, firstly, through advertising, associating slim, beautiful women with 'glamorous' products; secondly, through pictures of thin women in women's magazines; thirdly, through the media's joint work with the fashion world, promoting models and supermodels as the bodies 'in fashion'; and lastly, through the media's employment process, employing slim attractive women to be in the public eye.

Some of the women talked about whether media images were beginning to change, for example with larger women such as 'Jo Brand ... being out there and saying that to be big is o.k. (Diet, 1). However, the consensus was that undermining such positive changes is the ubiquity of the 'supermodel' or 'waif' body:

> you've got magazines ... saying 'Well, it's o.k., for women to be these shapes ... we're all different' ... but I think underlying it all you've still got the fact that ... in fashion is the waif, the supermodel (Diet, 2).

Image and reality

The third theme to emerge was the extent to which media images reflect the 'reality' of women's bodies. There was consensus among all of the women in each group that the media fail to reflect what the majority of women's bodies are 'really' like: 'I don't think they really reflect what women are like at all' (Alternative Identity, 1). The underlying reason for this failure was the narrowness of the representations of women's bodies, which takes several forms: the media only portray slim women who are unlike the majority of 'real' women; they fail to acknowledge the diversity of women's bodies; and they only present perfection, ignoring the 'imperfections' of real women's bodies:

> the media emphasise people like Claudia Schiffer and most women aren't that size, aren't that shape, so it's totally illogical (Alternative Identity, 3).

> women are all different shapes and sizes ... there's very few people like that [supermodel], six foot and seven stone..it's not the way we are at all (Diet, 2).

> most women have got bodies that are imperfect, slightly overweight or they're a bit out or proportion somewhere ... they're not in this ... ideal proportion (Alternative Identity, 1).

So, there was a perceived 'gap between what women are and what the media images are' (Diet, 2), and two very different pictures of the female body emerged: the 'media body': 'slim, long legs', 'the supermodel, very tall, very thin', 'Claudia Schiffer type ideal proportion'; and the 'real body': 'imperfect', 'slightly overweight', 'a bit out of proportion', 'probably size 14 plus' with 'lumps and bumps'.

Media images and women's body images

Having considered the women's perceptions of the female body in the media, what impact were these images perceived to have on women's attitudes towards their own bodies? When the women talked in a general way about the influence of the media on their 'body image' some differences between the three groups emerged. While there were differences between the women within the groups, overall the 'alternative identity' women seemed the least sensitive to influence from media images. A key theme which emerged was the comparison of one's own body with media images of the female body, which seemed to feature more strongly for the diet and fitness women:

> You might think 'I'm not going to aspire to being six foot and seven stone, but you do ... you're bombarded with ... that same image ... you're constantly comparing yourself ... and you're thinking, 'Do I fit into that category?' (Diet, 2).

> Kate Moss ... compared to her I'm huge, and I think, 'I'd never be like that'... I just look at magazine pictures and think 'I'd kill to look like that' (Fitness, 4).

> It's a standard that sometimes I compare myself to, but I think I value other stuff more ... I don't think my worth should come from how I look ... It isn't a major bugging factor (Alternative Identity, 4).

When the women were probed for more specific responses, the differences between the three groups became more subtle and complex, and three further themes emerged: 'living up to' media images; the media's impact on women's feelings about their own bodies; and the importance of body appearance.

'Living up to' the image

Firstly, many of the women in the three groups discussed whether they felt that they tried to 'live up to' media images of the female body. No clear differences between the groups emerged. Some of the women in each group, but particularly those in the diet and fitness groups, said that they did strive to achieve the media 'ideal'. This seemed to be driven by the prevalence and prescriptive nature of such images:

> I hate myself because I know I'm falling into the trap of the media ... but the images are all around you ... it's all to do with having the perfect body ... I am manipulated because the media's telling you what you should look like, so you stupidly try to look like that (Diet, 2).

> Yes ... you open a magazine ... and they're always there..how to diet this, and how to look good ... and I want to do it (Fitness, 2).

> I'd say to an extent, but not to an extreme, and it would just be in trying to maintain a certain level of attractiveness ... but it's not something which is always on my mind (Alternative Identity, 4).

Conversely, some of the women in all three groups did not feel that they should 'live up to' media images of the female body:

> Well, I'd like to be thinner, but I know I'm never going to end up looking like a supermodel, so no not really (Diet, 4).

> No, not really, I just look at them and think 'Well, she looks nice, I'd like to look like that' but I don't try to do anything about it. You are the way you are really (Fitness, 1).

> 'Alternative Identity': No, I don't think [I try to live up to media images] ... I think I see it as an impossibility ... it's not really real (Alternative Identity, 2).

These women viewed living up to media images of the female body as an 'impossibility', as 'unrealistic'. While they were aware of the images, and in some cases did express a desire to be thinner, they recognised and accepted the futility of using them as 'standards' for their own bodies. For these women 'you are the way you are' (Fitness, 1).

Feelings about your body

The second theme to emerge was whether media images of the female body influence women's feelings about their bodies. Some of the women in all three groups felt that on occasions media images of the female body do shape their feelings, although this perceived influence seemed more common among the diet and fitness women:

> They don't make me feel good because if I look at a supermodel, if I saw her on telly ... I'd feel 'Ugh, it's not fair' ... I'd think 'I wouldn't mind looking like that', so I'd try to lose weight (Diet, 4).

> I think sometimes they can make you feel bad ... when you get these thin women and they look really nice on the catwalk, you think 'Oh, I'd like to look like them (Fitness, 1).

> Sometimes they do ... I think your confidence level can, if you're feeling particularly insecure and then you see a picture of a supermodel I think it can accentuate your moods (Alternative Identity, 1).

For these women, the constant portrayal of slim, perfectly-proportioned women in the media sometimes makes them feel dissatisfied with their own bodies and wish to look like the women portrayed. For one diet woman the solution is clear: 'try and lose weight' (Diet, 4).

However, some women in all three groups said that media images of the female body do not influence their feelings about their own bodies.

> No, not really ... when I'm at my ideal body weight and when I'm happy about myself, I don't think the media plays much to do with it (Diet, 3).

> No ... nine times out of ten I feel fine and I feel quite happy with myself and good about myself ... I don't compare it to anything in the media (Fitness, 3).

> No, not really ... just because I'm happy with who I am (Alternative Identity, 3).

These women perceived little influence from the media on their feelings about their own bodies largely because 'I'm happy with myself'. However, some differences between the groups of women do emerge in the reasons given for this contentment. For one diet woman, her satisfaction with herself seems to be contingent upon her body weight: 'when I'm at my ideal weight ... I don't think the media plays much to do with it'. In contrast, for an 'alternative identity' woman, it seems to derive from her personal faith, which in her view 'transforms her thinking' to feel positive about her outward appearance. Her 'resistance' to media images of the female body seems to be rooted in her belief system which acts to constrain and, in her view, enrich her perception of her own body:

> to me it's what's on the inside that counts, and ... for me the basis of that is my self-image is based in God and ... how God feels about me ... and that transforms my thinking to think 'It's ok to be me, to be how I am, how I look' (Alternative Identity, 2).

Body appearance

Lastly, the importance of body appearance emerged as a theme from the women's comments about the media and their own body image. All of the women in each group felt that the appearance of their bodies was important to them to a certain extent, but it seemed particularly so for the diet and fitness women:

> How my body looks is important to me ... if I'm overweight I feel miserable with myself (Diet, 2).

> I'd like my body to be fit ... because if my body feels good ... then I feel more confident. If I think I look horrible and fat, then I won't talk to anybody, or I'll hide in a corner ... Some days I just hate myself (Fitness, 4).

> If I think I'm looking really drab and feeling fat, it might make ... my mood slightly lower, but I'd probably just get on with life and forget about it. So just in the moment I look in the mirror (Alternative Identity, 4).

The diet and fitness women in particular seemed to attach considerable importance to body appearance, and certain values were associated with the body, namely a 'good' body is one which is slim, fit, toned and free from visible cellulite and wrinkles. However, for the 'alternative identity' women, the concern with body appearance seemed more fleeting and momentary, 'just in the moment that I look in the mirror' (Alternative Identity, 4).

Media images and women's body-related behaviour

Having considered the impact of media images on the women's perceptions of their own bodies, did the women feel that the media influence their body-related behaviour? When the women talked about their dieting or fitness activities and what shaped this behaviour, three main themes emerged: reasons for dieting or participating in fitness activities; trying to achieve a particular body size or shape; and the influence of the media on their body-related behaviour.

Reasons for body-related behaviour

Firstly, the women from all three groups gave a range of reasons for their participation in dieting and exercise activities. The most common reason was for health and fitness ('I'd like my body to be more fit', Diet, 1). Other reasons included social reasons and 'enjoyment' ('aerobics is a good social event', Fitness, 1); stress and energy release ('aerobics, if you're really stressed out ... it's nice to just go and forget about everything' Fitness, 1); self-respect or 'looking after my body as I should be' (Alternative Identity, 1), and in response to comments from a partner ('my husband said "You're getting a little bit chubby", so I went on a diet' Diet, 3). However, it also seems that there are some 'identity' factors at play. The value that the majority of the women, particularly the diet and fitness groups, placed upon achieving a healthy, fit body suggests that working on the body plays a key role in maintaining a positive self-view. This is reflected in the comment of one fitness woman who said:

> I do a lot of keep fit and it's got to the stage now if I don't go I feel really let down in myself ... I'm thinking 'You should have gone tonight, that's terrible, why didn't you go' (Fitness, 3).

In contrast, 'self-respect' as a reason for body-related behaviour was given uniquely by some of the 'alternative identity' women. This arguably reflects an attitude of 'stewardship' towards the body: the body as an entity which these women feel they have a responsibility to care for. Such an attitude perhaps mirrors aspects of the relationship between body and identity for these women, which consists, in part, of caring for the body and 'respecting' the self. This constrasts with the relationship between body and identity proposed for some of the diet and fitness women, for whom maintaining and working on the body seems important for sustaining a positive self-identity.

Striving for body types

The second theme to emerge was striving towards a particular body size or shape. The majority of the women in all three groups said that they had tried to achieve a particular body size or shape through dieting or fitness activities, although this quest seemed more important for the diet and fitness women. For the diet group, the predominant body type desired was the 'slimmer' 'supermodel' body: 'like a supermodel ... I'm trying to achieve that ultimately' (Diet, 2). The majority of the 'alternative identity' women also desired a 'slimmer' body, but overall 'it's no big thing' (Alternative Identity, 2), 'I'm happy with the way I am' (Alternative Identity, 3). The particular 'type' of body desired by the fitness women was rather different: a body that is not only slim but firm and 'well-toned', a 'fit' physique: 'all I'm interested in is toning up what I've got '(Fitness, 4).

Two further intertwined themes which arose out of this discussion of desired body size or shape were futility and control. Particularly with regards to body shape, many of the women pointed to the futility of trying to change one's body. There was acknowledgement that the desire to achieve a body like that epitomised by the supermodel is fruitless. Thus, there was an apparent conflict between the desire to change one's body appearance, and the realisation of the futility of such a desire:

> I know in my heart of hearts that I'm never going to look like a supermodel, but that is the thing you look up to ... I'm never going to be like that ... yet you still try and aspire to it (Diet, 2).

Further, some of the women acknowledged a conflict between the control they aim to exert over their body size or weight and the controlling effect of their desire to change the body. These women recognised that the very desire to control one's body can itself have a governing or regulatory influence:

> I started to lose weight, and then it's like ... a drug ... you've got to be careful because it can get addictive ... it can get to the stage where it takes over (Fitness, 3).

> It's good to have a goal but not be totally dominated by it. You are in control. This impulse to diet or be a certain weight doesn't have a hold on you, you have a hold on it, and that's the way it should be (Alternative Identity, 2).

Media influence

The final theme to emerge was the extent to which media images of the female body influence the women's dieting or fitness activities. Overall, there were no clear differences between the three groups. Some women in each group felt that media images do influence their behaviour:

> Media images do influence me ... I mean if I was around in the fifties then I'd have ... been ok because the fashion then was more curvaceous and plump, so there wouldn't have been any need to diet, whereas ... now we're oriented to being slim and have a nicely toned body (Diet, 2).

> With exercise the media influences me because I think the more exercise I do, I'm going to lose weight and ... my body's going to look fitter (Fitness, 4).

> 'Alternative Identity': I think they do affect ... my confidence in myself, in my body, and what I decide to do about it (Alternative Identity, 1).

Conversely, some women across the three groups did not feel that media images shape their dieting and fitness activities:

> Maybe if I was size 18, size 20, I'd see the women and think 'Yes maybe I should do something', but as it is I'm not massively overweight and I'm happy with how I am in general (Diet, 3).

> You know yourself you couldn't be like that, so I don't look at the media and think 'I want to be like that' ... A lot of people would though (Fitness, 3).

> No, because the exercise I do anyway and that would be the only thing I really do (Alternative Identity, 3).

However, there are certain implications in the comments of the diet and fitness women who perceived little influence from media images. Their comments suggest a potential influence from the media, particularly if the 'gap' between media images and one's own body became greater. They also recognise that while they personally do not desire a body like that in the media, 'a lot of people would'.

Discussion

How can this research on the media and women's body image contribute to a sociological understanding of the body and embodiment? The implications of the research will be considered in relation to theoretical work on the body, feminist approaches to the media and women's embodiment, and methodological approaches for studying the body.

In relation to the theoretical work on the body in consumer culture or 'late modernity', the data provide insight for a sociological analysis of the relationships between the body, 'body image' and self-identity. Turner (1996) has argued that the emergence of the modern self is not only tied up with developments in consumerism and consumption, but further 'the notion of self in consumer society ought to be seen in terms of the body-image that plays the distinctive role in the understanding and evaluation of the self within the public arena' (p.7). This notion of a 'representational' self (cf. Goffman, 1969) conceptualises identity as intimately intertwined with body-image and the public display of exterior body surfaces.

In the light of this theoretical work, it could be suggested that the diet and fitness women in this research reflect both the drawing in of the body to identity (Giddens, 1991), and the importance of outward 'body image' as representational of self in social interaction in late modern society (Turner, 1996). While there were differences between the women within these groups, overall the importance they attached to body regimes and the appearance of the body (for some mediated by the cultural ideals portrayed in the mass media) arguably reflects how for some individuals the body has become a site of discipline and labour, a 'project' fundamental for self identity.

In contrast, the 'alternative identity' women in this research perhaps indicate that religion, rather than being a traditional identity source which has been eroded in the process of modernisation, is an important feature of life in late modern society. These women arguably reflect the significance of 'external reference points' for self-identity for some individuals. While, in the same way as the diet and fitness women, they interpreted and gave meaning to media images, their external source of identity seemed to mediate their 'body image' and relationship with their bodies in a unique way. Their religious faith precipitated a certain attitude to the body, mediated and (in their view) positively constrained the impact of the media on their own body image and body-related behaviour, thus precluding the body as an important source of identity. This provides a contrast to those sociological and feminist theories of religion which have evaluated religious institutions and thought (particularly Judao-Christian theology) negatively, as tools of female bodily oppression and control (e.g. Foucault, 1987; de Beauvoir, 1972). Thus, the data from the 'alternative identity' women contribute to arguments that a sociological analysis of the body in late modern society should consider the key and highly complex role of religion in shaping relationships between the body and self-identity (Mellor and Shilling, 1997; Turner, 1991, 1996).

The research reported in this paper also makes a contribution to feminist debates about the media and women's embodiment. From a feminist perspective, the concept of agency is central to an analysis of relationships between the media and women's experiences: are women passive, unresisting victims of an oppressive patriarchal media culture, or are they active, negotiating, interpreting agents in their reactions to media images of the female body? An over-simplistic feminist reading of the data could suggest that the women who expressed an influence from the media on their 'body image' and body-related behaviour (most notably the diet and fitness women) are beguiled casualties of the beauty system in western consumer society. However, the women working to 'beautify' their bodies in this research are not deluded 'cultural dopes' (Davis, 1995). Rather, they are an active, interpreting, knowledgeable and diverse audience, who attribute meaning to cultural images of female 'beauty', and negotiate their relationships with their own bodies within the constraints of the 'fashion-beauty complex' (Bartky, 1990).

Further, the data contribute to feminist debates about the diversity of women's experiences, by indicating that as an audience of the media, women differentially interpret, give meaning to, and assimilate media messages. For some, the images had meaning for their own experiences of embodiment, and they acknowledged that they applied these standards of beauty to their own bodies and often strived to conform to such ideals. Some of these women expressed feelings of frustration with themselves in 'falling into the trap of the media'. However, others recognised the potentially constraining effects of the media and cultural images and expressed decisions to work on their bodies in ways that are unrelated to ideals of femininity. These women showed relative lack of concern with media ideals, interpreting messages about how the female body 'should' look as unrealistic, bearing no relation to the reality of their experiences, and choosing not to apply these standards to their own bodies.

Finally, the research described in this paper also contributes to a methodological debate about ways of researching the body. It illustrates how a qualitative approach, consistent with interpretive epistemologies, can provide a rich and detailed account of women's experiences of embodiment, in contrast with the 'rigorous' yet decontextualised accounts of the impact of media images on women's body image provided by experimental studies. Quantitative approaches, drawing on positivist epistemologies, have focused on obtaining 'objective' measures of cause-effect relationships between media images of the ideal female body and women's over-estimation of, and dissatisfaction with, their own body size. However, what is also needed is qualitative research, drawing on interpretive epistemologies, which explores the processes by which women develop 'images' of their own bodies, the social and cultural contexts in which they do so, and the meanings which women attach both to media images of the body and to their own bodies. Such an approach provides a richer account of the impact of the media on women's body images. By obtaining detailed subjective accounts of experiences of embodiment this research contributes towards a greater sociological understanding of the complex relationships between the media, the body and self-identity for women in late modern society.

References

Allan, J.D., Mayo, K. and Michel, Y. (1993), 'Body Size Values of White and Black Women', *Research in Nursing and Health*, Vol. 16, pp. 323-333.

Altheide, D.L. and Johnson, J.M. (1994), 'Criteria for Assessing Interpretive Validity in Qualitative Research', in N.K. Denzin and

Y.S. Lincoln (eds), *Handbook of Qualitative Research*, Sage, London.
Bartky, S.L. (1990), *Femininity and Oppression: Studies in the Phenomenology of Oppression*, Routledge, New York.
Bloor, M. (1983), 'Notes on Member Validation', in R.M. Emerson (ed.), *Contemporary Field Research*, Little Brown and Co., Boston.
Brodie, D.A., Bagley, K. and Slade, P.D. (1994), 'Body Image Perception in Pre- and Post-Adolescent Females', *Perceptual and Motor Skills*, Vol. 78, pp. 315-319.
Chapkis, W. (1986), *Beauty Secrets: Women and the Politics of Appearance*, South End Press, Boston.
Chernin, K. (1983), *Womansize: The Tyranny of Slenderness*, The Women's Press, London.
Craik, J. (1994), *The Face of Fashion: Cultural Studies in Fashion*, Routledge, London.
Davis, K. (1995), *Reshaping the Female Body: The Dilemmas of Cosmetic Surgery*, Routledge, London.
De Beauvoir, S. (1972), *The Second Sex*, Penguin, Harmondsworth.
Fallon, A.E. and Rozin, P. (1985), 'Sex Differences in Perceptions of Desirable Body Shape', *Journal of Abnormal Psychology*, Vol. 94 (1), pp. 102-105.
Featherstone, M. (1993), 'The Body in Consumer Culture', In M. Featherstone, M. Hepworth, and B.S. Turner (eds), *The Body: Social Process and Cultural Theory*, Sage, London.
Ferguson, M. (1983), *Forever Feminine: Women's Magazines and the Cult of Femininity*, Heinemann, London.
Foucault, M. (1987), *The Use of Pleasure. The History of Sexuality, Vol 2.*, Penguin, Harmondsworth.
Garner, D.M., Garfinkel, P.E., Schwartz, D. and Thompson,M. (1980), 'Cultural Expectations of Thinness in Women', *Psychological Reports*, Vol. 47, pp. 483-491.
Giddens, A. (1991), *Modernity and Self Identity: Self Identity in the Late Modern Age*, Polity Press, Cambridge.
Goffman, E. (1969), *The Presentation of Self in Everyday Life*, Doubleday, Garden City, New Jersey.
The Guardian (1997), 'Mummy I'm Fat', Wednesday April 23, p. 15.
Hamilton, K. and Waller, G. (1993), 'Media Influences on Body Size Estimation in Anorexia and Bulimia: An Experimental Study', *British Journal of Psychiatry*, Vol. 162, pp. 837-840.
Harding, S. (1987), *Feminism and Methodology*, Open University Press, Milton Keynes.

Hill Collins, P. (1990), *Black Feminist Thought: Consciousness and the Politics and Empowerment*, Routledge, New York.

Jacobs-Brumberg, J. (1988), *Fasting Girls: The Emergence of Anorexia Nervosa as a Modern Disease*, Harvard University Press, Cambridge, Mass.

MacSween, M. (1993), Anorexic Bodies: A Feminist and Sociological Perspective on Anorexia Nervosa, Routledge, London.

Mellor, P. and Shilling, C. (1997), *Reforming the Body: Religion, Community and Modernity*, Sage, London.

Myers, P.N. and Biocca, F.A. (1992), 'The Elastic Body Image: The Effects of Television Advertising and Programming on Body Image Distortion in Young Women', *Journal of Communication*, Vol. 42 (3), pp.108-133.

Orbach, S. (1978), *Fat is a Feminist Issue: The Anti-Diet Guide to Permanent Weight Loss*, Paddington Press, London.

Shilling, C. (1993), *The Body and Social Theory*, Sage, London.

Stanley, L. and Wise, S. (1983), *Breaking Out: Feminist Consciousness and Feminist Research*, Routledge and Kegan Paul, London.

Stannard, U. (1971), 'The Mask of Beauty', In V.Gornick and B.K.Morgan (eds), *Women in Sexist Society*, Basic Books, New York.

Strauss, A.L. (1987), *Qualitative Analysis for Social Scientists*, Cambridge University Press, Cambridge.

Streigel-Moore, R., Silberstein, L. and Rodin, J. (1986), 'Towards Understanding the Risk Factors for Bulimia', *American Psychologist*, Vol. 41, pp. 246-263.

The Times (1996), 'Vogue Model Too Thin for Omega', Friday May 31, p.1.

Turner, B. (1991), *Religion and Social Theory, 2nd ed.*, Sage, London.

Turner, B. (1992), *Regulating Bodies: Essays in Medical Sociology*, Routledge. London.

Turner, B. (1996), *The Body and Society: Explorations in Social Theory, 2nd ed.*, Sage, London.

Wolf, N. (1990), *The Beauty Myth*, Vintage, London.

2. The model of a man: masculinity and body image in men's lifestyle magazines

Angus Bancroft

Introduction

In recent years sociologists have increasingly come to recognise the importance of studying the embodied nature of human experience and social relations. Gender has received particular attention as an embodied aspect of human life. Discourse around the gendered body is one part of the complex interlinking that binds individuals to society: this discourse has become more intense over the course of the century. It has the peculiar ability to link the public with the intimate and does so in the arena of lifestyle culture. As a researcher I am particularly interested in the part body image plays in the establishment of masculinity, or male-ness, on a social and an individual basis. So the recent development of lifestyle magazines for men caught my attention, as it brings to the fore many of the issues around embodiment that are of interest to social researchers. The following chapter is a study of the formation of masculinity through the representations of body image in men's lifestyle magazines, and what it can tell about the interrelationship of maleness, display and dominance. I consider the implications for a sociological understanding of the body, and the possibilities for further qualitative research into the formations of masculine embodiment. I also provide some reflections on the role of qualitative methods in researching the body.

Men behaving normally? Masculinity in the 1990s

In our society, young men are the object of a large amount of regulative discourse and, disproportionately to their numbers, coercion. Groups of young men have been at the centre of most 'moral panics', a recurring one of which is the 'crisis of masculinity' to which British society returned in the 1990s. Problems with the masculinity of young men were identified in the early 1990s in the context of a series of riots on housing estates across England and Wales (Campbell, 1993). The disturbances appeared in themselves to admit little in the way of sociological explanation in terms of social conflict models of class or race. Specific grievances were not apparent as causal factors; there seemed to be no symbolic or concrete objective. In explaining the wave of violence both the conservative right and the feminist left identified young men, and implicitly masculinity, as the problem. Both political wings took the view that young men were in need of some form of external control. A lot of feminist commentary took the violence as yet further evidence that masculinity was impoverished: prone to assertion of self through violence, either symbolic or actual. There has always been a body of feminist thought that has come to similar conclusions as those on the political right, implying the existence of an inherent violence and destructiveness in men and in masculinity (e.g. Cline and Spender, 1987).

In this paper I wish to challenge the assumption that masculinity is impoverished. Rather, I argue that its strength lies precisely in its richness. It is doubtful whether men would adhere to masculinity as a personal practice if it did not have some direct emotional rewards that go beyond the generalised, abstract and increasingly irrelevant benefits of patriarchal dominance. Sociological theorisation of masculinity needs to take into account the fact that men adhere to masculinity even when the rewards are not obvious. For example, male unemployment in the UK is now higher than female unemployment and women are outstripping men in most of the education stakes (Office for National Statistics, 1997, p.55). These facts by themselves do not prove that women are achieving a dominant position in the labour force - many of those jobs are part time or insecure - but they do suggest that the direct rewards of masculinity are uncertain. The resultant conflict, *contra* theorists of the male backlash against women (Faludi, 1992), is not primarily between men and women but, I suggest, between status groups of men.

If male power is as uncertain as this, especially the power of individual men rather than any putative 'patriarchy', then its assumed existence requires some explanation. Farrell (1994) proposed that male power had become a myth, to which both men and women adhered despite the passing of its reality. Farrell's work is largely polemical, and the evidence he presents is perhaps not sufficient to warrant the conclusion that male dominance is a myth, in the sense of having no foundation in human experience. However, it may be helpful for sociologists to view male power as a mythological system. I drew on this notion of male power as a mythological system when examining the representation of the male body in men's lifestyle magazines. For example, many of the forms of representation, especially those in *Arena* and *GQ*, draw directly on body representation in neo-classical sculpture.

It is important, nevertheless, to recognise that there are multiple masculinities. One of these, which we can call 'traditional' masculinity, is based largely on dominance, homophobia and self-mastery. These social practices are assumed to be part and parcel of male body practice (Connell, 1995). However, this is not the whole story, since the pleasurable aspects of traditional masculine identity have been under-recognised by theorists. They neglect the element of desire and pleasure that exists between bodies. It is the embodied aspect, the enjoyment of the male body, which intertwines masculinity and sexuality. The gay movement, for example, has contributed to the understanding of masculinity in part through its emphasis on the pleasures of embodiment, and the politicisation of pleasure. Pleasure is central to the cultural success of gay politics, whose militant hedonism has drawn in many 'straight' heterosexual men - termed 'strays' - towards the gay subculture. The influence of the gay movement is reflected in some of the magazines studied here, especially *GQ* and *Arena* in their early years, both of which used homoerotic imagery. In contrast to the body-politics of the gay movement, much feminist activism and theoretical work has tended to focus on the oppressive/regulatory aspects of women's embodiment under patriarchy. However, perhaps recognising some of the lessons of the success of the gay movement, more recent feminist work has sought to celebrate the female body and emphasise the pleasurable aspects of women's embodiment. I shall now place these theoretical arguments in the context of the development of the lifestyle magazine as a genre.

The emergence of the lifestyle magazine

The term 'lifestyle magazine' is used to denote a set of periodicals which embody and promote an ideal reader. The first mass circulation lifestyle magazines were founded in the late Victorian period (Winship, 1989). But it was the development of a mass consumer economy after the Second World War which boosted the circulation of lifestyle magazines, aimed predominantly at women. During this period these magazines became part of a mass lifestyle culture which covered aspects of daily life which are at once public and personal: relationships, sex, appearance, diet. But the content of lifestyle publications has changed with the times, for instance towards a greater sexual explicitness and hedonism which began with the launch of *Cosmopolitan* in the early 1970s (McRobbie, 1996).

In the 1960s and 1970s, social movements prefiguring the politics of the women's, gay and environmentalist movements also contributed to the upsurge in lifestyle culture, which expanded to include the development of a male body culture. These developments emphasised the abandonment of social behaviour derived from institutional discourse, and influenced radical and progressive political movements. During the 1980s cultural theorists such as the *Marxism Today* group embraced the politics of consumption, spin-doctoring style as subversion and couture as critique. But postmodern theorists have taken different standpoints on the politics of identity and consumption. Consumption has been considered as either radical cultural appropriation and resistance (McRobbie, 1994) or the glazed-eyed absorption of the commodity code into which the individual's identity is submerged (Baudrillard, 1994). Such developments in lifestyle culture may be regarded as progressive and liberating, for example, potentially recasting the boundaries of what is acceptable male and female behaviour and practice. However, an alternative Foucauldian framework would take them to be part of a generalised discourse around the body which produces power networks, implicating specific subjectivities of sexuality, with movements based around sexual politics themselves being a part of the production of discursive networks of body practice (Foucault, 1987).

Where there is agreement among theorists is that identity is increasingly based on consumption choices. Moreover, people increasingly apply themselves to consumption as if it is an ethical obligation. Such intense consumption practice develops its own culture, a 'style' culture. This style culture developed from the 'lifestyle' culture which was a feature of mass consumer society from the 1950s to the 1970s. A crucial differentiating factor between these two cultures is that the former includes men. The style culture was heralded by *The Face* magazine, which during the 1980s established style as serious, and consumerism as important business (Nixon, 1996). It helped to legitimate men's liking of fashion, not as dandyish frippery but a statement of being a man. *The Face* laid the ground for a full blown male lifestyle magazine, *Arena*, launched in 1986. Central to these magazines was a strong emphasis on male style, on display and meaningful consumption.

Men's lifestyle magazines: the market

My research into men's magazines was conducted in two six-month periods. The first was in 1994 when *GQ* dominated the market and *Loaded* had just been launched. The second was in late 1996 to early 1997, when *Loaded* and *FHM* were vying for dominance of a rapidly expanding market. For the most part I focused on *GQ* and *Loaded*, partly because they were both market innovators. I analysed the magazines, collected media research information on their impact, and collated newspaper interviews with the magazines' publishers, editors and writers. I also spoke to the media officers of *GQ*, *Loaded*, and *FHM* and collected the publicity material used by each magazine. In reading the magazines I looked at the individual style of each publication, the representations of men and women in them, and specific points of comparison with women's magazines.

The main players in the men's lifestyle magazine market in the UK are *Loaded*, *GQ*, *FHM*, *Arena*, *Esquire*, *Men's Health*, *Maxim*, and *XL*. The market as a whole is small compared to women's magazines but is growing rapidly and has a high profile, partly because it saturates the media village. Total sales number 1.3 million copies per month. The broad demographic profile of readers is weighted towards the middle class more strongly than for women's magazines (Smith, 1996). Class is a stronger marker than age for the readers of this sector of the magazine market. Its class boundaries are more tightly drawn than that of women's magazines, where age for the most part is a more important factor than class in differentiating a magazine's readership. *GQ* has a more affluent readership than average, *Maxim* much less so. However, despite the expectations of affluence contained in advertising prospectuses a large proportion of working class men do read the magazines and adopt a style ethic.

Loaded, which styles itself 'the magazine for men who should know better' had the highest sale of these magazines until 1997, when *FHM* achieved the surprising coup of overtaking both it and the best selling women's magazines. *Loaded* states its target readership to be single men in their twenties in social classes ABC1. It adopts a very 'laddish' tone and places a lot of emphasis on hedonism, especially of an alcoholic and sexual kind. In 1996 the *Loaded* team launched a food and drink magazine, *EatSoup*. *GQ*, as 'the men's magazine with an IQ' was the market leader until the launch of *Loaded*. It aims for a more affluent, conservative and slightly older readership than the rest of the market, and it was the first magazine I examined in depth.

GQ: the essential male

'The *GQ* reader is stylish, intelligent, open-minded, sociable and adventurous' (Conde Nast, 1997). Launched in 1988, *GQ* was for a long time the market leader among men's lifestyle magazines. It is not so any more, and instead stakes its claim on being - along with its readers - a cut above the rest. Its advertising prospectus describes the readers of *GQ* as more affluent and better educated, as well as being, crucially, 'better' consumers than men in general. It boasts of the extent to which '*GQ* men' spend more on clothes, grooming and holidays when compared to other men. It is, of course, the job of the magazine to sell its readers to its advertisers, and it sells them as practical consumers. The body is the focus of this consumption.

During the 1980s and early 1990s *GQ* was nicknamed 'Gaily Queerly', because it portrayed the male figure in a manner which bore more than a passing resemblance to gay male erotica. From its inception to the early 1990s, its cover images were entirely of men: actors, businessmen, and occasionally pop stars. From the 1990s it was remade somewhat to be more overtly heterosexual, foregrounding the male gaze and the female body. Covers now feature women much more often that they do men. Under the influence of *Loaded*, *FHM*, *Esquire* and to a lesser extent *Arena*, have also altered their visual style and magazine covers now almost never feature men. This is ironic as *Loaded* quite often has men on its cover. A selection of cover stars from the first half of 1997 includes model Melinda Messenger (*FHM*), actresses Jennifer Aniston (*GQ*), Pamela Anderson (*Esquire*), and Sophie Dahl (*Arena*). Unlike women's magazines the cover star is a public person rather than a model. One long-standing norm holds: men are allowed to be old or not conventionally sexy and still make it onto the cover, whereas the women featured on the covers of men's and women's magazines are universally young and conventionally attractive. The exception to that latter rule is, surprisingly, *Loaded*, which has had women like actress Kathy Burke and comic Jo Brand on its cover, women who are celebrated for their force of personality rather than their adherence to a conventional ideal of beauty.

As the magazines' advertising prospectuses illustrate, and as economics dictate, they have to sell readers to advertisers and commodities to readers. The increased importance of the advertising system in image, textual production and commodity circulation in our society has led to a greater aesthetic content in commodities and the ever faster turnover of those commodities. The promise of masculinity is promoted within the aesthetic of commodities targeted at men, especially so in advertising. Goffman

(1979) offers a brilliant analysis of the symbolic conveyance of masculine authority in adverts. He analysed how conventions such as relative size and the ritualisation of subordination are used to convey the power relations of gender. In the men's lifestyle magazines of the 1990s conventions have altered away from the domination of women: in *GQ* the most common pose of the male figure is cool, confident, staring out of the page, a permanent fixture, more often than not alone. In the adverts Goffman studied the male figure was a patriarchal one, carrying responsibility for and authority over women and the family. The adverts in men's lifestyle magazines show the male figure as far more individuated, and less family obligated, than those examined by Goffman.

Following on from the relative absence of patriarchal relationships in its adverts, the social landscape of *GQ* does not feature personal relationships with the opposite sex as central, in contrast to women's magazines. The world view represented is a public one, reflecting the construction of its reader as an informed and confident operator in the public arena. Hence, male cover stars are not male models but public men, men with an established role outside the self-perpetuating bureaucracy of style: actors, politicians, pop stars. Reflecting their general focus, none of the men's magazines have problem pages dealing with relationship issues. There are none of the self revelatory stories of the problems of private life that feature so strongly in women's magazines. In men's lifestyle magazines like *Arena* and *GQ* the care of the self is the perfection of style, rather than the insertion of the self into the milieux of personal relations.

GQ is a component of that discourse which constructs gender symbolism in male body image. Each image in the magazine is loaded with meaning for body culture. It is a commonplace assumption that women are more concerned than men about having a coherent, presentable, body image. Qualitative research into the daily amount of time spent on maintaining personal appearance appears to falsify this assumption (Biltman, 1988). Men on average take almost as much time on body care as women do. Body awareness is underscored by the decline of the male breadwinner wage and employment, whereby masculinity is decreasingly drawn from men's role as autonomous producers, and is increasingly a part of men's role as autonomous consumers. It is this role that *GQ* had a key part in establishing.

Loaded: the blokelash

Loaded was launched in 1994 with a projected monthly sale of 35,000 copies. It now sells ten times that number. It has had an enormous impact on men's magazines and as part of a new bloke-ish culture, introducing the 'new Lad', the backlash against the failed 'new Man'. The new Lad is supposed to enjoy football, drinking, is comfortable with soft porn, is generally pleased with himself, but is dignified by ironic awareness of his clownish nature. *Loaded's* content is fairly hedonistic, the men featured in its articles typically being represented as 'hard living'. 'Each edition involves such excess - whether that be of an alcoholic, narcotic or energetic nature' (James Brown, *Loaded* editor until 1997, interview with *The Independent*, 29 September 1996). The excess is highly body orientated, both in what is put into the body and what is done to the body. The care of the self is not a feature of *Loaded's* content as it is of that of *GQ*. In fact it is explicitly denied by it: the magazine has no time for the body-rigour of its elder siblings. One feature - from the February 1997 issue - was the 'Toast Olympics', carrying the by-line that toast and beer are the mainstays of the diet of modern man. Whereas the readers of the thirty-something magazines like *GQ* live in terror of the oncoming beer belly, those of *Loaded* care about it only to the extent of revelling in their disdain. Sports featured are as likely to be darts or snooker as anything offering outdoor exertion to punish its readers. It is possibly this semi-realism about what they can expect from their bodies that has made the formula so successful across such a wide range of men. The new Lad - as far as he is a *Loaded* reader - is a cross class figure to a larger extent than the new Man of *GQ*, as shown by the fact that *The Guardian*, a liberal quality broadsheet, is the *Loaded* reader's second favourite newspaper, the first being *The Sun*, a popular tabloid.

Despite its reputation as something one should purchase in a paper bag, an image the magazine revels in, the soft-pornography in *Loaded* is far more soft than it is graphic. It actually has a far less rigid adherence to both male and female beauty ideals than most of the other men's magazines. Reflecting its affected informality, the photomontages and writing style tend to be deliberately slapdash. The gay influenced iconography used during the 1980s by *GQ* and *Arena* has been completely rejected by *Loaded*, and in this all the other magazines have fallen into what they perceive to be the *Loaded* line: 'We've never published an issue without a girl on the cover' (Eric Fuller, *Maxim* editor, interview with *The Observer*, 11 August 1996).

The *Loaded* advertising prospectus sells the magazine on its circulation and media impact - with the phrase '*Loaded* man' used as demographic shorthand by media commentators. It makes less of the affluence of its readership than does *GQ* - they are less affluent - and more of their loyalty and identification with the magazine (IPC, 1997).

To summarise these developments: in the 1980s a style culture emerged, fuelled by the newly confident class of young professionals. On the basis of this market, publishers were able to launch a lifestyle magazine for men, *GQ*. Its success allowed other publishers to move into the market. The surprise success of *Loaded* has changed the emphasis of most of these men's magazines to reflect a highly (hetero)sexualised body imagery, though in fact *Loaded* itself carries some visual challenges to this form of body imagery. I now turn to developments in the longer established market of women's magazines, as a point of comparison with men's magazines.

Tanned bodies: a comparison with women's magazines

There is a wealth of fascinating research into women's magazines by feminists and media researchers (e.g. Budgeon and Currie, 1995; Rich and Cash, 1993). This allows comparisons to be drawn between body image construction in men and women's lifestyle magazines. The landscape of social life in women's magazines is more restricted, private and individual than that of their male equivalents. Admittedly the influence of magazines such as *Cosmopolitan* has expanded that landscape to include public arenas like work, but on the whole these are still dealt with in a highly personalised manner. The representation of work situations in women's lifestyle magazines eroticises the operations of labour market and work space, in which responsibility lies on the woman to change herself, rather than be an agent of change. The standard of beauty is a tool for use in the labour market: an article on workwear combines the appearance of sexuality with the appearance of efficiency. Men in men's magazines tend to represent agency in the labour market: women in women's magazines are expected to turn their bodies into capital, an object for consumption (Bourdieu, 1984).

The advertising of tanning products in women's magazines can be taken to represent a paradigmatic area of interface between consumerism and body practice, which has several implications for the gendered distribution of responsibility, agency and the body as a product bearing symbolic capital. Skin colour management has a long history in the West. Make-up products in the early modern era tended to be skin lighteners, from the white lead that was the death of many Elizabethan ladies to the Dandies' paling powder. To be upper class, one demonstrated the lightness of one's skin colouration. The relationship between class and skin colour has inverted somewhat: as with the leisurisation of physical exertion, so the browning of the skin has come to be taken as representing health and wealth. Hence the promotion of tanning products as desirable lifestyle accessories. These can be taken as a point of comparison between men's and women's magazines.

Coupland and Coupland (1997) in their study of the advertising of tanning products in women's magazines find that women regard a tan as an artefact or object - 'I like to get a tan'. Whereas one might assume that tanning is a natural process working on an object (the individual's body), in fact individual women turn themselves into the agent and the tan into the project, the end product being an attractive body. Adverts in women's magazines emphasise the agency of the individual operating on her body, with the suncare products as instruments to facilitate the achievement of a body tan. A lifestyle choice is taken concerning the equation of desirability and physical colour. The lifestyle culture asserts the body as a commodity, an exchange item, a form of symbolic capital that requires work to have its exchange value reproduced.

In women's magazines the responsibility of women is asserted with regard to the tanning of children and the avoidance of skin cancer in male partners. Reflecting this division of labour in regard to the body there are no adverts for tanning products in mainstream men's lifestyle magazines. Only the most health conscious of the magazines - *Men's Health* - carried a few adverts for tanning products. Men are encouraged to work on 'chat up' technique, style, wealth display, and not directly on their body. It would appear that looking after the body, for example protecting men's and children's skin, is still primarily women's responsibility.

More generally, the emphasis in men's magazines is on being a man, with little reference to women, whereas women's magazines insist that being a woman has to be done in reference to men: specifically to *a* man. In contrast *Loaded*, *FHM*, and *Maxim* speak of women in the plural. Body advice is given so that 'you can be more attractive to women/girls'. There is certainly little encouragement in men's lifestyle magazines to generate the body as symbolic capital in itself. Body centred men's magazines make aesthetic appeals couched in functional ideals, such as that of fitness. Exercise in *Cosmopolitan* is oriented to the end of squeezing the female body into an ideal shape corset, whereas in *GQ* it is about fitness and sport, the body mastering and exercising power in public space. As highlighted earlier in this chapter, the role of the individual as a consumer is of ever increasing importance. The body is both an object of that consumption, and a project, to be produced through specific forms of consumption. It is in this process that the body is gendered. I now return to the meaning of changing masculinities for men, and how this could provide a fruitful avenue for qualitative research.

Qualitative research and male body image

'What makes a man?' was the question I asked when I chose to study these publications. It is also a question that is increasingly important for many men. Adult men who find themselves locked into long term unemployment or insecurity of job tenure, boys academically outpaced by girls, all have to face this previously unasked question and develop some sort of response that does not rely on assumptions of the inevitability of paid work and domestic dominance. A partial response was the emerging cult of the perfect male body in the 1980s, as represented in *GQ* fashion features and adverts from that time. However, this was a highly exclusionary and class based masculinity, and it appears to have created something of a backlash in the form of *Loaded*.

The most significant and potentially progressive development which men's lifestyle magazines represent is that men are being spoken to as men. Men have become the subjects of the lifestyle discourse, or, more exactly, their bodies have. The development of an information economy and the decline of manual labour has meant that the male body has lost its place as the locus of commodity production. The male body is now sold as the focus of commodity consumption and the lifestyle magazine sells the body of the reader to the advertiser as an ideal consumer. But, as the body politics of the gay movement have shown, there is potential here for new identities to be developed, which allow for the pleasurable aspects of embodiment to be emphasised over its controlling/repressive aspects.

Goffman (1990) outlined a way of understanding how social actors develop what are implicitly body practices and how they interrelate with others through these practices, through the practical arrangement of bodies. Much of behaviour and action is intercorporeal, between bodies. Men have in successive times and places utilised differing body practices in the formation of masculinity. With the development of body culture and body politics these are undergoing rapid change. The emergence of men's lifestyle magazines and the associated body culture represents a development in the body practices that men need to 'be' men. It is this development that could usefully be pursued further, in particular the question of how this prefigures progress towards a non-dominating masculine identity.

Analysis of men's magazines seems to suggest that much of the competition which is a key feature of masculinity is competition between men. Crucially, it is the study of how men relate to each other and to their bodies that can move researchers on from examining the representation of the male body, as I have done here, to a consideration of the interaction of masculine bodies within social relations. Part of that project could include the way in which men read these magazines, and how that informs body image and body practice. Qualitative research has potential in gaining access to subjective understanding and experience, and to the processes by which men develop images of their bodies. The use of focus groups has been highly productive in researching masculinity (Connell, 1995), and is one that could be used with this end in mind. The focus group is particularly apt because of the nature of masculinity, which is for the most part established in relation to other men. Focus groups allow for this 'demonstrative' part of masculinity in social relationships to be shown, but also to be cut beneath. In allowing for reflection and explication the focus group can encourage men to provide what they are far too seldom asked for: an account of themselves.

To date research on men has tended, for perfectly good reasons, to focus on delinquent men, especially violent males (Dobash and Dobash, 1992), or on 'minority' men such as gays (Weeks, 1997). More research on mainstream or core masculinity and the formation of maleness would be of use, as it is this which is increasingly being drawn into question by social and economic changes throughout the last quarter of the twentieth century. One aspect of future research should be the enjoyable aspect of men's bodies, the pleasure of embodiment. Sociology has tended to prefer describing the networks of repression and domination that feed into male power. However, what may be the key to the strength of masculinity is that as an embodied ideology it can offer a degree of direct pleasure to both men and women.

References

Baudrillard, J. (1994), *Simulacra and Simulation*, University of Michigan: Ann Arbor.

Biltman, M. (1988), 'Service Provision, Women and the Future of the Household', *International Research Group on Time Budgets and Social Activities Conference*, Edinburgh University 1988.

Bourdieu, P. (1984), *Distinction,* Routledge and Kegan Paul: London.

Budgeon, S., and D. H. Currie (1995), 'From Feminism to Post-feminism, *Women's Studies International Forum*, vol. 18, no. 2, 173-86.

Campbell, B. (1993), *Goliath,* Methuen: London.

Cline, S., and Spender,D. (1987), *Reflecting Men*, Andre Deutsch: London.

Conde Nast (1997), *GQ Advertiser's Prospectus*, Conde Nast Publications: London.

Connell, R. W. (1995), *Masculinities*, Polity: Cambridge.

Coupland, J., and N. Coupland (1997), 'Competing Discourse Resolved', *Media, Risk and the Environment Conference*, Cardiff University 1997.

Dobash, R. E., and R. P. Dobash (1992), *Women, violence and social change*, Routledge: London.

Faludi, S. (1992), *Backlash: The Undeclared War Against Women*, Chatto & Windus: London.

Farrell, W. (1994), *The Myth of Male Power: Why Men are the Disposable Sex*, Fourth Estate: London.

Foucault, M. (1987), *The History of Sexuality*, vol. 1, Penguin: Harmondsworth.

Freud, S. (1979), *Civilisation and its Discontents*, Hogarth: London.

Goffman, E. (1979), *Gender Advertisements*, Macmillan: London.

Goffman, E. (1990), *The Presentation of Self in Everyday Life*, Penguin: Harmondsworth.

IPC (1997), *Loaded Media Information*, IPC Magazines: London.

McRobbie, A. (1994), *Postmodernism and Popular Culture*, Routledge: London.

McRobbie, A. (1996), 'More!: New Sexualities in Girls' and Women's Magazines', in Curran J., Morley D., and Walkerdine V. (eds), *Cultural Studies and Communications*, St Martin's Press: New York.

Nixon, S. (1996), *Hard Looks,* University College London: London.

Office for National Statistics (1997), *Social Trends*, The Stationery Office: London.

Rich, M. K., and T. F. Cash (1993), 'The American Image of Beauty', *Sex Roles*, vol. 29, no. 1, 113-24.

Smith, P., (ed.) (1996), *Key Note 1996 Market Report: Men's Magazines*, Key Note: Hampton.

Weeks, J. (1997), *Coming Out,* Quartet: London.

Winship, J. (1989), *Inside Women's Magazines*, Pandora: London.

3. Bodybuilding and sexual attractiveness

Lee Monaghan, Michael Bloor, Russell P. Dobash and Rebecca E. Dobash

Introduction

Following the 1980s fitness boom, a strong and fat-free body is often deemed aesthetically superior (Glassner, 1990; Monaghan, 1995). The dieted and exercised soma is increasingly associated with beauty and sexual attractiveness. Athletically muscular 'Jock chicks' (Bolin, 1992) and sculpted male pinups (Dyer, 1989) are familiar images in popular culture, representing somatic ideals and new markers of sexuality and desirability. These popular images have helped to make 'bodywork' and the consumption of bodybuilding technologies more acceptable in contemporary society. Featherstone (1991) notes that the body is increasingly seen as a reflection of the inner self, and so bodily neglect lowers one's acceptability as a person. Small wonder, then, that bodybuilding and weight-training have increased in popularity in recent years.

Admittedly, the levels of muscularity and 'vascularity' (i.e. prominence of veins) displayed by physique competitors are regarded by some people as stigmatising. Bolin (1992) comments that the ideal for the competitive bodybuilder may be seen as 'pronormative' (i.e. they have pushed body toning too far). Muscle has traditionally been considered antithetical to femininity (Aoki, 1996), and bodybuilding has been dismissed as a 'shadowy subculture and a fertile ground for the innuendoes of the amateur psychologist' (Thirer and Greer, 1978). Nevertheless, male and female bodybuilding activities are becoming increasingly popular (Klein, 1993). One reason for this is the identification of muscularity with ideals of the sexually attractive body:

> 015: I mean, to me it's got a sexual basis I think. You feel good about yourself, you look good, you feel, you know, you think: 'well if I look at myself and look good

then girls must look at me and think I look good' […] Yeah, it's a very sexually based thing I'm sure with most people, whether they know it or not. It certainly is for me.

LM: So a muscular physique, you think it makes a person more sexually desirable?

015: Yeah, yeah, and if you feel better about yourself you feel sexier anyway, definitely.

(Formal interview with male bodybuilder).

I think the athletic look for a woman is sexy and is in at the moment. You can see that by the number of women who come to my aerobic classes who want a body like mine! (Field-diary: fitness instructor/female bodybuilder at *Olympia Gym*, 10.7.95).

Of course, sexual attractiveness is simply one meaning among many which may be ascribed to the body. But the sexual attractiveness of muscular bodies is nevertheless an important and under-researched topic in the sociology of the body. This chapter aims to compensate for this neglect by focusing on bodybuilders' *embodied understandings* of sexual attractiveness. Another aim of the chapter is to demonstrate the value of ethnographic methods in researching bodily matters. These methods allow a sensitive exploration of the diverse meanings and motivations of participants in bodybuilding subculture. They help to provide a phenomenological or 'carnal sociological reading' (Crossley, 1995) of the representational significance of the muscular/sexual body, in a way which illuminates the lure of bodywork. Among other things, this exploration highlights the limitations of accounts of bodybuilding which attempt to explain it in terms of a 'masculinity-in-crisis' (White and Gillett, 1994). In short, this research casts doubt on feminist accounts which simply view bodybuilding as an attempt to work through gender insecurities by constructing an 'imposing exterior' signifying 'hegemonic masculinity' (Klein, 1993). Before reporting and analysing the data, however, a brief description of the research methodology is appropriate.

Methods

The data presented here were obtained during a two year ESRC funded project on bodybuilding, steroids and violence (Dobash et al., 1996; Bloor et al., 1998). This study included both ethnographic work and in depth interviews. The pilot work involved visits to twelve towns across South Wales in order to locate suitable fieldwork sites. During this pilot phase, overt participant observation was undertaken at fifteen gyms, twelve leisure centres, three needle exchanges and a Well Steroid User clinic. Bodybuilding competitions were also visited. The ethnographer (L. Monaghan) also mixed with research subjects outside of the gym context in settings such as night clubs and subjects' homes. Bodybuilding gyms were eventually selected as the main ethnographic site, and the main study was conducted on a time-sampling basis at four 'hard-core' gyms (Olympia, Pumping-Iron, Al's and Temple).

An interview schedule was devised to tap members' tacit taken-for-granted understandings. Sixty seven depth interviews were then conducted with a range of bodybuilders and weight-trainers, both men and women. While most of the interviewees were recruited through ethnographic contacts, efforts were made to recruit some of the sample by other means, including visits to a group of prisoners who worked-out with weights. Posters were also placed in three needle exchange facilities, and advertisements were placed in a national bodybuilding magazine, *Bodybuilding Monthly*.

All the interviews were transcribed. The transcripts and ethnographic fieldnotes were then indexed using *Ethnograph*, the most commonly used coding software package in qualitative studies. Indexing of the fieldnotes and transcripts allowed a systematic approach to data analysis, helping to develop analytical propositions which applied to the entire universe of data carrying indexed codes. This approach is variously termed 'analytic induction' or 'deviant case analysis' (Bloor, 1978).

Bodybuilding and the mate market

This section presents data gathered by means of the research tools described above. The data suggest that many of the interviewees were motivated by the prospect of improving their sexual attractiveness. Sex is a common topic of conversation among gym members and it is clear that a muscular body has great sexual significance as far as participants are concerned. Whether the individual is male or female, heterosexual or homosexual, muscle is generally believed to have an important sexual dimension.

Male attitudes

Since most of the subjects contacted during the study period were male heterosexual bodybuilders, most of the research data refers to this group. Ethnographic fieldwork reveals that, for them, muscle is indeed correlated with sexual attractiveness. Consider the following extract:

> Taz was in the changing room. He was planning on a quick training session since the gym was about to close in forty minutes. He'd just 'popped in' after some sort of outing since he had his two young children with him [which is unusual] - a boy aged about eight and a girl of ten. The boy was in the changing room with his father, while the girl was outside. I asked the youngster whether he'd be lifting weights in a few years time. Taz laughed and said to him: 'that depends on how much pussy [vagina] you want doesn't it son?'
> (Field-diary: *Temple Gym*, 18.6.94).

The owner of Pumping Iron Gym claimed that muscle evokes favourable sexual reactions from women:

> 018: I've actually been in a pub now where women have walked up and grabbed my arm and gone 'ooh! What a hunk' and pinched my backside, you know! And so I would say that they do find you a lot more desirable…I think to be honest, over the past couple of years where Schwarzenegger brought muscle to the box office films whatever, people find it a little bit more acceptable that there are big bulging biceps on some of us men. And I also think the Chippendales have sort of helped as well […] Once women have been to a variety act and seen them stripped off and then they're in a pub and they sort of see somebody clothed, the real thing, then yeah, they definitely will accept it more. In fact I sort of played a bit of a joke in the pub over Christmas time. I was in condition, it was the end of my course [he'd just completed a steroid cycle and looked at his best] and this girl was giving me the eye. And it was Christmas and I thought 'well' you know 'I'll give her a bit of a treat'. So I walked over to her and dropped my trousers, lifted my shirt up and showed her my abs [abdominal

muscles or 'six-pack' as it is commonly referred to in popular culture], and I was tanned as well. And at first she thought I had a latex body-suit on. And then she actually sort of felt my abs and she said 'oh my god!' and sort of grabbed me and sort of mauled me!

Clearly, many gym members are motivated by the desire to enhance their sex appeal in a way that facilitates access to sexual partners. Moreover, this seems to apply to homosexuals as well as heterosexuals. One homosexual bodybuilder highlighted the sexual significance of his trained body:

025: I expect it to be more attractive to the sort of man I'd want to attract, yeah, you know. I like muscular men, so I would expect, you know, that to be important to another muscular man.

Of course, it has to be recognised that there are various 'orientations' to lifting weights and bodybuilding. Whilst the wish to improve sexual attractiveness may be considered an important reason for training, this motive should not be ascribed to gym members without reference to their own ideas, intentions and emergent dispositions. For instance, one of the men interviewed denied that he trained in order to attract women. This man, an international competitor, stressed that his main motivation was the excitement and pleasure of athletic competition:

021: I know people [men] who develop their body just to go out and pick women up, yes. But from my own personal point of view, no. I married my wife when I was about nine and a half stone [he now competes at around fourteen stone]...so she remembers me like that, so to me personally no, it doesn't play a part. I mean it's great when you get other women passing comments on you, yeah. It's only the same as me seeing Pamela Anderson and saying 'cor, yeah!' And you do get some comments from other girls the same way, so to some people yes, it is, but from my own personal point of view with my sexual relationship, no it's not important.

LM: So would you say a muscular physique makes a person more sexually desirable?

021: Yes.

LM: But for you personally that's not an important reason why you train?

021: No […] It's nice to have compliments, but that's not why I train. I train to be a successful athlete.

Thus, whilst it is clear that enhancing one's sexual appeal is a source of considerable satisfaction for some males, this is less important for others. The visual appeal of a muscular physique may matter more to men seeking new partners than to men in long term monogamous relationships. Established partners become 'desensitised' to exaggerated musculature and tend to take it for granted. But many interviewees stated that in the context of the bedroom it was usually 'new' lovers who expressed a positive reaction to their physique:

015: With a partner that you know well it [the body] has a lesser effect 'cause they're used to it and again they adapt. You know, they don't see it really. They don't even notice probably half the time. I think it's best with somebody you've first met. You know, the first time you sort of strip off in front of them and they're like 'fucking hell, I wish my husband looked like that' type of thing.

It would be a mistake to think that the relationship between muscle and sexual attraction is straightforward. Mostly the men felt that a muscular body aided a healthy and active sex life, but some of them expressed fears that it left them open to sexual exploitation:

009: Some girls really appreciate the fact that they know you because you're a bodybuilder and they can't wait to get you into bed because of your shape […] A lot of people will tend to use you, if you allow them to use you, because you've got a good body and perhaps they're married and perhaps they're courting or perhaps whatever. But if you let them use you they'll just use you as a bit on the side, because they want to try you, someone with a good body. So in other words you'd be a gym accessory to them like. They'd just be using you like a bench-press machine. To them they won't care like. They'll just have a crack at you and then just knock you on the head. It's surprising the amount of people there are around like that.

Such a comment was unusual among younger interviewees since it runs counter to male heterosexual ideology where promiscuous sex devoid of romantic attachment is considered an index of masculinity and a source of self-esteem. However, many bodybuilders are conscious of the way they are ridiculed for their presumed narcissism (Aoki, 1996). Although they associate muscle with male beauty, they are aware that some outsiders may regard them as conceited and thus unsuitable as lovers. In this respect, muscle may become a handicap. The following statement is illustrative and is also noteworthy since it highlights the fact that there will inevitably be variance in opinion concerning whether or not bodybuilders are considered attractive by those outside the subculture:

039: If you're out people notice you straight away. And again you get your different comments. What did happen, I didn't want to go out really. You know. It would all depend on whether she likes bodybuilders or not. And also you get approached by different girls. You get different comments off different boys. Yeah, it does affect your social life.

LM: What sort of comments then?

039: Well, you know, you get, with your mates, 'oh, look at the size of him', or they tend to think that you're something that you don't think you are yourself. So, when they [males] say [to females] 'look at him, duw, he's good, he's the one you want to see love for the body'. And you're thinking, 'well, no', so they're automatically setting you up, without knowing it, that you're a poser. So you think a lot of yourself, whereas you don't but they're setting you up for that. So that then, a girl, even if she did like you she'd think: 'oh, you're a bit of a poser. I won't bother with you'. You lose out then. And the number of times that has happened. So yeah, it does affect your social life a lot.

Another fear among bodybuilders is the impact that lack of training will have on their physique and, subsequently, sex life. A muscular physique is generally believed to build sexual confidence and high self esteem, but this is threatened if the training regime is ceased and muscle atrophies. Muscle, after all, is a reversible form of body marking (Falk, 1995.) Muscular decline, in turn, may have implications for the bodybuilder's standing in the mate market. These fears were expressed by one participant who sustained an injury and who thus stopped training for a while:

> *Soccer*: With my body going to pot I'm starting to look more like a 'normal' human being. I don't stand out so much […] Even though I fit in more now I don't enjoy the feeling because I feel out of shape. I don't look as I want to look. Because I don't look, in my eyes, good, I don't feel good about myself. Now, I may not be going out to pull the women but it's nice to think if you wanted to you could. Feeling like a bag of shit, though, means that you're awkward and you just don't feel attractive. (Field-diary: *Pumping Iron Gym*, 2.8.95.)

Women's views

This section reports the views of the female bodybuilders and trainers in the research sample. Generally, these female heterosexual interviewees (none claimed to be lesbian or bisexual) felt that their developed bodies gave them an advantage in the mate market or enhanced their existing sexual relationships. They considered a low-fat, muscular body to be sexually appealing and empowering. Hence, bodybuilding had a strong sexual component for these women. This view came across in an interview with a Ms Physique Welsh bodybuilding champion:

> 011: I haven't got the looks of a beauty queen but I have a lot better body than one, that's my attitude. I'm not, you know, an oil painting but I can look at a lot of women that have got beautiful faces but they've got horrible bodies and I think 'well, give me her head and stick my body under it'.

This view of muscle as sexually attractive was endorsed by another international bodybuilding competitor:

> 019: He [my bodybuilding husband] said to me the other day 'there's not many men been married nearly twenty years

and their wives turn them on as much as ever'. I think that says it all quite honestly.

These sexual connotations seem to explain some of the attractions of bodywork for women. However, female bodybuilders, just like their male counterparts, attach different degrees of significance to this. For example, consider the following casual exchange between a male and female in the gym. Although *Monique* concedes that her trained body signifies sexuality and desirability, she is ambivalent about this. She seems to fear that men will value her only for her looks, or, alternatively, may not regard a well trained female body as sexually desirable:

Soccer: Why do you keep yourself covered up? When training with us I think you should get rid of them baggies [loose fitting trousers] so we can see your legs…I'm a believer in the saying 'if you've got it, flaunt it'.

Monique: I've never been one for wearing stretch lycra and tight clothes in the gym. Even when I go out I wear jeans and a top that keeps me covered. My friends say I'm stupid. They say I should show it off. I do when I take my aerobics class but when out I don't. I don't think I need to show my body off. [Tongue in cheek] I like to think that I've cultivated my personality to the extent that people are attracted to me for me, the whole person, rather than my body.

Soccer: Yeah, but you can have both. You wouldn't be doing yourself a disservice if you showed yourself off a bit. You look good so why not?

Monique: I don't know about men. I can't work it out. You'd think that if men trained and took a pride in their bodies then they'd want a woman with a good body as well, but you see bodybuilders at competitions with their girlfriends and they're a right state. Big fat arses. You think: 'what's he doing with her?'

Soccer: The thing is, most men go for quantity rather than quality. (Field-diary: *Olympia Gym*, 28.3.95)

Some female trainers reported negative feedback concerning the way they looked. The woman quoted below once competed as a bodybuilder but she was unsure whether to resume training after a spell of illness:

Dawn: Whereas before I was training regularly and developed a fair bit of muscle, now I've lost it all. Then again, I'm not sure if I prefer the way I look now to how I did before.

LM: Do you mean, because how you look now [fairly athletic as opposed to muscular] fits in more with conventional ideas about how a woman should look?

Dawn: Yes. When I trained regularly with weights I was muscular. My boyfriend hated it. In fact, he didn't want me going to the gym full-stop. When I went I told him I was seeing my friend. Once I was on the phone, I had my arm bent with the phone to my ear, so I was basically doing a bicep pose in a way. My boyfriend immediately cottoned on that I'd been training. He grabbed hold of my upper arm and said: 'you've been lifting those bloody weights again haven't you'. Once he said going to bed with me was like going to bed with Mike Tyson. He hated it … So, you can see why I might prefer the way I look now since my lay off. (Field-diary: *Dawn's home*, 10.9.94)

For Dawn, looking sexy was not the main motivation for bodybuilding. Rather, her bodywork made her feel invulnerable and strong and heightened her confidence in dealing with her potentially violent boyfriend. Nevertheless, Dawn believed that a moderately muscled and fairly lean body is perfectly compatible with ideals of sexual beauty. It is only when weight-training and body-shaping is taken to extremes that it threatens their sexually desirable image. This issue, which applies to both male and female bodybuilders, is dealt with in the following section.

Sexual attractiveness and excessive muscularity

Excessive muscularity can diminish the bodybuilder's sexual attractiveness. The general public probably regard athletically muscular and fairly lean bodies such as those of the Chippendales as sexually appealing, but the types of bodies displayed by elite male bodybuilders who are in 'competition shape' are another matter. Likewise, if a woman aspires to look like a physique bodybuilder - rather than the moderately muscular Ms Figure-Fitness competitors (cf. St Martin and Gavey, 1996) - then she runs the risk of being judged negatively by outgroups. In that case her motive for training is likely to be independent of the wish to enhance sexual attractiveness. Consider the following remarks by a female bodybuilder:

> 030: It would be nice to think that it looks sexy to everybody because everybody would be doing it then wouldn't they? But yeah. I'd like people to look and think 'oh, she looks sexy' but I don't think a lot of people think like that do they? They think: 'Oh God, look at her. She's got loads of muscles!' So to a lot of people it would be a turn off wouldn't it really?
>
> LM: So really that's not an important reason why you train? Looking sexy is not a big motivation?
>
> 030: No, I'm not really bothered whether people like it or people don't or whether people think it's sexy or not because I don't care. I do it for me because I want to look good for myself, you know.

It is sometimes difficult for bodybuilders, whether male or female, to gauge when their muscle becomes 'pronormative' (i.e. beyond acceptable limits) rather than simply normative (i.e. conforming to a generally shared ideal). Perceptions of the body are relative, and so muscle enthusiasts come to realise that their bodies will not necessarily have the same meaning for everyone:

> LM: You're looking good. What does your wife think about the way you look?
>
> Rod: Funnily enough, the first time she's seen me properly was the other day. I'd just come out of there [the weights room] and my wife was stood here [the reception]. I had a vest on and I was pumped to fuck [muscles engorged with blood following exercise]. She looked at me and her mouth dropped: 'Oooow. What the fuck have you done to yourself?'
>
> LM: So she doesn't appreciate it then?

Rod: No. I was just amazed at that comment. I mean, I just didn't know what to say. What do you say? It's the total opposite of what you expect. What the fuck am I slogging my guts out in there for if I'm just gonna get that sort of reaction from my own missus?…It's strange. The other day I was in a vest and I'd just finishing training and my delts [shoulder muscles] were well pumped. I had to do some business with a woman from a catalogue company who came here. She was talking to me and she said: 'I hope you don't mind me asking, but how long have you been training for then? I said: 'Oh, about four or five years.' She was looking me up and down and said: 'Well, fair play to you. You look the part, you look really good.' I could feel my face blushing...Then she came out with 'are you married then?' I said: 'yeah, I've just got married.' Then she said: 'Oh well, never mind. If you went down town with your vest on like that you'd give all the women a treat.' (Field-diary: *Pumping Iron Gym*, 8.3.95).

Rod nevertheless continued building his body in spite of the negative views expressed by his wife. Although bodybuilders prefer to think that their bodywork enhances their sex appeal, it is not always an overriding concern. A number of them gradually develop an 'ethnophysiological' appreciation of bodybuilding, in which the main pleasures come from the intense feelings associated with training, the excitement of competition, the feeling of well-being and the pride in physical strength and shape. Neophyte bodybuilders and their sexual partners may start out regarding 'excessive' muscularity as outlandish but gradually, through a process of interaction with others, they learn to appreciate it:

031: … then you start looking at bodybuilding shows and then you see it as a sport then. You don't so much look at it as 'I'm gorgeous. I want to be good looking.' The sport takes over the vanity bit.

LM: I suppose there's an idea of men looking muscular just to look attractive. If you went to a bodybuilding competition it's like the bodybuilder's physique isn't really the same as a Chippendale's physique is it?

031: No, that's right. Women would be more attracted to Chippendales than they would a bodybuilder. But that's what I'm saying … I don't care about the Chippendales, I prefer to look like a bodybuilder.

LM: Does that change over time?

031: Yes. I mean they go to the extreme of looking like a bodybuilder at the competition. You go past the vanity bit then. If you were that vain you would want to look like a Chippendale, you'd stop there. But you don't because you go past it and so it becomes like less important as a vanity thing.

024: I've been out with lots of girls over the years and I've always been a bodybuilder since I was sixteen and the first reaction you get with a girl is: 'oh my God, that's gross. That's gross!' But then they're being exposed to something that is almost a culture shock. And they've never seen guys with veins and arms as big as their other boyfriends' legs and things. And then I think after looking at magazines and hanging around with bodybuilders and going to shows, it gradually becomes acceptable to them. It becomes the norm. And then you find a lot of girls who have been involved in the bodybuilding - you know, by way of boyfriends or whatever - they tend to accept that as the norm and then a guy with pipe stem arms and legs and a beer belly is gross.

For others, the wish to appear sexually attractive - as judged by the out-group's more moderate standards - may be the overriding motivation. In that case they adjust their physiques accordingly:

Soccer: At the end of the day I just want a body beautiful which is impressive to the average person on the street. To someone with a trained eye there'll be flaws in my physique. A bodybuilding judge may say to me: 'Yeah, you've got a good foundation but you need to work on this, this, and that.' Well, I couldn't give a fuck what a bodybuilding judge would say. If I was good in his eyes I'm pretty sure the average woman on the street would think I'm fucking disgusting because to be good in a bodybuilding judge's eyes you have to look like a freak, especially today in the 1990s. I don't want to look like a competitive bodybuilder, I'm not gonna compete. No, I want what is considered a sexy physique like a Chippendale. Now, if a Chippendale entered a bodybuilding show they'd get pissed all over [beaten]. A Chippendale wouldn't really stand a chance. Even so, I bet 98% of the population would agree that a Chippendale physique is far more pleasing to the eye than Dorian Yates [current professional world bodybuilding champion]. Whereas bodybuilders who are no more than 2% of the population would rate Dorian Yates. Now, you have to decide what you want to aim for, but personally I'll go with 98% who say the Chippendale has got the best physique. (Field-diary: *Olympia Gym*, 19.3.95)

Conclusion

Bodybuilding is in many respects a highly individualistic world, and there is certainly heterogeneity among gym members. There are different reasons for lifting weights, and different levels of muscular development. Sexual attractiveness is simply one meaning among many for consuming bodybuilding technologies. Indeed, within postmodernity bodybuilders' physiques become conterminous with the fit-looking body, representing polysemic cultural texts which blend and blur various gender-wide insignia. For example, other overlapping meanings such as health, youth and social status may be ascribed to bodies fashioned through exercise and diet (Glassner, 1990). For these reasons, the fit and trained body is highly valued by many 'outsiders' as well as by bodybuilders themselves (Schulze, 1990).

The research data nevertheless suggest that sexual attractiveness is certainly a common theme in bodybuilding circles. Many muscle enthusiasts tend to associate muscularity with sexual attractiveness, and they feel that this view is shared by many outsiders. However, they also recognise that the connection between muscle and sexual desirability becomes more problematic when bodybuilding exceeds normative standards and enters a pronormative stage. 'Excessive' muscularity approximates a stigmatised model of physicality as judged by outsiders. Some hardcore bodybuilders insist that even 'excessive' muscle is physically attractive, but most of them accept that it is widely regarded as sexually undesirable. In that case, how can we explain their continued participation in the more demanding forms of bodybuilding? The research suggests that many hardcore bodybuilders acquire an ethnophysiological appreciation of 'outlandish' bodies which is analogous with various indigenous peoples' somatic codes and aesthetic preferences (cf. Brain, 1979; Polhemous, 1978). Learnt through a social process of becoming, this way of looking at bodies is not antecedent to the individual's affiliation to bodybuilding subculture. Hence, ongoing practical involvement in the cult of muscularity may in fact be independent of a masculinity-in-crisis, psychocultural anxieties or gender inadequacy.

Lastly, it should be stressed that bodies are sentient beings rather than simply physical entities or surfaces upon which culture writes its meaning. No doubt, future work on the sociology of the body in general, and bodybuilding in particular, will benefit from recognising that whilst bodies are social the social is also embodied (Crossley, 1995). In this respect it is to be appreciated that qualitative research has an important role to play in embodying social scientific studies of the human body.

References

Aoki, D. (1996), 'Sex and Muscle', *Body & Society*, vol. 2 no. 4, pp.59-74,

Bloor, M. (1978), 'On the Analysis of Observational Data', *Sociology*, vol. 12, pp.542-552.

Bloor, M., Monaghan, L., Dobash, R.P. & Dobash, R.E. (1998), 'The Body as a Chemistry Experiment: Steroid Use Among South Wales Bodybuilders' in Nettleton, S. and Watson, J. (eds) *The Body in Everyday Life*, Routledge, London.

Bolin, A. (1992), 'Vandalized Vanity: Feminine Physiques Betrayed and Portrayed' in Mascia-Lees, F. and Sharpe, P. (eds) *Tattoo, Torture, Mutilation, and Adornment,* State University of New York Press, New York.

Brain, R. (1979), *The Decorated Body*, Harper and Row, New York.

Crossley, N. (1995), 'Merleau-Ponty, the Elusive Body and Carnal Sociology', *Body & Society*, vol. 1 no.1, pp.43-63.

Dobash, R.P, Dobash, R.E., Bloor, M. and Monaghan, L. (1996), 'Roid Rage: Bodybuilding, Steroids and Violence', *Criminal Justice Matters*, no. 23, pp.5-6.

Dyer, R. (1989), 'The Right to Look' in McRobbie, A. (ed.): *Zoot Suits and Second Hand Dresses: An Anthology of Music and Fashion*, Macmillan, Basingstoke.

Falk, P. (1995), 'Written in the Flesh', *Body & Society*, vol. 1 no. 1, pp.95-105.

Featherstone, M. (1991), 'The Body in Consumer Culture' in Featherstone, M. Hepworth, M. & Turner, B.(eds), *The Body: Social Process and Cultural Theory*, Sage, London.

Glassner, B. (1990), 'Fit For Postmodern Selfhood' in Becker, H. and McCall, M. (eds), *Symbolic Interaction and Cultural Studies*, University of Chicago Press, Chicago.

Gillett, J. and White, P. (1992), 'Male Bodybuilding and the Reassertion of Hegemonic Masculinity', *Play and Culture*, no. 5 pp.358-369.

Klein, A. (1993), *Little Big Men: Bodybuilding Subculture and Gender Construction*, State University of New York Press, New York.

Monaghan, L. (1995), *Becoming a Steroid User: A 'Phenomenological' Approach to the Activity of Steroid Use Amongst Bodybuilders*, Salford Papers in Sociology No. 16, University of Salford.

Polhemus, T. (1978), *Social Aspects of the Human Body*, Penguin Books, Middlesex.

Schulze, L. (1990), 'On the Muscle' in Gaines, J. and Herzog, C. (eds) *Fabrications: Costume and the Female Body*, Routledge, London.

St Martin, L. and Gavey, N. (1996), 'Women's Bodybuilding: Feminist Resistance and/or Femininity's Recuperation?' *Body and Society*, vol. 2 no. 4, pp.45-57.

White, P. and Gillett, J. (1994), 'Reading the Muscular Body: A Critical Decoding of Advertisements in *Flex* Magazine', *Sociology of Sport Journal*, vol. 11, pp.19-39.

4. Ei gwrol ryfelwyr *. Reflections on body, gender, class and nation in Welsh rugby

(* a line from the Welsh national anthem, translated as 'its brave (or manly) warriors')

Sally Holland and Jonathan Scourfield

> there persists between the Welsh and the men who represent them on the rugby field a deeper, more personal bond (McIlvanney, 1995, p.16).

It is fitting for a volume in a series of Cardiff papers on qualitative research to have a Welsh dimension. There could perhaps be no more obvious a place to begin a sociological analysis of the body in Wales than with the sport of rugby. Since rugby is often said to be central to Welsh identity, a critical perspective on contemporary Welsh society ought to attempt to deconstruct the social meanings of the game. It is, however, a relatively under-researched feature of Welsh life. Much of the prominent scholarly writing on Welsh rugby in recent years has been by relatively uncritical enthusiasts (Smith and Williams, 1980; Williams, 1991). Whilst we are not unenthusiastic about the game as an exciting spectacle, we will begin to critically explore some possibilities regarding rugby's social meaning in Wales, particularly in the light of recent insights into the sociology of the body and the sociology of masculinities. It is unfortunate that, despite some major recent theoretical work on the body, there has been a relative dearth of empirical research into 'concrete incorporating practices' (Wacquant, 1995). This chapter's aim is to begin to suggest some of the complexities involved in a sociological analysis of the body in Welsh rugby and to highlight some opportunities for qualitative research.

There are two different rugby codes in the UK. Rugby league has a professional history and is played mainly in the North of England. Rugby union has been an amateur sport until very recently and its traditional strongholds are private schools throughout the UK, and popular participation in industrial South Wales. Before rugby union's amateur status was officially changed, there was a drift of first class players from Wales to professional English rugby league teams, which has resulted in success for the Welsh rugby league team in recent years. However, when discussing Welsh rugby in this chapter we refer to rugby union, and specifically to men's teams. Although participation in women's rugby is growing, it has neither the hegemonic position in the culture of many Welsh communities nor the symbolic importance to national identity that men's rugby has. For brevity we will only use the term 'rugby' from now on.

We do not intend to suggest homogeneity in Welsh life. Rugby playing is, broadly speaking, more rooted in industrial South Wales than in the rural West and North, and these regions have very different histories and cultures. However, to avoid potential pedantry, we often use the terms 'Wales' and 'Welsh' in relation to rugby. Recent research has questioned whether rugby is currently a primary leisure activity in traditional rugby-playing areas (Adamson and Jones, 1996). Our assumption in this chapter, based on our own experience of South Wales, is that the sport still has a major cultural importance. Brian Roberts' research (1995) found that rugby was very often cited as an image of 'Welshness' by residents of the South Wales valleys. This is an area which was rapidly populated in the nineteenth century in order to serve the coal mining industry. This industry has declined to the extent that it is now an insignificant part of the local economy, albeit still powerful in the local cultural imagination. The valleys constitute an area of high social deprivation according to all the standard indices. At several points in the discussion below we make reference to the South Wales valleys.

Some issues with potential for future qualitative research on rugby will be discussed. There is currently a dearth of such research on the sport in Wales, and perhaps qualitative methods are best placed to illuminate the social meaning and social organisation of rugby. We refer primarily, though not exclusively, to potential work on the body. The body can be seen as central to any discussion of sport in society. As Frank writes, 'the sociology of the body understands embodiment not as residual to social organisation, but rather understands social organisation as being about the reproduction of embodiment' (Frank, 1991, p.42). The discussion will be organised into three sections: rugby as training for bodily practices, rugby and social stratification, and rugby as embodied national identity.

Rugby as training for bodily practices

When a sport has a powerful position in a local culture, it will probably influence the embodiment not only of those who play it, but also those who watch, those who choose not to play or watch, and those who are not expected to do either. People learn to orient their bodily practices either in support of or in opposition to the hegemonic model (Connell, 1995). In this section we argue that attention needs to be paid to rugby's influence on the bodily practices of its players, of boys and men in general, and of women.

Masculinities

There is potential for research on the embodiment of first class rugby players, who are often high profile figures in the Welsh media and in local communities. Wacquant (1995) has analyzed the 'bodily labour' of professional boxers, based on an ethnographic study in Chicago, and describes them using their bodies as a form of 'capital': their bodies are their livelihood. The rich data in Wacquant's study are an example of how in-depth qualitative research can illuminate the detail of embodiment and generate theoretical ideas about bodily practices in sport. Some comparison may be made with Welsh rugby, since both it and boxing could be seen as working class combat sports. Rugby union has an ostensibly amateur history; that is, players were not officially paid until 1995, when the sport was opened up to professionalisation, although in fact for many years some first class players had received financial support from a variety of sources (Dunning and Sheard, 1979). This history would predict a different emphasis on the body as capital and the sport as work from that found in Wacquant's boxers. The professionalisation of the sport may provide new avenues for research into rugby as bodily labour. Wacquant's discussion of boxers' risk-taking also has something to offer the study of rugby. Risks, and the acceptance of pain are a significant feature of rugby culture. In Schacht's study (1996) on the gendered world of rugby, the coach was described by players as 'a man's man' because he carried on playing with a broken collar bone. Schacht's research highlights the importance of a gendered analysis of the body in sport. When taking an in-depth look at rugby players, gaining a perspective on masculinity appears to be central.

Qualitative research might focus on players 'doing' masculinity on the rugby field (West and Zimmerman, 1987). Dunning (1986) has written that in many sports the aggressive competition of the match is centrally about the expression of masculinity. In rugby, amongst the most aggressive of team sports, this might be particularly true, and this aggression could be an important part of the players' identities as men. One of the authors recalls from his work as a probation officer in the South Wales valleys a client declining a game of football on the basis that it is 'a poof's game' in comparison with rugby. It might be fruitful to explore different masculine identities associated with different sports. For example, it would be interesting to compare the embodiment of body-builders (Monaghan's chapter in this volume) with that of rugby players, particularly since body-building has become very popular for men in industrial South Wales in recent years. Research could also explore the link between the toughness that is expected in playing the game and violence off the pitch, or explore how people construct explanations of violence. There is a powerful discourse in Welsh folklore which claims that, in contrast to the 'hooligan' (and English) football culture, rugby is 'respectable' and the game itself channels all violent impulses. The meaning and significance of this construction of 'Welshness' could be examined through qualitative research.

Research into the production of masculinities in Welsh rugby runs the risk of an unproblematised presentation of working class men as macho and aggressive. If researchers were to find in rugby culture the subordination of the 'other', this should be understood in the context of a framework of gender relations that takes into account other axes of power. Connell's work (1995), for example, provides such a framework. It has to be remembered that less conspicuously embodied and more middle class masculinities can also be oppressive to women and to other men; for example, some white collar crime (Levi, 1995) and the psychological abuse of women (Jukes, 1993).

There is scope for qualitative research to explore the complexities, ambiguities and contradictions of men's embodiment in rugby. Much research has focussed on male body 'ideals' as represented, for example, in the media, and particularly in relation to notions of consumerism (e.g. Edwards, 1997). However, the bodies of some rugby players, forwards in particular, with their vast bulk, thick necks and occasionally cauliflower ears, are in contrast and contradiction to such 'ideals'. They could be understood in terms of the concept of the grotesque male body (Morgan, 1993), and be seen as representing resistance to certain ideals of male embodiment, such as those perpetuated by the fashion industry. They do also, however, represent some traditional aspects of hegemonic masculinity, such as physical power and domination: the body of the warrior. An analysis of images of male rugby players in the Welsh media would contribute to the literature on representations of gendered bodies in the media (Sabo and Jansen 1992; see also Bancroft's chapter in this volume).

Qualitative research on the body in sport provides the potential for the further development of existing theoretical work on the body. Frank (1991) conceptualises sport as a practice of the 'dominating body'. This connects with the notion that sport is a site for the production of hegemonic masculinity, although as Connell (1990) has pointed out, this production is not without contradictions and ambiguities. These and other pertinent theoretical insights could be tested through detailed empirical work. Ethnography in particular might be well suited to this kind of theory building. A qualitative study which focussed on the bodily practices of Welsh men and rugby players in particular might shed some light on our understanding of the multiplicity of masculinities and how they intersect with other power structures and other identities, including national identities (Hearn and Collinson, 1994). Dunning (1986) proposes that sport is less important than the wider social structure in defining masculinity. This highlights a theoretical debate about the relation between body and social structure that rugby research might illuminate.

Regulation of the body

In parts of Wales where rugby is the dominant sport, and often the only approved sport in secondary schools, rugby also provides training for boys and young men in masculinising bodily practices. Connell has argued that to learn be a man is to learn to project a physical presence that speaks of latent power (cited in Whitson, 1990). Sport is a crucial part of that learning, with physical education in schools as a process of schooling the body (Hargreaves, 1986). Institutional sport can be understood in terms of Foucault's concept of the disciplining of the body (Rabinow, 1991). Research conducted in Wales by Sutton et al (1996) illustrates how boys are encouraged to partcipate in sport to a greater extent than girls, especially team sports. This division is produced through the social structures in Welsh schools and communities such as sports clubs, playground space and the expectations of family, peers and physical education teachers. Theberge (1991) makes a link between the social organisation of sport and the 'naturalizing' of gender difference in physical performance, which in turn is used to justify a social hierarchy. She sees sport as constructing 'frail' women, which contributes to the embodiment of women's subordination and the embodiment of assertiveness in men (see also Whitson, 1990). Messner (1994) illustrates this aspect of gendered embodiment nicely with his discussion of throwing a ball 'like a girl'. There is also an element of generational initiation into these gendered bodily practices. Fathers taking sons to watch matches, and encouraging them to play is an important part of the culture of many sports (Fine, 1987). There is much potential for research into the 'socialisation' of body practices in sports such as rugby, with qualitative methods such as ethnography, life histories and focus groups likely to be useful means for such studies.

Sexualities

The sexuality of rugby could provide a productive avenue for research. Homophobia is likely to be mainstream in rugby culture, as it is in most all-male company where heterosexuality is assumed (Sabo, 1994). There may, however, be homoerotic elements to rugby culture. Certainly, nudity can play a major part in rituals such as post-match communal baths or showers and drunken games. White and Vagi's (1990) claim that rugby provides a safe outlet for homosexual desire in an all-male setting warrants further exploration. If there is homoeroticism, there is also considerable ambiguity in such post-match rituals as the 'game', recounted to one of the authors, of putting coins under the foreskin.

Potential research questions arise about how gay men negotiate their identities in a culture where rugby is dominant. Helpful theoretical insights might include Connell's (1995) notion of subordinated masculinity, and the idea of bodily resistance. Another research area might be the kinds of relationships between men that are fostered by the camaraderie of shared enjoyment in watching and playing games such as rugby. The sport may provide a means for emotional closeness between men, perhaps the nearest they get to this kind of relationship with other men.

All the above questions about rugby as training in bodily practices lend themselves to qualitative research and many of them require the detailed intensive observation of cultural practices that qualitative research can offer (Hammersley and Atkinson, 1995). The ethnographic study of rugby clubs provides one of the most fruitful possibilities for qualitative research. Schacht decided early on in his American study to participate in a team. This allowed him privileged access both to the dynamics of the game and the 'play' off the pitch. There are clearly ethical dilemmas involved in such research, some of which he discusses in a recent article (Schacht, 1997). King (1997) attended every Manchester United football match for a season, studying the masculinity of the male football fans. Similar studies in Wales would allow the ethnographer to explore specifically Welsh masculinities. Surprisingly, there has been very little research published to date that critically analyses ways of being a man in Wales, and how these relate to notions of 'Welshness' or 'Britishness'. Boyd's discussion of Scots men in literature begins to do this for another part of the United Kingdom (Boyd, 1994). Thurston's work highlights some Welsh men's understanding of their violence towards those they see as coming from a different country and class (Thurston, 1995). However, perhaps subordinated masculinities within Wales, and within the heartland of rugby, need to be explored as well. Such research might reflect on processes of power and resistance within the gender order.

The potential that participant observation offers for researching rugby as training in bodily practices has already been discussed. A variety of other qualitative methods could be employed, including interviewing, collective case studies and documentary analysis (Denzin and Lincoln, 1994). There is further scope for the analysis of literary, artistic and musical aspects of rugby culture, which might include an examination of the representation of rugby players and supporters in newspapers, magazines, cartoons and songs.

Rugby and social stratification

Having discussed rugby as training in practices for the body, in this section we outline some possible areas for qualitative research into the body and social control, and the complexities of class and gender in the sport and its culture. Rugby in Wales has traditionally been a working class sport when compared with its social base in the rest of the British Isles, where it has been rooted in public (fee-paying) schools. The class status of the sport in Wales requires further exploration, however. There is clearly more to be said about rugby and class in Wales than the rather glib summary that it is a working class sport. For many Welsh people, support for Welsh rugby also connotes class loyalty, especially when playing against England, and many are proud to see the sport as popular culture. However, a visit to the sacred national stadium, Cardiff Arms Park, during an international match reveals the apparent abundance in the crowd of the middle class professional trappings of sheepskin jackets and hipflasks. There has traditionally existed a form of class divide within rugby teams, between working class forwards and 'clever' middle class backs (Smith, 1984), and a superficial inspection of Welsh international players suggests a general shift towards the professional middle classes.

There are several research questions raised by the class status of the players and followers of Welsh rugby, many with connections to theories of the body. Is the toughness of the sport related to the traditional occupational base in industrial South Wales with its emphasis on men's physical labour? If so, is this changing with the evolving job market, and the decline of deep mines in particular? Further, how should we theorise class and sport? Cashmore's overview of the sociology of sport reminds us that some

Marxists have branded sport as just another opiate for the people, whilst Gramscians have concentrated on its teaching of values necessary to capitalism, such as obedience to authority, respect for rules, loyalty, courage and teamwork (Cashmore, 1996). Bourdieu (1978) has provided some preliminary theories of class and sport. He suggests that there is an instrumental relation to the body in working class sport, as opposed to his notion of the body as an end in itself in the sport of the privileged classes. These theoretical perspectives could be explored through qualitative research on the relationships between embodiment and class in Welsh rugby.

Furthermore, to go beyond an analysis based only on class, we need to consider relations between men and women, and relations between men, in the context of rugby's role in Welsh communities. Whitson (1990) describes two types of male hegemony in sport: it is male-dominated, and its social acclaim confirms men's privilege and the subordination of women. To relate this analysis to rugby, Sheard and Dunning (1973) and Schacht (1996) have described the rugby club as a male preserve with a culture of misogyny. Sutton et al (1996) describe how women provide a supportive role in Welsh rugby clubs such as making tea and doing secretarial tasks. Women also provide the necessary childminding and domestic work to allow many men to take part in a team. A thirteen year old boy commented of his Welsh town 'Maesteg is a rugby town so it hasn't got much going for girls' (Sutton et al, 1996, p.232). Hargreaves writes that 'sports compensate working-class men for their subordination at the expense of working-class women' (Hargreaves, 1986, p.215).

For many years feminist writers (e.g. Firestone, 1979; Oakley, 1981) have provided critical analyses of female embodiment in patriarchal societies. More recently social theorists have tried to go beyond these feminist analyses by theorising a different form of social control of women's bodies in the late twentieth century. Turner (1996) argues that the system of patriarchy has collapsed, and has been replaced with what he calls 'patrism'. Turner differentiates between the two systems by defining patriarchy as an objective social structure enforced by the legal and political exclusion of women. Patrism is a system of men's prejudicial beliefs and practices towards women without systematic institutional backing. Qualitative research on rugby could illuminate this and other theoretical debates about the body and gender relations. Some women do participate in rugby culture, of course, by watching games and by playing in women's teams. An empirical study of Welsh rugby with attention to gender relations, using qualitative methods such as semi-structured interviews and observation, would no doubt reveal complexity, tensions and ambiguities. It could potentially contribute to a theoretical model of the embodiment of gender which encompasses such complexity.

Sport plays an important part in the hierarchy of masculinities (Connell, 1990). Rugby can, perhaps, be seen as one resource for the accomplishment of respectable masculinity in Wales. For middle class men, whose class status provides automatic social respectability, involvement in, or even an interest in rugby can signal identification with the powerful male body. For working class men, for whom the status of respectability can be of paramount importance, membership of the rugby club can constitute affiliation to a powerful community institution that stands for pro-social manly values. An example from one of the author's probation experience might help illuminate this.

One crucial significance of crime in working class communities is as a marker of unrespectability: the slide into 'roughness'. Staff in the probation office who lived locally were often horrified when a 'boy' (often very much a man - the presentation of South Walian men as eternally youthful is interesting in itself) from a 'good family' presented himself at the office for a pre-sentence report. From the limited observation of a probation officer, the culture of the village of 'Glan-yr-afon' divides its population into the respectable majority in the private terraced housing, the questionable residents of the small council estate, and the most definitely unrespectable, and marginalised 'Spar boys', so called after the shop outside which they 'hang about'. The Spar boys can be contrasted with the respectable men who play or drink in the rugby club. One court case from the village involved the attack on an apparently speeding car by a respectable local man on his way back from a night in the rugby club. He had presumed the car was being driven by one of the Spar boys. When he realised it was in fact an 'innocent' young woman, he was full of remorse. The perceived respectability of rugby club men, preservers of the community's social order, had no small part to play in that exchange. The physical domination of public spaces in this village by macho young men (Campbell, 1993), sometimes accompanied by admiring young women, seemed to threaten the established hierarchy of the community.

The recent launch in South Wales of an organisation called Rhondda Rugby Challenge, specifically designed to keep young men on the 'straight and narrow', illustrates the popular belief that manly sport can harness young men's aggressive and competitive 'urges' in a pro-social way. The Spar boys of Glan-yr-afon reject the dominant respectable masculinity of the rugby club. They represent Connell's marginalised masculinity (Connell, 1995). Their bodily practices constitute a display of powerful masculinity. Unlike the fuller figures of most rugby club men, they are thin and wiry, and they display an exaggerated machismo in contrast to the often restrained and even reserved machismo of many of the respectable rugby men. The Spar boys' bodies are primed with unsanctioned drugs, whereas the rugby club men will only drink beer. They take risks, whereas the respectable men play it safe. Many of both groups of men do not have jobs, but the Spar boys are constructed as not wanting to work anyway.

The exploration of the cultural aspects of social divisions such as these could be said to require qualitative research methods. In depth community studies have a great deal of potential for researching social stratification, and its reflection in sport and its bodily practices. Two recent studies by anthropologists provide possible models. Wight's work (1995) in central Scotland discusses masculinity and respectability in a working class community, and Dunk's in Ontario (1991) reflects on the place of sport, amongst other things, in a 'working man's town'.

Rugby as embodied national identity

Having looked at the research possibilities for rugby as training in bodily practices, and rugby and social stratification, we now examine the potential for researching the sport's relationship with national identity.

In the 1996 film *Twin Town*, set in Swansea, there is a cameo where several characters freeze and relive a great Welsh rugby victory against Scotland in reverential tones. This is perhaps the moment of the film that most conspicuously sets out to construct an overt agreed Welsh identity. A neighbour of ours recently said that he had helped his grandson invent a story for school homework with the theme of 'Cardiff'. In the story, the dragon (Wales' national emblem) which is sculpted on top of the City Hall, escaped and was running rampage in the city. It took a hero to tame it, and the appropriate hero that our neighbour came up with was Gareth Edwards, the 'legendary' scrum half rugby player. There is potential for sociological work here on how people, both Welsh and non-Welsh, understand 'Welshness' or Welsh identity. How is it represented in imagery? Welshness as men's bodies on the rugby field? Welshness as aggressive masculinity? Body and nation becoming one?

When Roberts (1995) asked residents of a former mining valley the question 'Do you consider yourself Welsh?' the usual reply, he writes, 'was a mundane statement of Welsh national identity as located in rugby competition, communal singing, and (rather less now) the chapels' (p.84). He goes on to dismiss this as merely a 'symbolic shorthand' for 'the reality of identity' (p.84). He is clearly right that there is more to be said about identity than a simple reference to popular local or 'national' images. However, where his analysis can be seen to be lacking is in failing to deconstruct these images that are so commonly cited that they must be seen to have important social meaning as regards identification with imagined communities. Qualitative research methods provide means of exploring and uncovering such meanings behind shared and individual taken-for-granted assumptions and constructions (Schwandt, 1994).

Andrews (1996) claims the rugby-Welshness link was deliberately created at the turn of the century by an industrial bourgeoisie who drew on a selective reading of Celtic history to construct rugby's Welsh roots at a time when high immigration threatened the unity of a potentially disruptive working class. The national anthem, 'Hen Wlad Fy Nhadau', formed part of this invention of tradition. It has become associated with rugby internationals since its first public airing at the famous 1905 Wales v. New Zealand match. For many years the International Days have certainly eclipsed St. David's Day (Wales' patron saint's day), and arguably too the National Eisteddfod (the most significant Welsh language cultural festival) as constituting the most prominent public expression of Welshness, with the singing of the national anthem before the game being the moment of the greatest intensity. This intensity is, of course, both social and embodied. You are expected to sing your Welshness and feel your Welshness in the physical thrill of massed voices. It is emotional patriotism, but not connected with political nationalism. It is perhaps a politically acceptable declaration of difference within the British state. Within Wales, as the McIlvanney quote which opens this paper argues, there is considered to be a 'deeper, more personal bond' between the men of the national rugby team and the 'people'.

National identities may also have other complex relationships with gender and class identities, which are expressed through rugby. Beddoe (1986) has outlined the limited images of Welsh women in our culture and outside. She identifies the Welsh mam, the sexy Welsh woman, the Welsh lady in national costume, the pious Welsh woman and the funny Welsh woman. The dominance of rugby in many communities has not helped women. Andrews writes that in Wales at the turn of the century 'culturally women were little more than passive participants in the national cultures being selectively invested in at that time' (Andrews, 1996, p.52). The debate in the Welsh media in 1995 and 1996 about whether the appropriate Welsh millenium project should be a rugby ground or an opera house mostly centred on the issue of class. The rugby ground was assumed to coincide with working class interests, and the opera house with middle or upper class interests. In all the debate about exclusivity, little concern was expressed about the relative exclusion of women from the leisure activity (rugby) promoted as 'national' and 'genuinely popular' that won the millenium funds. As well as women, other Welsh masculinities and other types of male embodiment are excluded from the popular imagery of national identity which relies so heavily on rugby. There may be some change, however. Whilst the game does not appear to soften and rugby men are still very much 'hard' men, some women are playing too. The Welsh national rugby team is in a long period of decline, but Welsh sportsmen and women are successful in ice-hockey, cricket and athletics. This expansion in Welsh sport may have some impact on imagery of Wales and Welshness and how people identify themselves in relation to it.

Qualitative research which explored national identities, and their relationship with gender and class identities through rugby in Wales could provide an empirical investigation of the theoretical analysis of nationality provided by, for example, Yuval-Davis (1997), and Adamson (1991). Adamson suggests that any analysis of nationalism in Wales must include an explanation of the role of class and the means of production. Yuval-Davis provides a many-layered theory base for studying gender and nationhood. She warns against oversimplifying notions of nationalism, with movements differing widely between each other and within themselves. She suggests that the cultural level is a rich area in which to explore gender and nationhood: 'In this culturalized discourse, gendered bodies and sexuality play pivotal roles as territories, markers and reproducers of the narratives of nations and other collectivities' (p39).

Several qualitative research methods could lend themselves to exploration of these concepts. In-depth interviews, as used in Brian Roberts's study (1995), of a range of Welsh men and women could explore embodied images of Wales, people's understandings of their Welsh identities, and their relation to gender identities and bodily practices. Also, again, images of Welshness in media and popular art, literature and music could be a fruitful source of data. In any attempt to explore the more complex notions of class, gender, sexuality, race and the body which may underly people's individual understandings of 'Welshness' it would be important to undertake a systematic analysis of qualitative data, rather than falling into the trap of using data to provide interesting illustrative examples of pre-formed ideas (Silverman, 1993).

Conclusion

In this paper we have presented some initial thoughts about the complex intersections of class, gender, sexuality, identity and the body in Welsh rugby. We have suggested several avenues for qualitative research, recommending community studies, participant observation, semi-structured interviewing, focus groups and the analysis of written documents and cultural media. Qualitative methods such as these, with their attention to rich detail, process, meaning and context, offer the potential for researchers to get beyond what is taken for granted. They can potentially give greater understanding into relationships between the body and rugby. Turner (1996) has called for the development of a research agenda for the body. This paper has tried to contribute to such an agenda. The social meaning of rugby in Wales is an under-researched area. As we have argued, there are many opportunities for qualitative research into a sport which has been seen as central to Welsh life. Such research could enhance a sociological understanding of the sport as training for bodily practices, its relation to social stratification, and the meaning of rugby in relation to Welsh identities.

Acknowledgements

We would like to thank John Horne, Scott Fleming and Alison Shaw for their helpful advice during the preparation of this chapter.

References

Adamson,D.L. (1991), *Class, Ideology and the Nation. A Theory of Welsh Nationalism*, University of Wales Press, Cardiff.

Adamson, D. and Jones, S. (1996), *The South Wales Valleys: Continuity and Change*, Treforest, University of Glamorgan, Occasional papers in the Regional Research Programme.

Andrews, D. (1996), 'Sport and the masculine hegemony of the modern nation: Welsh rugby, culture and society, 1890-1914' in Nauright, J. and Chandler, T. J. L. (eds) *Making Men: Rugby and Masculine Identity*, Frank Cass, London.

Beddoe, D. (1986), 'Images of Welsh women' in Curtis, T. (ed.) *Wales: The Imagined Nation: Studies in Cultural and National Identity*. Poetry Wales Press, Bridgend.

Bourdieu, P. (1978), 'Sport and social class', *Social Science Information*, 17, 6.
Boyd, S.J. (1994), 'A man's a man: reflections on Scottish masculinity', *Scotlands*, 2.
Cashmore, E. (1996), *Making Sense of Sports* (Second Edition), Routledge, London.
Connell, R.W. (1990), 'An iron man: the body and some contradictions of hegemonic masculinities' in Messner, M. A. and Sabo, D. F. (eds) *Sport, Men and the Gender Order*, Human Kinetics Books, Champaign, Illinois.
Connell, R.W. (1995), *Masculinities*. Polity, Cambridge.
Denzin, N.K. and Lincoln, Y.S.(1994), *Handbook of Qualitative Research*, Sage, London.
Dunk, T.W. (1991), *It's a Working Man's Town: Male Working-Class Culture in Northwestern Ontario.*
Dunning, E. (1986), 'Sport as a male preserve: notes on the social sources of masculine identity and its transformation', *Theory, Culture and Society*, 3, 1.
Dunning, E. and Sheard, K. (1979), *Barbarians, Gentlemen and Players. A Sociological Study of the Development of Rugby Football*, Martin Robertson, Oxford.
Edwards, T. (1997), *Men in the Mirror: Men's Fashion, Masculinity and Consumer Society*. Cassell, London.
Fine, G.A. (1987), *With the Boys: Little League Baseball and Preadolescent Culture*, University of Chicago Press, Chicago.
Firestone, S. (1979), *The Dialectic of Sex: The Case for Feminist Revolution*, Women's Press, London.
Frank, A.W. (1991), 'For a sociology of the body: an analytical review' in Featherstone, M., Hepworth, M. and Turner, B. (eds) *The Body: Social Process and Cultural Theory*, Sage, London.
Hammersley, M. and Atkinson, P. (1995), *Ethnography: Principles in practice*, (Second Edition), Routledge, London.
Hargreaves, J, (1986), *Sport, Power and Culture*, Polity, Cambridge.
Hearn, J. and Collinson, D.L. (1994), 'Theorizing unities and difference between men and between masculinities' in Brod, H. and Kaufman, M. *Theorising Masculinities*, Sage, Newbury Park, CA.
Jukes, A. (1993), *Why Men Hate Women*, Free Association Books, London.
King, A. (1997), 'The Lads: Masculinity and the New Consumption of Football' *Sociology,* May, Vol 31, pp.329-346.
Levi, M. (1995), 'Mascuinities and white-collar crime' in Newburn, T. and Stanko, (eds) ***Just Boys Doing Business***, Routledge, London.

McIlvanney, H. (1995), 'Ieuan enters the kingdom of legends', *Sunday Times*, 11 February, section 2, p.16.

Messner, M. (1994), 'Ah, ya throw like a girl!' in Messner, M.A. and Sabo, D.F. *Sex, Violence and Power in Sports*, The Crossing Press. Freedom, CA.

Morgan, D. (1993), 'You too can have a body like mine: reflections on the male body and masculinities' in Morgan, D. and Scott, S. (eds) *Body Matters: Essays on the Sociology of the Body*, The Falmer Press, London, pp.69-88.

Oakley, A. (1981), *Subject Women*, Martin Robertson, London.

Rabinow, P. (ed.) (1991), *The Foucault Reader*, Penguin, London.

Roberts, B. (1995), 'Welsh identity in a former mining valley: social images and Imagined communities', *Contemporary Wales*, 7, pp. 77-95.

Sabo, D. (1994), 'The politics of homophobia in sport' in Messner, M.A. and Sabo, *Sex, Violence and Power in Sports*, The Crossing Press, Freedom, CA.

Sabo, D. and Jansen, S.C. (1992), 'Images of men in sport media: the social reproduction of gender order' in Craig, S. (ed.) *Men, Masculinity and the Media*, Sage, Newbury Park, CA.

Schacht, S.P. (1996), 'Misogyny on and off the "pitch". The gendered world of male rugby players', *Gender and Society*, 10, 5, pp. 550-565.

Schacht, S.P. (1997), 'Feminist fieldwork in the misogynist setting of the rugby pitch. Temporarily becoming a sylph to survive and personally grow', *Journal of Contemporary Ethnography*, 26, 3, pp.338-363.

Schwandt, T.A. (1994), 'Constructivist, Interpretivist Approaches to Human Inquiry' in Denzin, N.K. and Lincoln, Y.S. (eds) *Handbook of Qualitative Research*, Sage, London, pp.118-137.

Sheard, K. and Dunning, E, (1973), 'The rugby football club as a male preserve', *International Review of Sport Sociology*, 3, 4, pp.5-21.

Silverman, D. (1993), *Interpreting Qualitative Data: Methods for Analysing Talk, Text and Interaction*, Sage, London.

Smith, D. (1984), *Wales! Wales?,* George Allen and Unwin, London.

Smith, D. and Williams, G. (1980), *Fields of Praise. The Official History of the Welsh Rugby Union, 1881-1981*, University of Wales Press, Cardiff.

Sutton, M., Hutson, S. and Thomas, J. (1996), 'The boys have taken over the playground' in Betts, S. (ed.) *Our Daughters' Land. Past and Present*, University of Wales Press, Cardiff.

Turner, B. (1996), *The Body and Society* (Second edition), London, Sage.

Theberge, N. (1991), 'Reflections on the body in the sociology of sport', *Quest*, 43.

Thurston, R (1995), *Men, Masculinities and Violence. A Leverhulme Trust Study*. University of Glamorgan, Pontypridd.

Wacquant, L.J.D. (1995), 'Pugs at work: bodily capital and bodily labour among professional boxers', *Body and Society*, 1, 1, pp.65-93.

West, C. and Zimmerman, D.H. (1987), 'Doing gender', *Gender and Society*, 1, 2.

White, P.G. and Vagi, A.B. (1990), 'Rugby in the British boarding-school system: a feminist psychoanalytic perspective', in Messner, M.A. and Sabo, D. F. (eds) *Sport, Men and the Gender Order*, Human Kinetics Books, Champaign, Illinois.

Whitson, D. (1990), 'Sport in the social construction of masculinity' in Messner, M.A. and Sabo, D.F. (eds) *Sport, Men and the Gender Order*, Human Kinetics Books, Champaign, Illinois.

Wight, D. (1995), *Workers, Not Wasters: Masculine Respectability, Consumption and Unemployment in Central Scotland*, Edinburgh University Press, Edinburgh.

Williams, G (1991), *1905 and All That: Essays on Rugby Football, Sport and Welsh Society*, Gomer, Llandysul.

Yuval-Davis, N. (1997), *Gender and Nation*, Sage, London.

5. 'You need the leotard': revisiting the first PE lesson

Sara Delamont

Introduction

The paper takes its title from a remark made by a PE teacher, Mrs. Dartnell[1], at Melin Court Secondary School, to a group of new first year girls in their initial encounter with secondary PE. The lesson opened with a check of clothing, starting with the leotard, which was deemed essential. Mrs. Dartnell said: 'You need the leotard for gymnastics and dance'.

This paper revisits the double lesson which opened with this ruling, to draw out implications for the collection, analysis and publication of ethnographic research on physical education in the light of the 'literary turn' which has swept through sociology and anthropology in the last decade. The paper is in five sections. First it sets out the theoretical and methodological background to the exercise, then it presents the data, and analyses those data in the light of the theoretical and methodological background.

Methodological background: the literary turn

In 1986 Clifford and Marcus published a seminal collection of papers on the textual production of social anthropology. In this volume the authors became self-consciously reflexive about how anthropologists 'wrote up' their 'findings' for publication: that is, how the texts of the discipline were constructed. Recognising that all disciplines are, at one level, rhetorical in that all arguments have to be framed to convince, or try to convince, the reader, the contributors to Clifford and Marcus began the task of reflecting critically upon the ways in which anthropology had been, and was being written. Clifford and Marcus (1986) is now seen as the landmark volume, but there had been precursors such as Boon (1982) Edmondson (1984) and

Fabian (1983). Since the Clifford and Marcus book there has been a steady growth in analyses of all aspects of sociological and anthropological texts from fieldnotes (Sanjek, 1990, Emerson et al, 1995) to publications (Atkinson, 1990, 1992, 1996). For example, Sanjek (1990) collected a series of papers in which anthropologists reflected upon their use of fieldnotes: how they wrote them, what they wrote, why they were especially private, how they moved from fieldnotes to other varieties of text. As Jackson (1990) argued, fieldnotes were a liminal variety of text, on the borderline between 'the field' and 'home', between 'data' and 'results', between 'private' and 'public' records. Fieldnotes are not a closed, completed, final text: rather they are indeterminate, subject to reading, rereading, coding, recording, interpreting, reinterpreting.

One of the consequences of the literary turn has been the revisiting, or reopening, of ethnographers' accounts and analyses of their fieldwork. Wolf (1992) for example, revisited her fieldnotes, her journal, and a short story she had written while doing fieldwork in a Taiwanese village. Reflecting on those materials Wolf realised:

> that the fieldnotes, the journals and the short story represented quite different versions of what had happened (p.2).

She recognised that all three texts had

> become data, interesting data that should be analysed and shared with my intellectual community in the usual academic format (p.3).

The three texts, drawn from fieldwork in the little village of Peihotien, all concern the mental illness (or spirit possession) of a young mother, in the early 1960s. Wolf (1992) published a fictional account of this event, selections from the fieldnotes taken at the time, and an academic journal article together in one book, which rapidly became a best seller, partly because she uses the three texts as a basis for an argument about feminism, postmodernism, orientalism and the future of anthropology.

Atkinson (1992, 1996) has been inspired by the same debates to revisit his own data on the teaching of surgery in a Scottish medical school. He wrote (1996, p.111):

> It is clear that my own fieldnotes are in no sense complete records of what I observed 'in the field'. They are very partial records. They 'made sense' when they were written, and make

sense now, insofar as I bring to bear my tacit knowledge of those settings, and can evoke general and particular features of them. They also make sense in that I bring to them sociological interests whereby meaning and significance may be read into them.

What now strikes me as I review the notebooks is that I find contrasting possible ways of doing that reading. And we have to bear in mind at this juncture in the argument that in doing the kind of work I am referring to, we are engaged in complex processes of writing and reading. The construction of fieldnotes, diaries and the like, reading and re-reading those documents, writing analytic notes and memos, working papers, theses, journal articles and monographs - these all imply completed processes of textual construction and interpretation.

Atkinson contrasts two ways of reading and analysing fieldnotes. The first, which can be labelled 'traditional' and is embodied in Lofland (1971), depends on breaking the fieldnotes up into small chunks, often physically. The researcher codes small pieces of data, and physically disperses them: by cutting up the written record and filing the separate bits in different shoeboxes, folders or envelopes; or, more commonly today, by separating them electronically into different software files. Lofland's (1971) advice, to make multiple physical copies of the notes, and then cut them up, dispersing the material into *thematic* files was followed by three generations of ethnographers. Noticeably Lofland stressed breaking up the chronological ordering or narrative, in order to create an analytic order, a theorised social scientific account. Since the wide availability of software packages (Tesch, 1990, Weaver and Atkinson, 1994) many ethnographers have used a text analysis program to perform this task: 'tagging' segments of text and gathering cognate chunks together.

Atkinson (1996, pp.113-115) contrasts this traditional method of analysing and writing up fieldwork data with a more holistic approach. As he puts it:

Rather than working on the filed and indexed fragments, I have gone back to the original notebooks. This has proved an interesting exercise in re-reading: [...]. What I find on re-reading is that I am now much less inclined to fragment the notes into relatively small segments. Instead, I am just as interested in reading episodes and passages at greater length,

> with a correspondingly different attitude towards the act of reading, and hence of analysis. Rather than constructing my account like a patchwork quilt, I feel more like working with the whole cloth (115).

In the 'new' analysis, Atkinson presented much longer extracts from his fieldnotes, searched for the surgeons' narratives, and treated these as important elements in the socialisation of medical students. Surgeons engaged in the bedside teaching of medical students routinely produce stories to make pedagogical points.

In his conclusion, Atkinson (1996, p.123) points out that the two strategies of analysis are complementary and he was not praising one and rubbishing the other. Rather he wished to make three methodological (and theoretical) points.

> In the first place, it is important to realise that, just as 'data' are not fixed, so there is no one best way of reading them. On the contrary, there is every advantage in canvassing different approaches. Secondly, there is merit in trying different analytic strategies on the same ethnographic data. We engage too rarely in secondary analyses or meta-analyses of ethnographic materials. There may be much to be learned from such methodological exercises. Third, the exercise forces us to treat our taken-for-granted methods and analyses as problematic. We should not fall into analytic approaches that are employed routinely, mechanistically and uncritically. Given the current popularity of certain computer-based analytic strategies, a constant questioning of our analytic practices is especially important and timely (126).

Theoretical background: the contested body

Frank (1990, 1991) argued that sociology had fallen behind other spheres of academic discourse because sociologists were neglecting to afford 'centrality to the body'. Frank then divided the literature into substantive categories, those of the *talking* bodies, *disciplined* bodies, *sexual* bodies, and *medicalized* bodies. Of these four approaches to the body, it is the disciplined body which is central to the leotard lesson. The 'disciplined body' is an ideal type, based on responses to four issues: other-relatedness, self-relatedness, desire, and control: all deriving from the theories of

Foucault (1979). Frank (1991) argues that the disciplined body describes one style of body use and body-to-object relatedness around these four dimensions. Frank himself illustrates the disciplined body with examples from military drill, holy anorexia in medieval mystics, and professional dance, but in this paper the teachers' plan to create disciplined bodies from classes of twelve year old girls will illustrate the same concept/ideal type.

The four dimensions of the disciplined body need to be briefly explained. First on the dimension of control, the disciplined body is regimented, displaying predictable skills (other types of body are unpredictable, unregimented). On the dimension of desire the body is either lacking or producing desires, and the disciplined body is lacking desire. On the dimension of other-relatedness the disciplined body is focused in upon itself (monadic) not constituted through relations with others (dyadic). The dimension of self-relatedness turns on whether the body dissociates itself from its corporeality, or embraces it, and Frank argues that the disciplined body dissociates itself. Thus the disciplined body is focused on itself, lacks desires, is dissociated from corporeality and is regimented displaying predictable skills. In the leotard lesson we will see the teachers holding up the ideal type of the disciplined body to the class, and it will be analysed in those terms, drawing also on the feminist arguments of Hughes and Witz (1997).

The leotard lesson then

Just as Wolf (1992) felt that the 'madness' of Mrs Tan in Peihotien was a critical incident which crystallised many issues that arise from fieldwork, textual production and indeed anthropology, I had always remembered the 'leotard lesson' for reasons I had never seriously examined. It exemplified for me everything that was depressing about the experiences of girls in the six comprehensives studied for the ORACLE project (Delamont and Galton, 1986) compared to classes observed at St. Luke's, an elite girls' school (Delamont, 1984, 1989). I could recall it, I thought, quite clearly. Inspired by Wolf's (1992) and Atkinson's (1996) return to their data, I decided to revisit the Melin Court material.

The data at the centre of this paper are fieldnotes (and publications deriving from them) taken originally in September 1978 at Melin Court School in Coalthorpe, a city in the north of England. Melin Court was a mixed comprehensive school for pupils aged 12 to 18, studied as part of the ORACLE project (Delamont and Galton, 1986). The leotard lesson was a double period in the girls' changing room which I observed in the first week of the Autumn term. Forty-odd girls from several first year classes were gathered together to be taught by two women PE teachers, Miss Sugnett and Mrs. Dartnell. The equivalent boys were elsewhere with two PE masters probably having 'the same' lesson. Although 'the leotard lesson' has stayed vividly in my mind, only small extracts from it have been published. The original analysis and publication is recapitulated first, and then rendered problematic, before an exploration of the fieldnotes in which the complete event was recorded.

The data from the lesson have been analysed and published only in the disembodied chunks which were the results of normal analytic strategies in the early eighties. In Delamont and Galton (1986) the fieldnotes were used predominantly in a chapter about interfaces between the home and the school. The published extract reads:

> PE teachers explain what clothes are needed for PE. Included is a skirt for hockey and dance. 'If your mum's quite handy at needlework there's no reason why you shouldn't make your own.' Later when they are examining the kit the girls already have, one teacher says to one girl 'Your mum made this?' Girl nods. 'Right, that's fine'. (Delamont and Galton, 1986, p.192).

This brief extract was used to illustrate the ways in which schools explicitly demanded that parents fulfil their duty to send children to school in the correct uniform, but recognised that money could be a problem, and so accepted or welcomed the home-made alternatives to the expensive shop-bought clothing that some girls produced.

Later in the chapter comes a longer extract from the same lesson, used to illustrate several ways in which the girls' current and future family lives were invoked in the school. This reads:

> The girls were told they needed a leotard for dance and gymnastics, plus a short skirt.
>
> If you don't wear a leotard you must buy decent knickers for hockey because there are boys on the top pitch ... Jewellery must all come off for PE except sleepers. One girl says her ring won't come off. She is told that tight rings are dangerous when you get swelling in pregnancy. If they have a ring that is too tight they should get it cut off ... Teacher asks what can go into socks to protect your legs when playing hockey? 'Shin pads', 'foam rubber', 'Miss, newspaper'. 'Yes, borrow your dad's

page three from *The Mirror'* ... (Later) if the girls buy a skirt with an adjustable waist ... it will last them throughout their school life, and when they leave school, if they work in an office and want to play in the badminton team, it will do for that (Delamont and Galton, 1986, p.207).

Noticeably, although the leotard lesson has remained vivid in my mind, relatively little of it was reported in the (long) book. Nothing from it was reported in the three earlier chapters (Delamont, 1983) based on the ethnographic fieldwork, nor in later papers. Although I remember it as a significant, critical lesson, most of the interaction lies unpublished, even unanalysed in the fieldnotes and the 'out of field' diary.

The publications from this fieldwork were all based on the traditional analytic method of taking desegregated snippets of data and assembling them into mosaics which tell stories. Delamont (1983) and Delamont and Galton (1986) presented many small fragments of data from six schools woven into a thematic analysis with chapters on danger, time, movement, formal groupings, informal groups, the interface of home and school, initial encounters, and the pre-transfer programmes. There are also three papers which use the snippet mosaic technique to focus on pretransfer anxieties (Delamont and Galton, 1987), aesthetic activities (Galton and Delamont, 1987) and initial encounters with science (Delamont, Atkinson and Beynon, 1988).

The leotard lesson now

In 1996 I went back to the original fieldnotes, 'out of the field' diary, and list of pseudonyms, and produced the following account of the whole double period modelled on Atkinson (1992). This is presented in full, before an analysis is attempted, but with a commentary on differences between 'the original' and the extracts already quoted. For subsequent convenience I have numbered the paragraphs.

1. The PE lesson took place in the girls' changing room with two teachers, Miss Sugnett and Mrs. Dartnell and the girls from several first year classes. Mrs. Dartnell tells them she got married in the summer, their brothers and sisters may have told them about Miss Verity -'that was my name - now I'm Mrs. Dartnell'.

2. Miss Sugnett and Mrs. Dartnell began the lesson by showing the girls examples of the kit they would need for PE. They held up new garments borrowed from the school shop and explained what they were, their purpose and price. The first garment to be inspected was a leotard. The teachers had two styles to show off. Mrs. Dartnell said 'If you've got one, any colour, that's OK!' If they did not already have a leotard, 'You can buy one from the school shop, in the school blue, they're £2.05 or £2.45 for this style. You need the leotard for gymnastics and dance'. The leotard was the most important garment, the highest priority.

3. The next item is a short skirt and again two styles were passed around, which cost either £2.00 or £4.00. One (the £4.00) was a wrap around style with an adjustable waist, so it would adapt as they grow. Miss Sugnett points out that because the skirt is adjustable, it will last beyond the girls' school lives.

   'When you leave school and work in an office, if you join the badminton club you can wear the skirt to play in.'

   'If your mum's quite handy at needlework, there's no reason why you shouldn't make your own wraparound skirt.'

4. For netball 'you wear the skirt over the leotard with white socks and pumps. For hockey it's blue socks and boots'. The hockey boots cost £2.10 and the socks are 91 pence. A girl asks 'If you don't want to buy hockey boots can you wear black plimsolls?' She is told 'no', shown the 'studs' on the hockey boots, and the need for grip on grass is explained.

5. Miss Sugnett warns: 'If you don't wear a leotard you must buy decent knickers because of the boys on the top field'. Finally there is a white PE blouse (again two styles at £2.50 or £4.00) and a towel. Both teachers stress the crucial matter of naming the kit.

6. The lesson moved on to showers and swimming. For swimming they need a swimsuit. (There was no uniform swimsuit. Girls could wear whatever costume they owned.) The PE teachers keep a record of who has a shower and who goes swimming, when you are 'on period' they put 'P' on the record. If you cannot swim you go to the baths, but tell the swimming master you're 'on period'. The girls were reassured: 'he won't be embarrassed, he's a married man'.

7. When it is cold they can wear a track suit if they have one. The teachers are both in smart track suits. A few girls say they have one at home, they are encouraged to bring it on cold days.

8. No jewellery - at the beginning of the lesson they must put it in the jewellery box - no jewellery to be worn during PE - 'except sleepers'. One girl (ginger hair, high heels) says she 'can't get this ring off - it's too tight to come off'. She has had it on since she was a baby. The teachers say immediately 'tight rings are dangerous'. They talk of how tight rings can cut off the circulation 'when your fingers swell when you're pregnant'. The girls are told to get tight rings cut off, because they are dangerous. Failing that they should use soap to ease them off, or cover them with sticking plaster during PE lessons.

9. The next phase of the lesson was checking the clothing that the girls had brought, and inspecting their feet. Each pupil had to come up when her name was called and show the teachers the particular garment with her name in it. The pupil was then ticked off on a list. Thus each girl brought up her leotard, then every girl brought up her skirt, then her shoes or boots and so on.

10. All but one of the girls has got kit of some kind to be checked, today. They have to show name tags in the kit and have their feet inspected. Nothing happens if they haven't named their kit - just told gently to get it done for next time.

11. The teachers see them in alphabetical order, while inspecting their feet the teachers ask then if they know about athlete's foot and verrucas. Mrs. Dartnell finds a verruca - the girl says it has been 'cured' by a chiropodist. Mrs. Dartnell says: 'it hasn't'. The girl argues 'Miss, the chiropodist cut it out.' The girl is told to go back to the doctor/chiropodist. Mrs. Dartnell finds an odd little toe. Brings them all round to see the verruca - and to see another girl's webbed feet.

12. Mrs. Sugnett tells them in the summer they will have athletics, rounders and tennis, while sometimes in the winter they'll have badminton in the sports hall. (The school has a sports hall for weights, trampoline, badminton, gymnastics and five a side football.)

13. Tricia asks: 'Miss, is it all right to wear a Fred Perry badminton skirt for tennis?'

14. Most are praised for having brought something temporary to do PE in. Miss Sugnett asks what can go into socks to protect legs during hockey? Girls volunteer the following:
'Shin pads'
'Foam rubber'
'Miss, newspaper'
This last gets the cheerful response:
'Yes, borrow your dad's Page Three from *The Mirror*'

15. Typical dialogues between the teachers and a pupil are:
(a) 'Your Mum made this?' (nod) 'Right, that's fine'
(b) 'Got your name in everything?' 'Miss, no'
(c) 'That's a nice little skirt: where did your Mum buy that?'
'Miss, I don't know'.
One girl has brought some shorts instead of the skirt which Miss Sugnett says are fine to start off with, but 'We'd prefer you not to wear just shorts on their own', because girls 'get fatter as you get older and a skirt will cover your Dr. White's better.'

16. Mrs Dartnell asks who has played hockey before (about six girls put their hands up) and netball (all but one put their hands up).

17. The school operates a two week timetable with two double periods for PE in each of the weeks. On a Monday in the double lesson in Week 1, the girls will play netball, in Week 2, hockey. On the other day they will do gymnastics, trampolining, dance or badminton in the hall. So Mondays is an outdoor lesson, the other is indoors. It is not clear to me, from this explanation, when they go swimming.

18. The bell goes. The girls left excited about learning badminton.

19. In retrospect it is immediately striking that I wrote very little for a double lesson that lasted 80 minutes. As Atkinson (1996, p.115) comments on revisiting his old fieldnotes:

In the first place, the notes themselves are very patchy. There must have been a host of more or less implicit decisions which influenced what I noted, and how I did it. Some of the notes are left as 'jottings'- brief notes consisting only of key words, phrases and fragments of conversation. They were scribbled down 'in the field' or immediately afterwards. Others are worked up into 'processed' notes, with more extended reconstructions of scenes, actions and words (cf. Hammersley and Atkinson 1983, pp. 145-161). The extended, polished notes were written up away from 'the field', usually later the same day. The notes are evocative (cf. Lederman 1990). Incomplete though they are, they trigger a variety of memories: with no guarantee, of course, that those 'memories' are faithful reconstructions of what actually occurred. The written record and memory interact to produce new reconstructions of social settings and persons. Some characters can still be 'heard' and conjured up; others remain shadowy. Unnamed individuals make fleeting contributions and are now quite lost to view. In some ways, after the passage of time the notes are alien in some ways. One comes to them 'cold'. Reading them is, however, different from the reported experience of working with someone else's field data (Lutkehaus 1990). For they can still evoke a lived experience.

Immediate contrasts

A comparison between the few snippets published in Delamont and Galton (1986) and the full lesson leads me to reflect, immediately, on some of the points I seem to have missed in the eighties. Until I revisited the leotard lesson I had forgotten that there were two distinct phases: first the display of 'mint', official garments from the school shop and then the inspection of the motley collection of clothing owned by the pupils. In the actual chronological sequence, the contrast is much sharper than I remembered it.

Several noteworthy features of initial encounters (Ball, 1980; Beynon and Atkinson, 1984) are not explicitly recorded in these notes. In Paragraph 9, for example, there is nothing in my notes, but it is clear that this longwinded procedure, which brought each girl up to where the two teachers were sitting six times, to show a garment and be ticked off on a list, *or* confess they did not have a garment and be not ticked off, was one strategy to help the PE teachers learn the girls' names. Unlike many other staff, who could, and did, insist that pupils always sat in the same seat, and even made them sit in alphabetical order, until they had learnt their names, PE staff have to learn to name 'moving' children. I 'knew' this in 1978, but did not comment on it in the notes or the diary - even though other seating/naming strategies were the focus of attention, such as the male craft teachers' practice of marginalising the girls in woodwork, metalwork, and technical drawing rooms (see Delamont, 1990, p.57).

In Paragraphs 5 and 6 I recorded very little of what was said about showers - only noting that the girls had to bring a towel which had their name label on. This, in retrospect, is distinctly odd, given the disquiet about showers which these same girls had revealed in their pre-transfer interviews (Galton and Delamont, 1986) and in the 'urban legend' material (Pugsley *et al.*, 1996) on secondary schooling. Girls facing secondary PE are apprehensive about communal showers, and there are 'atrocity stories' in their folk culture about being spied on while naked by lesbian teachers and being humiliated in various (improbable) ways when without their towel.

Such reflections on the snippets are potentially infinite. Instead of drawing out more and more isolated chunks, I turn now to a different kind of analysis which treats the lesson as a whole, and shows how the two teachers invoke the four dimensions of the disciplined body.

The lessons of the lesson

When the lesson is treated as a whole: an extended lecture and performance by two teachers: the centrality of the disciplined body is readily apparent. Frank's model of the disciplined body is, when the lesson is seen as a whole, clearly visible in the aims that the two teachers set out for the pupils. The four dimensions of control, desire, self-relatedness and other-relatedness, can all be seen in the theory and practice of adolescent girls' school physical education as Mrs Dartnell and Miss Sugnett expound it to their new class. The new lesson is clearly focused on 'those doggedly fleshy, troubling matters of female embodiment' as Hughes and Witz (1997, p.56) characterise them. The leotard lesson displays discourse about four ways in which the adolescent body is to be disciplined (and in which the bodies of the physical education teachers themselves are already disciplined) which are embodiments of the four dimensions outlined by Frank (1991). The four ways in which the body is to be disciplined by physical education at Melin Court are:

A The techniques and skills of the different sports to be learnt at the school.

B The power of the hegemonic gaze of the male and the need for modesty in adolescent females.

C The differentiation of physical education from ordinary school and home life, and the internal differentations between physical education activities.

D The inevitability of the biological processes of the life cycle controlling female behaviours and lives.

These can be related directly to Frank's (1991) four dimension of the disciplined body: control, desire, other-relatedness and self-relatedness, which are illustrated by the four ways in which the teachers outline the future for their pupils. Theme A relates directly to Frank's control dimension, Theme B to desire, Theme C to other-relatedness, and Theme D to self-relatedness. Control (A) can be seen in the teachers' discourse about the regimented, predicable techniques and skills that will be learnt in the physical education curriculum. Desire (B) is manifest in the teachers' talk of male gaze on female bodies, and appropriate female modesty in dress and deportment during physical education. The dimension of relation to others (Theme C) in which the body is focused in upon itself - monadic - is displayed in the discourse around the differentiation of physical education from the rest of school life and life outside school. The internal differentiations within the physical education, which turns on whether the body dissociates itself from its corporeality is apparent in the Theme D discourse by the two teachers.

A. The techniques of the body

The disciplines of the physical education itself are not demonstrated in this lesson, and are only hinted at in the recorded speech and activities. Indeed, the lesson is notable for its seated, static, non-physical character just as many art lessons had less drawing in them than 'academic' classes (Delamont and Galton, 1987). However, the teachers' *talk* foreshadows a range of activities which will produce, or be designed to produce, the regimented, predictable skills Frank (1991) argues are central to the disciplined body. Thus in P2 the teachers mention gymnastics and dance, in P3 badminton, in P4 netball and hockey, and in P6 swimming. Later, in P12, the summer activities of athletics, rounders and tennis are contrasted with badminton, trampolining and gymnastics. (Weight training and football were clearly labelled as boys' activities, and it is clear that I took this so much for granted that I did not even record the sex-typing of sports.) In P14 hockey is again mentioned, and it reappears, with netball, in P16 and 17. The body of the girl who learnt all the physical disciplines associated with these sports, such as the standard raquet strokes of tennis and badminton, the techniques of hockey and netball, the four swimming strokes, the routines of gymnastics and trampolining, and the basics of athletics, would indeed be disciplined.

B. Modesty and the male gaze

Frank (1991) emphasises that a disciplined body has a dimension of desire (whether the body is producing desires or is lacking them). That dimension is manifested in the leotard lesson through talk of modesty and the inappropriate display of female anatomy: that is the hegemonic power of the male gaze: *not* through any *recorded* mention of any desires that the pupils themselves may have. Let us trace male hegemony through the lesson, or rather through the teachers' discourse. In the opening paragraph, Mrs Dartnell tells us she used to be Miss Verity, but that she has got married and taken her husband's name. In paragraph 5 the girls are warned that they must dress modestly in 'decent knickers' or the leotard, because of the gaze of the boys (cf. Mahoney, 1985; Wolpe, 1988; Herbert, 1989). In paragraph 6 the menstrual calendars of the girls are to be scrutinised by not only the female physical education teacher, but also by the man at the swimming pool. In paragraph 14 the father, 'Dad', makes his only appearance - gazing at topless women in his tabloid paper.

C. The differentiation of the physical

Throughout the lesson there is a clear thread of emphasis about the marking off, or setting apart, of the physical education activities, not only from everyday life at home, but from each other by the specialist clothing and equipment. Each activity has its own clothes, which are specially designed for that activity and its location. P2 emphasises the leotard, to be worn on its own, in the gymnasium, a private, female only space, for dance (trampolining?) and gymnastics. In P3 and P4 the leotard becomes a form of underwear, worn with a skirt and blouse (P5) for two outdoor games, netball and hockey. These are differentiated by their footwear, 'pumps' (plimsolls) and white socks for the former, boots with studs and blue socks for hockey. The girls now learn of the existence of grass covered pitches for hockey (P4) swimming has got a swimsuit (P6), a tracksuit is also allowed, (P7) and while these can be the same garments worn at home, for school purposes like the towel (P5), they all have to be named. Additionally, no jewellery is allowed to be seen: it is either removed or covered up. Throughout this catalogue only badminton appears to be related to life outside Melin Court: the girls seemed to anticipate it with excitement (P18), at least one girl has a garment she likes ready (P13), and the teachers enthuse about badminton in the girls' later life (P3). Arguably badminton is the only sporting activity where the posited body relation is dyadic (constituted through relations with others) rather than monadic.

D. Physiology as destiny

Self-relatedness, and hence, corporeality, is the aspect of recent sociological writing on the body which concerns Hughes and Witz (1997). In this lesson, the teachers stress the inevitability of biology/anatomy as destiny, in ways that reflect the patriarchal discourse of female bodies as flawed and limiting. Hughes and Witz (1997) argue that feminism in the first twenty five years after 1945 stepped back from 'women's bodily being' (p.57), while in the poststructuralist era the body was made central to feminism but corporeality was denied. In the leotard lesson the corporeality of female experience is pre-feminist: anatomy is destiny. The young women must deny their corporeality to attain the desired, disciplined body.

From these extended notes the teachers appear fixated on modesty, menstruation, marriage and pregnancy. The lesson opens with the announcement of Mrs Dartnell's marriage, in Paragraph 5 the girls are warned that their underwear will be visible to male pupils when they play hockey. Then in Paragraph 6 menstruation is seen as a reason to avoid swimming, and yet these twelve year old girls are expected to tell a man - who they will only see at the baths, so he is a stranger - that they are 'on period' and reassured that *he* is married. Their embarrassment is not addressed - nor the possibility of using tampons and going swimming anyway (even though this may have been the teachers' plan for the pupils). In Paragraph 8 pregnancy appears, as a time when one's fingers swell. Then in Paragraph 15 we once again get the warnings about disguising underwear and menstruation (again without any mention of tampons as an alternative to bulky 'Dr White's').

Conclusion

A reanalysis of the original fieldnotes has proved to be theoretically productive because a complete, sequential review reveals that there was a Foucauldian dimension to the lesson which was not properly addressed by the former snippet, mosaic technique. The vivid recollection of the lesson as important in the establishment of the gender regime of Melin Court was grounded in the discourse of that lesson. Exercises of this sort are open to various misinterpretations, and they need to be addressed before the more positive conclusions are briefly reaffirmed. The exercise of re-reading fieldnotes (or any other data) in this way is *not* intended to be a Whiggish one: I have not revisited these materials in order to remedy an earlier misunderstanding. My intention has certainly not been to dismiss the first use to which the field data had been put, and so to 'get it right' the second time round. Equally, this is not meant to be a gratuitous act of self-congratulation: I have not undertaken this analysis in order to celebrate how 'insightful' or 'rich' were the original data, or my original and subsequent readings of them.

My positive intentions have been addressed to methodological and substantive issues. Methodologically, it is important to recognize that fieldnotes - and indeed any other ethnographic data - are never fixed or determinate. They are not just inert and cold. They are texts, or other forms of representation, that we create in order to think with. The processes of reflection and analysis are therefore grounded in our active interactions with those materials. There is no single best interpretation of them, nor one single mode of analysis. Analysis is certainly not a mechanical process, constrained by one single orthodoxy. This is not a recipe for arbitrary or whimsical approaches to analysis, which must always remain principled and careful, but a recognition of the constructive dialogue between analyst and data.

A revision of field data in this way can therefore illustrate the possibility of alternative modes of working with the data. A careful reading of this initial encounter between a teacher and the class has shown how fruitful it can be to concentrate on extensive readings, rather than the common strategy of fragmenting field data into smaller and smaller thematic categories and codings. It remains important to reconstruct the shape and structure of social encounters and events - such as the school lesson. In the course of this paper I have developed such a perspective in order to re-trace the internal structure of the lesson as it unfolded. This involves a conscious effort to bracket previous uses to which those data were put, in order to interrogate them afresh.

Such exercises have their methodological value, not least as correctives to any uncritical adoption of analytic prescriptions and formulae. In the last analysis, however, such re-evaluations find their full justification if they raise substantive issues of some significance. Here I have used the field data to draw attention to the pervasiveness of the body in such educational encounters. For many years, however, the social body has remained largely implicit in most educational ethnographies. The embodied nature of educational work, the expressive body of teachers and taught, the disciplined body in the school or classroom regime, the embodied enactment of pedagogic performances - these have all remained part of the taken-for-granted background of educational research until recent years. Retrospective and secondary analyses of ethnographic data can help to rescue and render visible such embodied phenomena.

Notes and acknowledgements

The ESRC funded the original ORACLE project. Full details of all the researchers involved can be found in Delamont and Galton (1986). Marian Garside, Louise Perry and Jackie Swift wordprocessed this paper for me. Article originally published in *Sport, Education and Society* (1997), by Carfax Publishing Limited, 11 New Fetter Lane, London, EC4P 4EE.

1. All names are pseudonyms. A full list of all the schools, teachers and pupils can be found in Delamont and Galton (1986).

References

Atkinson, P.A. (1981), *The Clinical Experience*, Gower, Aldershot.

Atkinson, P.A. (1990), *The Ethnographic Imagination*, Routledge, London.

Atkinson, P.A. (1992), *Reading Ethnographic Texts*, Sage, London.

Atkinson, P. A. (1996), *Sociological Readings and Rereadings*, Gower, Aldershot.

Ball, S. (1980), Initial encounters in the classroom, in P. Woods (ed.) *Pupil Strategies*, Croom Helm, London.

Beynon, J. & Atkinson, P.A. (1984), Pupils as data-gatherers, in S. Delamont (ed.) *Reading on Interaction in the Classroom*, Methuen, London.

Boon, J.A. (1982), *Other Tribes, Other Scribes,* Cambridge University Press, Cambridge.

Clifford, J. & Marcus G.E. (eds) (1986), *Writing Culture*, University of California Press, Berkeley.

Delamont, S. (1983), The ethnography of transfer, in M. Galton & J. Willcocks (eds) *Moving from the Primary Classroom*, Routledge, London.

Delamont, S. (1984), The old girl network, in R.G. Burgess (ed.) *The Research Process in Educational Settings,* Falmer Press, Brighton.

Delamont, S. (1989), *Knowledgable Women*, Routledge, London.

Delamont, S. (1990), *Sex Roles and the School*, Routledge, London.

Delamont, S., Atkinson, P. & Beynon, J. (1988), In the beginning was the Bunsen, *Qualitative Studies in Education* 1,4.

Delamont, S. & Galton, M (1986), *Inside the Secondary Classroom*, Routledge, London.

Delamont, S. & Galton, M. (1987), Anxieties and anticipations, in A. Pollard (ed.) *Children and their Primary Schools,* Falmer, London.

Edmondson, R. (1984), *Rhetoric in Sociology*, Macmillan, London.

Emerson, R.M., Fretz, R.I. & Shaw, L.L (1995), *Writing Ethnographic Fieldnotes*, Chicago University Press, Chicago.

Fabian, J. (1983), *Time and the Other*, Columbia University Press. New York.

Foucault, M. (1979), *Discipline and Punish*, Vintage, New York.

Frank, A. W. (1990), Bringing bodies back in, *Theory, Culture and Society* 7,pp1,131-62.

Frank, A. W. (1991), For a sociology of the body, in M. Featherstone et al., (eds) *The Body*, pp.36-102 Sage, London.

Galton, M. & Delamont, S. (1987), The ORACLE and the muses, in L. Tickle (ed.) *The Arts in Education*. pp34-56, Croom Helm, London.

Hammersley, M. & Atkinson, P.A. (1983), *Ethnography.*, Routledge & Kegan Paul, London.

Hammersley, M & Atkinson, P.A. (1995), *Ethnography*, Routledge, London, 2nd edition.

Herbert C. (1989), *Talking of Silence*, Falmer, London.

Hughes, A. & Witz, A. (1997), Feminism and the matter of bodies, *Body and Society* 3,1, pp.47-59.

Jackson, J.E. (1990), Deja entendu, *Journal of Contemporary Ethnography* 19,8, pp.8-43.

Lederman, R. (1990), Pretexts for ethnography, in R. Sanjek (ed.) *Fieldnotes*, Cornell University Press. Ithaca, N.Y.

Lofland, J. (1971), *Analysing Social Settings*, Wadsworth, Belmont, C.A.

Lofland, J. & Lofland, L. (1984), *Analysing Social Settings*, Wadsworth, Belmont, C.A.

Lutkehaus, N. (1990), Refractions of reality, in R. Sanjek (ed.) *Fieldnotes,* Cornell University Press, Ithaca, NY.

Mahoney, P. (1985), *Schools for the Boys*, Hutchinson, London.

Pugsley, L., Coffey. A. & Delamont, S. (1996), Daps, dykes and five-mile hikes, *Sport, Education and Society*, 1,2.

Sanjek, R. (ed.) (1990), *Fieldnotes*, Cornell University Press, Ithaca, NY.

Tesch, R. (1990), *Qualitative Research*, Falmer, London.

Weaver, A. & Atkinson, P.A. (1994), *Microcomputing and Qualitative Data Analysis*, Avebury, Aldershot.

Wolf, M. (1992), *The Thrice Told Tale*, California University Press, Berkeley.

Wolpe, A.M. (1988), *Within Schools Walls*, Routledge, London.

6. Workplace bullying

Duncan Lewis

Introduction

Many people view bullying as a simple matter of physical violence being perpetrated on a hapless victim, with the act usually being committed in the school playground. But this stereotype does not cover the full range of bullying in society. This chapter draws attention to the various forms of bullying and harassment which are located in the workplace. According to some reports, this kind of bullying is increasing both in frequency and in intensity. Moreover, evidence suggests that the problem often involves bodily considerations. It is true that workplace bullying does not always entail a direct physical assault on the body of the victim, although such cases are not unknown. It can also take the form of verbal abuse, threatening behaviour or the imposition of stressful deadlines and workloads. But even in these more 'subtle' forms of bullying there is a kind of assault on the victim's body. Bullying can be a deeply unpleasant experience which has damaging physical and emotional consequences. Even in milder cases the victims tend to feel that their bodily space is somehow being 'invaded', their bodies are no longer quite their own. For these reasons, workplace bullying poses interesting issues for the sociology of the body.

This chapter has two main aims. First, it attempts to clear away some of the confusion in what is a highly complex area of investigation. Although studies of workplace bullying are growing in number, so far there is little agreement on relevant terms, classifications and explanations. Estimates of the extent of the problem vary widely and are often based on anecdotal or unsystematic evidence. By critically reviewing the existing literature and empirical evidence, this chapter makes a modest contribution to assessing the current state of knowledge. The second aim of the chapter is to demonstrate the value of a qualitative approach to the study of workplace bullying. Much of the evidence in this field is based on quantitative data which are not appropriate for the exploration of the more sensitive aspects of the problem. Qualitative research methods, it is suggested, provide a more useful basis for developing grounded theory.

The chapter starts with an examination of some organisational changes which seem to have exacerbated workplace bullying. It then considers the available quantitative evidence, before proceeding to make a case for qualitative case studies as a particularly helpful way of identifying the underlying meanings of workplace bullying.

The organisational background

The problem of workplace bullying must be placed in the context of major changes which have swept though large UK organisations in the past fifteen or so years. Private and public sector organisations alike have faced major reforms in the way they operate. For example, increased competition has led to a fundamental shift in the normal pattern of work for most employees. The traditional adversarial roles adopted by British managers and trade unions have been eroded by pressures from the market and a growth of 'realism' in employment relations. Furthermore, this period has seen the introduction of new strategies such as downsizing, right-sizing, delayering, multi-skilling, empowerment, team working, flatter structures and shortened career spans. Many organisations were downsized in the late 1980s and early 1990s as a result of the recession and the relentless search for increased workforce flexibility. Initiatives such as downsizing and delayering have obvious consequences for those who are eliminated from the workforce but they also have serious consequences for those left behind, the 'survivors' (Doherty, 1996). It is largely the responsibility of the Human Resource or Personnel department to deal with the various problems of the remaining workforce. The debate over the apparent demise of 'personnel' and the rise in 'human resource management' (HRM) continues to occupy many academics. Some (e.g. Starkey and McKinlay, 1993; Mabey et al, 1993) argue that HRM has replaced personnel, while for others (e.g. Armstrong, 1987; Fowler, 1987; Legge, 1995) the change is merely one of title. But both sides are agreed that a different style of managing people has emerged.

One aspect of this is the devolution of traditional personnel functions to line managers who are increasingly taking on the roles of appraisal, recruitment and selection, training and team development (Legge, 1995). From an organisational perspective this shift of responsibilities might appear sensible, but it puts added pressures on line managers who have to juggle their new found role alongside their conventional duties (Marchington and Wilkinson, 1996). Storey (1995) fears that managers may restrict expenditure on personnel matters in order to stay within their budget limits. In addition, the strain caused by these increased duties may lead to stress, absence and exit.

Alongside the 'new line manager' is the 'new employee', someone who, in terms of HRM ideals, is supposedly empowered, flexible and self-reliant. However, the downsized, flatter organisation also brings with it fears of redundancy, additional workloads, longer hours of work and, for some, a need for 'presenteeism' (a need to work long hours as a way of demonstrating commitment). Sewell and Wilkinson (1992) also suggest that modern team working, a key part of HRM, can lead to oppressive and potentially humiliating forms of surveillance, not just from management but also from peers.

In line with these developments in the workplace, bullying at work has become a well publicised issue (cf. Adams and Crawford, 1992). As Spiers (1996) notes, the increased pressure on managers and their subordinates to reach targets can be considerable and can create a climate in which bullying is inevitable. Moreover, the problem is not confined to Britain. A European dimension has been provided by, among others, Einarssen and Skogstad (1996), Leymann (1990, 1992) and Randall (1997). Other international sources include Australian research (McCarthy and Sheehan, 1996) and American research (Bassman, 1992; Wright and Smye, 1996). Ashforth (1994), a Canadian academic, describes many of the bullying concepts under the banner of 'petty tyranny'.

Researchers have also studied the strategies adopted by organisations to cope with bullying. Some organisations have attempted to provide 'welfare' through the establishment of EAPs (Employee Assistance Programmes), although these are far from widespread. These schemes are intended to help employees cope with domestic problems, stress and drug abuse as well as bullying. But Resch and Schubinski (1996) report that anti-bullying programmes are largely ignored by management unless pressure is brought to bear from public exposure or from trade unions. Moreover, Cummins and Hoggett (1995) suggest that counselling, the 'traditional' personnel approach to combat bullying, may no longer be an effective solution. Rather, counselling, once thought of as progressive and humane, has been 'hijacked' by HRM and used to ensure compliance with narrow managerial objectives.

Quantitative evidence

The previous section suggested that the problem of workplace bullying may have become more prevalent as a result of changing managerial philosophies and work structures. But research into the problem is faced with formidable methodological difficulties. For example, there is little agreement on how bullying should be defined. How does it differ, if at all, from harassment and violence? American researchers tend to favour the term 'abuse', while Europeans prefer the term 'mobbing' and Australian scholars conduct research under the heading 'bullying'. Another problem is the absence of a literature base, which perhaps explains why UK researchers usually have to rely heavily on the pioneering work of Adams and Crawford (1992). The evidence of stress and its impact on employees is well researched and documented (e.g. Earnshaw and Cooper, 1996; Labour Research, 1994) but the evidence of bullying and its effects is less well documented. Moreover, legitimate criticisms can be made of some of the reports which have been published, since they often rest on unsubstantiated claims and slack methodology. For example, a survey (IPD, 1996) by the lead body for the UK Personnel and Training profession, the Institute for Personnel and Development, suggested that one in eight UK workers were victims of bullying. But this figure was released without any supporting evidence. It is clear, then, that UK researchers need to adopt a more rigorous, disciplined methodology for the investigation of bullying in order to lend credibility to their data.

Another feature of the research literature is its heavy reliance on quantitative data. It is the argument of this paper that quantitative research methods need to be supplemented by qualitative techniques in order to provide a comprehensive picture of workplace bullying. But the quantitative evidence is nonetheless valuable, and so this section provides a summary of some of the main results of quantitative research. This evidence has emerged mainly, but not solely, from within the public sector and largely at the initiation of trade unions (who have been marginalised by the modern philosophy of HRM and industrial relations). Particular interest has been displayed by public sector and white collar unions (e.g. MSF, NASUWT, RCN). The studies that follow include Rayner's 1994 study of mature students at Staffordshire University, and two studies involving the nursing profession: a 1995 study of nurses by McMillan for the journal *Nursing Times*, and a 1997 study conducted by the Royal College of Nursing, reported by Cox (1997). Also included is a 1995 study of teachers by the National Association of Schoolmasters and Union of Women Teachers (NASUWT). Together, these studies offer a broad picture of the main sources and types of bullying, as well as the main causes and consequences of this kind of behaviour. Each of the four studies uses a percentage of respondents as the basis for the evidence quoted. This evidence is summarised in the tables below:

Table 1: Source of bullying

Source of Bullying:	*% of respondents affected*
Line Manager, Senior Manager or Supervisor	51% (Cox) 71% (Rayner) 90% (NASUWT) 81% (McMillan)

Table 2: Types of bullying

Bullying Behaviour:	*% of respondents affected*
Work Overloading	41% (Rayner)
Exclusion	52% (Cox)
Set impossible deadlines	41% (NASUWT)
Criticised/Humiliated	42% (Cox); 66.5% (McMillan)
Shouted at in front of colleagues	46% (NASUWT)
Destructive innuendo/sarcasm	57% (NASUWT)
Questioned competence	50%(NASUWT); 55%(McMillan); 33%(Cox)
Abusive language/threats	39% (NASUWT); 25% (Cox, McMillan)
Physical violence	less than 2.5% (NASUWT, McMillan)

Table 3: Causes of bullying

Reasons for Behaviour:	*% of respondents reporting reasons*
Change of manager/Job change	38% (McMillan, NASUWT); 82% (Rayner)
Organisational change	43% (McMillan), 60% (NASUWT)
Change in job responsibilities	32% (McMillan)

Table 4: Consequences of bullying

Consequence of behaviour to victims:	*% of respondents affected*
Loss of confidence/anxiety	75% (McMillan); 75% (NASUWT)
Depression, poor work performance	50% (McMillan)
Loss of appetite, eating disorders, depression, vomiting	25% (Cox)
Left employment	20% (NASUWT), 25% (Rayner)

Note: Organisational changes cited in the NASUWT study were predominantly factors associated with the creation of Grant Maintained schools and post-16 Colleges, both subject to opt-out from local education authority control. In both sectors it was suggested that these changes in status had resulted in new management pressures and subsequent bullying behaviours. The RCN survey also revealed that respondents had 'voted with their feet' (i.e. left the service), although no figures were available.

The major symptoms of bullying appear to fall into two broad categories: emotional and physical. Several symptoms have been identified in each category, although it is important to point out that quite often these symptoms have not been substantiated by hard evidence. The following symptoms (Table 5) have been culled from a broad spectrum of writings from both media, trade union and journal sources, including UNISON, MSF, NASUWT, and the Swedish National Board of Occupational Safety and Health.

Table 5: Symptoms of bullying

Physical Symptoms	*Emotional Symptoms*
nausea, crying, disturbed sleep, loss of appetite, sweating, shaking, palpitations, loss of energy, headaches, stomach/bowel problems, increased dependency on alcohol, caffeine and nicotine, ulcers, skin rashes, irritable bowel syndrome, high blood pressure, various illnesses of organs such as the kidneys	feeling belittled, worry, anxiety, fear, low self esteem, confusion, depression, mood swings, lack of motivation, anger, over-sensitivity, loss of libido, loss of confidence, bursting into tears, contemplating suicide

More rigorous evidence of symptoms is provided by the Swedish authors, Leymann and Gustafsson (1996). They define 'mobbing' as ganging up on someone, bullying or psychological terror. Based on their interviews with three hundred and fifty victims, they identify the following symptoms (Table 6):

Table 6: Symptoms of mobbing

Factor Group	*Symptom*
Group 1 - Cognitive Effects	memory disturbance, concentration difficulties, low spirits, depression, lack of initiative, apathy, irritation, general restlessness, aggression, feeling of insecurity, sensitivity to setbacks.
Group 2 - Psychosomatic Stressors	Nightmares, abdominal pain, diarrhoea, vomiting, feeling of sickness, loss of appetite, lump in throat, crying, feelings of loneliness
Group 3 - Symptoms derived from production of stress hormones	chest pain, sweating, dryness of mouth, heart palpitations, shortness of breath, blood surgings
Group 4 - Symptoms derived from observations made by company health-care physicians	backache, neck pain, muscular pain
Group 5 - Symptoms concerning sleep problems	difficulties falling asleep, early awakening
Group 6 - unclassified	weakness in legs, feebleness
Group 7 - unclassified	fainting, tremor

Adapted from: Leymann & Gustafsson (1996), p.253

Leymann and Gustafsson suggest that Post Traumatic Stress Disorder (PTSD) corresponds with groups 1 and 5 above. But they argue that the victims of mobbing find themselves in both a prolonged stress-creating and a prolonged trauma-creating situation. Instead of a short, acute (and normal) PTSD reaction that can subside after several days or weeks, the reaction of mobbing victims is constantly renewed. The authors liken their study victims to women being raped: 'as long as the perpetrator is free, the woman can be attacked again and again. As long as the mobbed individual does not receive effective support, he or she can, at any time, be torn to pieces again' (Leymann and Gustafsson, 1996, p.273).

This attempt at providing a clear link between the victims of mobbing/bullying and health disorders is not restricted to Scandinavian literature. Randall (1997), a British academic, also classifies the symptoms of bullying under PTSD and also stresses the way victims have persistent re-experience of the trauma. Also, Australian evidence from McCarthy et al (1996) found that thirty four per cent of their respondents (victims of managerial bullying) took an average of fifty days' leave (half of which was sick leave) as a result of the bullying

This summary of quantitative evidence suggests that an important start has been made in documenting the nature and extent of workplace bullying. But there is a great need for further studies to build on the slim knowledge base. Also, it can be argued that there needs to be a shift away from the dominant emphasis on quantitative data. Qualtitative research methods have not been used to any great extent in this field, yet they have great potential for revealing the deeper meanings and experiences of bullying.

Towards qualitative research

The previous section showed that quantitative research has a valuable role in documenting the extent of workplace bullying and in listing its main symptoms and patterns. But quantitative approaches are subject to severe limitations. They are of little help in identifying the subjective meanings and experiences of the people affected by bullying. Yet there is an urgent need to find out how these people view their situations. The study of workplace bullying is still in its early stages, and little is known about the perceptions, motives, reactions and strategies of the people concerned. Qualitative methods are far more useful for the task of exploring these social realities and social constructions. Furthermore, by allowing people to 'speak for themselves' to a large extent, qualitative approaches are less likely to fall into the trap of imposing the researcher's values and reactions on to the situations being studied. Of course, this is not to argue that qualitative methods must replace quantitative analysis. Rather, the argument is that the use of qualitative testimony helps to 'flesh out' the quantitative data.

As a modest step towards the development of a qualitative approach towards workplace bullying, this section presents two selected case studies derived from intensive interviews. These case studies report the experiences of two members of NATFHE in Wales in 1996/7. The evidence presented forms part of a larger Welsh survey of NATFHE members by this author. This ongoing research includes a postal survey of eight hundred and thirty two further and higher education lecturers in Wales, as well as a series of semi-structured interviews with key informants. The research also involves intensive ethnographic work with the victims of bullying and action research with organisations concerned with workplace bullying.

Miss R (further education lecturer)

Miss R had been employed for some twelve years in further education in England before returning to Wales to take up an appointment in a further education establishment in 1992. Miss R enjoyed a successful period of employment within the institution until 1996 when a new department head (subsequently Dean of Faculty) was appointed. Miss R found her workload changing: the courses for which she was initially employed were removed from her timetable and substituted with what Miss R regarded as lower level teaching. She was also required to teach in four different geographical locations, set as far apart as twenty miles. The situation deteriorated further when she was required to teach in three different locations in one day. This had a bad effect on Miss R:

> I got very ill and ended up in hospital with very serious health problems and was in the first instance off work for 6 weeks. I went back too early and didn't really recover.

On return from illness, Miss R asked if her workload could be cut down to reduce her stress levels because she couldn't cope, but this request was turned down by the Dean of Faculty. After this, Miss R continued to miss days off with illness but she found little sympathy:

> the Dean followed up my absences on a couple of Wednesdays when I taught hairdressing. He decided that I was not ill and that I was making all of this up and I was deliberately not going to teach these students because I didn't like them. When I returned to work he called me in and he slammed his fists on the desk telling me I had a warped sense of reality, that I was unprofessional and not fit to be in the job. I got to the point that I took a union rep in every time. It didn't stop him ranting and raving even in front of the union rep, even to the point where

> she stopped the meeting and said "Right I think that's enough". I didn't see the need for that sort of behaviour.
>
> I was basically threatened with a verbal warning and told "Pull your socks up. We don't believe you are ill, we want a consultants report". So I had to get one which I had to pay for. By now if I was slightly ill I didn't push myself, whereas in the past I would have. I just stayed off. He would ring me at home and basically tell me that I'm not that ill - if I can answer the telephone, I can come to work. So when I took days off, I used to unplug the phone or leave the answer phone on and not answer it. I would be hassled all day if I was off.

In Miss R's final year she had to go into hospital for an operation and was told she had to take recuperative time off (an estimated eight to ten weeks of post-operative recovery). The campus manager and personnel specialist went to visit her at home to make sure she was genuinely ill.

> I had to see my GP - I made a decision never to walk through the college doors again. I fell to pieces. My GP said "I will sign you off indefinitely - this stress is making you very ill".

In July the Vice Principal and Director of Personnel invited her to discuss her future with them. She took a union rep.

> I didn't realise how that place had affected me until I went in and began shaking. The union rep had to speak for me. The Vice Principal offered me voluntary redundancy with one week to make my decision. I wanted to leave. I asked for a reference and was offered a bland reference from the Personnel department which is not good enough to get you a job. I was told not to even think about approaching another FE college in the region as my reputation had gone before me.

Miss R reports that her personality and outlook were deeply affected by her experiences:

> In the two years I had been pulled in for all sorts of reasons. I'm now bitter and twisted. There comes a point when you get beaten around by your management team so much that you give up. I felt it was me - (perhaps I am) cantankerous, inflexible

> and resistant to change. My Dean had made a decision as to what I was like as a person regardless of what I was like professionally. I am probably appearing quite paranoid but I don't care any more because I endured years of marginalisation and cruel behaviour and was treated in a despicable manner from the Dean and his personal value judgements. I put this down to his promotion to a position he was incapable of holding. Mentally my behaviour became antagonistic to other staff which is not how I used to be. I became intolerant, arrogant, ignorant and uncooperative in order to protect myself. Because every time I offered something they either rejected it or took it away from me which left me stressed. I did think I was going mad to such an extent that I thought I'm such a bad person I can't even hold down a job.

Miss R. is no longer employed at this institution

Dr. S (higher education lecturer)

Dr S had been employed as a lecturer for four years before encountering workplace problems:

> He (Dean of Faculty) bullied me for the first time over a health and safety issue I had raised with him in a chemistry laboratory. He called me in and had me in tears. I used to think we got on well.

Dr S started to notice the strategies adopted by his superior in order to gain and maintain control:

> On one occasion he met me and suggested we needed to meet to discuss an issue. I offered there and then but he set the time and venue. I have since begun to understand how he had summoned me and how he had psychologically set the scene to be intimidating - I was facing the sun, he was in his big chair and then he started. He was horrendous, incredibly sarcastic, intimidatory and would easily lose his temper. He has even squared up to colleagues, people I think are incredibly passive.

> Colleagues generally put up with him because he can make life incredibly difficult either through horrible timetables or with part time colleagues by not renewing their contracts.

The strain caused by this intimidating atmosphere eventually took its toll on Dr S's physical and mental health:

> It got to the point that I didn't go to any of his meetings for a whole year. The thought of meeting him used to give me migraines and pains across my chest. I built him up to be more frightening than he was. He also used to summon me on a Friday at 4 o'clock for a Monday morning meeting so I would worry about it all weekend.

But gradually Dr S learned to develop avoidance strategies and counter tactics:

> In the early days I was very stupid and would meet him on my own, I have since learnt that he will lie and deny things that I know he had said. Nowadays I only see him as part of my subject team. Interestingly he is now on the defensive and we feel a little more in control.
>
> I think I used to get bullied because I used to answer him back, now I just shut up for an hour. If I saw him in a corridor, I would walk the other way. I simply completely avoided him.
>
> I had thought about taking a union person in with me but I was afraid he would say that I was being paranoid and that we got on really well and make me out to be a fool.

Dr S also built up a social construction of the situation in which, reassuringly, the blame for the problem is firmly attached to his head of department:

> He is well known as a bully by our department, even making colleagues cry. He was known as a bully in his last job. (He) didn't just bully me, he bullied several people in our department. He was just untrained and incompetent to manage people. He can't simply ask for help from someone who is better qualified to help him with a problem - he has to steal

their ideas and make out they are his own. Whenever he was under pressure or anyone made demands of him he would bully people. He would openly bully people in faculty meetings where there would be over 30 of us present. In my observations he has bullied plenty of people.

Such a construction makes it much more likely that people will believe the worst of the bully. This creates an atmosphere where rumours are quickly spread:

> One of my colleagues left a meeting with him and was reported to have had a heart-attack. This was recently and we haven't heard whether this was really a heart attack or some other illness but it can't have helped.

Yet, in spite of the ordeals Dr S has apparently suffered at the hands of his tormentor, he is nevertheless still able to identify some redeeming features:

> Funnily enough, when I was off ill he was very supportive and apparently he is a good family man. Perhaps he's just not very nice to work with. I don't think he handles pressure well and I know he goes home early, quite often with illness.

Dr. S remains in the same institution.

Qualitative research and the body

Workplace bullying is, among other things, an attempt to regulate the body. For example, victims may find their physical mobility constricted by having to work long hours in the office. Alternatively, they may be forced to move around frequently (e.g. Miss R had to travel between distant sites). As a form of social control, bullying also operates through bodily mechanisms (e.g. the deliberate positioning of bodies and furniture gave Dr S's superior a psychological advantage). The resultant bodily stress sometimes makes it difficult for victims to resist bullying (e.g. Dr S's migraines and chest pains discouraged him from attending meetings). The toll on the body can even precipitate bodily symptoms and illnesses which might seem to justify the view that the victim is in some way incompetent or weak.

This chapter has demonstrated, therefore, that workplace bullying is a legitimate topic for the sociology of the body. But it has also argued that qualitative research methods provide valuable insights into the operative mechanisms and processes. Selected case studies, based on interview data, were used to reveal some of the feelings, perceptions and reactions of victims of workplace bullying. These subjective experiences are interesting in themselves, but they also shed light on the *strategies* adopted by bullies and victims (e.g. Miss R and Dr S increasingly resorted to avoidance measures). Moreover, they show that bullying is not a static condition but a *process* which has certain twists and turns. It seems safe, then, to predict that the use of qualitative methods has great potential for increasing our understanding of the problem of workplace bullying.

Conclusions

This chapter has reviewed literature which suggests that workplace bullying is an increasing problem, the increase commonly being attributed to major changes in organisational structures over the past ten or so years. Yet it has to be admitted that the available literature is sparse and, in some cases, highly speculative. Even the more systematic evidence is usually quantitative in nature, largely a matter of counting the frequency of bullying and the main reported causes and consequences. This quantitative evidence is certainly valuable, not least in identifying the wide range of bodily symptoms associated with workplace bullying. It is clear that this type of bullying triggers a great many symptoms of physical and emotional distress.

Nevertheless, quantitative approaches leave relatively unexplored the important subjective dimensions of workplace bullying. These approaches need, therefore, to be supplemented by qualitative investigations of meanings and experiences. This chapter has offered a modest contribution to this enterprise, by showing how case studies derived from interviews can yield rich data which develops our understanding of workplace bullying. Qualitative research in this area is still in its infancy but it seems to have great potential for exploring perceptions, behaviour and strategies. Of course, future researchers will have to exercise critical judgement in handling 'witness testimony', since the accounts of participants are invariably partial and selective. Also, it will be necessary to balance victim accounts with the accounts of perpetrators (or alleged perpetrators). But these are only some of the exciting challenges which lie ahead for qualitative researchers. If qualitative research does little else, it should at least make us more aware of the complexities surrounding workplace bullying and its impact on the emotional and physical well-being of individuals.

References

Adams, A. & Crawford, N. (1992), *Bullying at Work*, Virago, London.

Armstrong, M. (1987), 'Human Resource Management', *Personnel Management,* Vol. 19, no. 8 pp. 32-35.

Ashforth, B. (1994), 'Petty Tyranny in Organizations', *Human Relations,* Vol. 47. no. 7 pp. 55-778.

Bassman, E. (1992), *Abuse in the Workplace*, Quorum Books, Westport.

Cox, C. (1997), 'Bullying in the Workplace', *Nursing Standard,* Vol. 11 no. 35 pp. 22-26.

Cummins, A.M. & Hoggett, P. (1995), 'Counselling in the Enterprise Culture', *British Journal of Guidance and Counselling*, Vol. 23 no.3 pp. 301-312.

Doherty, N. (1996), 'Surviving in an Era of Insecurity', *European Journal of Work and Organizational Psychology,* Vol. 5 no. 4, pp. 471-478.

Earnshaw, J. & Cooper, C. (1996), *Stress and Employer Liability*, Institute of Personnel and Development, London.

Einarssen, S. & Skogstad, A. (1996), 'Bullying at Work', *European Journal of Work and Organisational Psychology*, Vol. 5 no.2.

Fowler, A. (1987), 'When chief executives discover HRM', *Personnel Management,* Vol. 19, no. 1 p. 3.

Institute of Personnel Development, (press release 28.11.96), 'One in Eight UK workers are victims of bullying'.

Labour Research (July 1995), 'Taking the Stress out of Work', pp. 15-16.

Legge, K. (1995), *Human Resource Management - Rhetorics and Realities*, Macmillan, Basingstoke.

Leymann, H. (1990), 'Mobbing and Psychological Terror at Workplaces', *Violence and Victims,* Vol. 5, no. 2 pp. 119-126.

Leymann, H. (1992), *Fran Mobbning till Utslagning: Arbeidslivet*, Publica, Stockholm.

Leymann, H. & Gustafsson, A. (1996), 'Mobbing at Work and the Development of Post-traumatic Stress Disorders', *European Journal of Work and Organizational Psychology,* Vol. 5 no. 2 pp. 251-275.

McCarthy, S. & Sheehan, M.(eds.) (1996), *Bullying: From Backyard to Boardroom,* Millennium Books, Alexandria, NSW.

McMillan, I. (1995), 'Losing Control', *Nursing Times,* Vol. 91 no. 15 pp. 40-43.

Mabey, C. & Salaman, G. (1993), *Strategic Human Resource Management*, Blackwell, Oxford.

Marchington, M. & Wilkinson, A. (1996), *Core Personnel and Development*, Institute of Personnel and Development, London.

MSF (1994), *Bullying at work,* Conference report, London.

MSF (1995), *Bullying at work: how to tackle it*, MSF, Bishop's Stortford.

NASUWT (1996), *No Place To Hide,* NASUWT, Birmingham.

Randall, P. (1997), *Adult Bullying: perpetrators and victims*, Routledge, London.

Rayner, C. (1995), 'The Incidence of Workplace Bullying', paper presented at Bruce Burns Memorial Trust Conference, Birmingham.

Resch, M. & Schubinski, M. (1996), 'Mobbing: Prevention and Management in Organizations', *European Journal of Work and Organizational Psychologist,* Vol.5 no.2 pp. 295-307.

Sewell, G. & Wilkinson, B. (1992), 'Empowerment or Emasculation?' in P. Blyton & P. Turnbull (eds): Reassessing Human Resource Management, Sage, London.

Spiers, C. (1996), 'Bullying at work' *Training Officer,* Vol.32 no.8 pp. 236-238.

Starkey, K. & McKinlay, A. (1993), *Strategy and the Human Resource*, Blackwell, Oxford.

Storey, J. (ed.), (1995), *Human Resource Management*, Routledge, London.

Swedish National Board of Occupational Safety and Health (1993), *Victimisation at Work.*

Wright, L. & Smye, M. (1996) *Corporate Abuse,* Simon & Schuster, New York.

7. Power, control and the gendered body

Emma Wincup

Introduction

Within traditional sociology, the body has often been treated as an 'absent presence' (Shilling 1993, p.9). Historically, the discipline has rarely focused on the body as an area of investigation in its own right, yet its concern with the structure and functioning of societies has inevitably led to an analysis of some aspects of human embodiment. In the main, individuals have been treated as disembodied decision-making agents (Featherstone et al, 1991). However, increasingly over the past decade, academic sociology has begun to recognise the centrality of the body for a sociological understanding of human life and social interaction. To date, sociologists have been predominantly concerned with developing theoretical analyses of the body (Falk, 1994; Scott and Morgan, 1993; Shilling, 1993; Turner, 1992). A key issue discussed within this literature is the ways in which individuals are able to control their bodies and at the same time have them controlled by others. This is a central theme of this chapter.

The development of theorizing around the body and embodiment has been to some extent inspired by the rise of second wave feminism and the subsequent feminist analyses of the multiple ways in which women's bodies are implicated in social relations of inequality and women's oppression (Davis, 1997). Feminist theories have brought the body in to academic conceptualisations of patriarchy (Firestone, 1971; Rich, 1981). Additionally, feminist research has highlighted the commodification of women's bodies (Russell, 1993; Wolf, 1990) and the ways in which the discourses of law and medicine have allowed men to increase their control over women's bodies and their lives (Oakley, 1993; Smart, 1992). Moreover, at a political level feminist activists have sought to reclaim women's bodies from male abuse and oppression. The insights offered by feminist perspectives have impacted upon the sociology of the body and embodiment to some degree, although there is scope for a more detailed gender analysis within the sociology of the body. As Shilling (1993, p.204) argues, 'the body is centrally implicated in questions of self-identity, the construction and maintenance of social inequalities, and the constitution and development of societies'. Whilst agreeing with the centrality of the body in social life and interaction, feminists have added a further dimension by suggesting that gender is an essential category of analysis for understanding human embodiment. Clearly, there is some theoretical consensus between the sociology of the body and feminist perspectives. However, it is important to acknowledge that a diversity of theoretical perspectives constitute both the sociology of the body (Shilling, 1993) and feminism (Tong, 1989). This provides scope for a lively debate about the gendered body, as well as wide-ranging empirical research.

This chapter draws upon qualitative research on the experiences of women awaiting trial in bail hostels. The data gathered is used to explore and illustrate the importance of a gendered analysis of the body for an understanding of the ways in which women cope with the stresses and problems shaping their daily lives. In addition, the chapter reflects upon the use of qualitative research techniques to develop an appreciation of women's lives, and particularly the themes of power, control and the gendered body.

Listening to women's stories

One of the main characteristics of qualitative research is that it allows empathic understanding through the collection of rich and detailed data about individual lives. The analysis here derives from semi-structured interviews with fifteen women residents and fifteen female hostel staff in three bail hostels (Victoria House, Carlton House, North Street Hostel), supplemented by ethnographic observation. This form of interviewing straddles the divide between what Hammersley and Atkinson (1995) describe as 'standardized' and 'reflexive' interviewing. This approach provides an opportunity for women to add their own frame of reference, but also allows interviewers to ask questions which they feel are important to cover. Questions are open-ended and need not be asked in the same order. The interview is not rigidly constrained by an interview schedule, but the interview does have a clear agenda and the interviewer retains some control over the interaction. This makes it different from a conversation, although its informal style makes it similar to a conversation in many ways. In practice, the women interviewed for this study (particularly the hostel residents) shared with me deeply personal and vivid narratives about their lives. The rich accounts offered by the women provide a strong basis for a sociological analysis of the gendered nature of experience and the importance of the body and embodiment in women's lives. Detailed descriptions of three of the women residents follow. The women, like the hostels referred to, are identified only by pseudonyms. This strategy allows the complexity of the lives of the women interviewed to be portrayed, whilst at the same time protecting the confidentiality of those who agreed to participate.

Clare

Clare is in her late thirties and charged with criminal damage, attempted burglary and breach of bail. For a number of years, she worked as a care assistant for people with learning difficulties. Following a serious attack at work, she had a nervous breakdown and was forced to retire from work on medical grounds. She spent six months in a psychiatric hospital and is still undergoing treatment as an outpatient. She is dependent on prescribed medication. In the past, she has harmed herself and attempted to commit suicide. She maintains her innocence and is angry that she has been moved away from her home town. Cut off from the support she had at home from the local psychiatric team and her family, coupled with the additional anxiety of waiting for trial, she is finding it increasingly difficult to cope and fears she will become ill again and attempt to take her own life.

Ruth

Ruth is charged with theft and breach of probation. Despite only being in her early twenties, she has been convicted of property and violent offences in the past. Before coming into the hostel, she had been sleeping on a series of friends' floors and was unemployed. She has been taking drugs since she was thirteen: cannabis, speed, ecstasy and rock. She also drinks heavily and during her stay in the hostel harmed herself to such an extent that she was taken to the accident and emergency department of the nearby hospital. She describes herself as 'screwed up' and notes how she is easily influenced by who she terms the 'wrong' people. Despite her future hope to continue with her education and perhaps set up her own business, she is pessimistic about the likelihood of giving up substance use and offending in the future.

Judith

Judith is in her early twenties and charged with burglary and breach of bail. She has two young children who she cares for alone. Her previous partners, the fathers of her children, have been violent towards her. Her use of drugs and alcohol in the past has often had a number of negative consequences, leading to her involvement in crime and damaging her health through aggravating her asthma and bringing on anxiety attacks. She has managed to give up illegal drugs and alcohol and is committed to staying off them. She also has a history of depression and now finds it difficult to deal with the stress of waiting for trial. As a result, she sought medical advice and was prescribed anti-depressants.

Common problems and coping strategies

The stories above illustrate how women awaiting trial are a diverse group in terms of background, experiences, personalities and current circumstances. However, common themes appear in the varied accounts of the fifteen women awaiting trial interviewed. These included being charged with a criminal offence, low self-esteem, and the development of 'coping strategies' in response to the difficulties that stem from their socio-economic position in a patriarchal society. Such difficulties include poverty, homelessness, unemployment, experiences of abuse (emotional, physical and sexual) and sole responsibility for the care of dependants. The term 'coping strategies' refers to the ways in which women manage the realities of their lives, a term of reference implied in the women's' accounts but not explicitly referred to by the women themselves. The women varied in the types of coping strategies they adopted. Many used substances including illicit drugs, alcohol, prescribed medication and food. A small number engaged in self-harm. Hence, as the accounts of Clare, Ruth and Judith illustrate, women awaiting trial vary in terms of the types of problems they are experiencing and their responses to these problems; yet a recurrent theme is the way in which women's bodies are used in responding to problems at an individual level which stem from their position in society. Whilst appearing as a positive strategy in the short-term to promote well-being, the search for power and control at the level of the body is ultimately flawed in the long term. For individual women, the use of substances exposes them to the surveillance and control of individuals and agencies such as criminal justice professionals, therapists, counsellors, social workers and psychiatrists. There are also implications for women in general. Responding to social problems in isolation through individualized rather than collective means seeks to depoliticize the issues affecting all women. The consequences of the search of individual women for power and control through the body can be illustrated through an analysis of the diversity of coping strategies adopted, dealing first with women's use of substances and secondly, their use of self-harm techniques.

'Abusing' women

Increasingly, there has been recognition amongst academics and health and social care practitioners that women are engaged in substance use, involving both illicit and licit substances. However, analyses often focus on women's use of particular substances thus glossing over the common aspects which characterize women's use of all substances. There are some important exceptions. Doyal (1995) draws parallels between women's use of a diversity of legal substances as part of her analysis of the relationship between gender and the political economy of health. She argues that millions of women consume legal and potentially hazardous substances in an attempt to sustain themselves. Ettorre (1992) adopts a similar position. She offers a feminist analysis of women's use of both legal and illegal substances which develops links between women's dependency of 'the subordinate kind' and women's dependency of 'the addiction kind'. Like Doyal, Ettorre emphasises women's use of substances as intricately connected to the search for pleasure and well-being, yet Ettorre offers a more explicit view that women's search for pleasure is also connected with a search for autonomy and empowerment. The discussion which follows examines women's use of different substances: firstly, illegal drugs and alcohol, secondly, prescribed medication and finally, food. Common themes will be emphasised and the compatibility between the research findings and the theoretical position offered by Ettorre discussed.

Illegal dugs and alcohol

Traditional explanations of women's use of illegal drugs and alcohol have often employed a deviance model to explain women's use of these substances. The emphasis of such models has been upon individual pathology, thus creating an image of the female substance user as emotionally unstable, weak, dependent and passive (Friedman and Alicea, 1995; Taylor, 1993). Neglected from this analysis is an understanding of the role of social, economic and cultural factors in women's lives. Hence, as Marsh (1982) illustrates, the public issues of women's lives are manifested most painfully as the private troubles of individual drug users. However, there are important alternative explanations. Ettorre (1992) argues that women's use of substances can be viewed as a maladaptive response to deal with life stresses, and in this way individuals are viewed as active agents who are trying to cope with their lives. Others have suggested a similar view. For example, Carlen (1983) argues that women imprisoned in Cornton Vale in Scotland had learned that alcohol could temporarily deaden the pain caused by difficulties in their domestic lives, primarily slum housing and violent men.

Drawing on their experiences of working with drug and alcohol users on a regular basis, the hostel staff interviewed also offered gender-specific explanations relating to women's lives, particularly women's vulnerability to male violence.

> But drugs and alcohol are not the problem. There is a problem why they are on drugs or have a drug problem: sexual violence, physical violence, emotional abuse. (Hostel support worker)

> The initial problem presented is the drug or alcohol use which has often brought them into the situation, but underneath that we are often dealing with people's past lives, which I presume they are trying to mask through drug use. The main issues in that are abuse during childhood into their adult lives, parent's violence, sexual abuse, women who have spent a lot of time in care. (Hostel manager)

These quotations provide an illustration of two important aspects of the research findings. Firstly, the comments of the two hostel workers strongly suggest that women's use of substances can be interpreted in a political way, stressing the interface between the agency of women and the constraints they face in a patriarchal social order. Women's use of substances are thus linked with patriarchal pain and 'the distressing ordeals which women experience both publicly and privately in the gendered system of domination' (Ettorre, 1992, p.153). Secondly, the two hostel workers point to the ways in which the pathways into drug use are gendered. This has important parallels with the work of Binion (1982). She argues that women's drug use is intricately connected to interpersonal problems experienced within the family, especially during adolescence. In contrast, she suggests that men's pathways into drug use relate more to difficulties with external societal forces such as school, poverty and street life. This argument can be criticised for offering an essentialist position, denying the differences and inequalities which exist between women shaped by social factors such as age, ethnicity, social class and sexuality. Nonetheless, it emphasises the need for a gender analysis of substance use rooted in the identity and consciousness of women substance users.

Listening to the stories of the women hostel residents who used illegal drugs or who defined themselves as heavy drinkers, an important theme was that they found it difficult to articulate the reasons behind their use of drugs and alcohol, although they saw clear links between their use of substances and their offending behaviour. Often, they gave vague explanations for their entry into substance use. For example, Siobhan, a heroin and crack user for a period of ten years, commented 'I don't know how I got involved. I was just very young and very impressionable'. Margaret, a former amphetamine user, offered a similarly imprecise reason: 'I don't know. I was with someone at the time and she was on them and so I went along with her'. For both Siobhan and Margaret, it was easier for them to explain why they continued to use illegal drugs. For both, it was not only the addictive nature of the drug they were taking, but also because of the central position that illegal drug use occupied in their different networks. Margaret was unemployed, staying temporarily with friends who were drug users, and struggling to bring up her son alone. Siobhan had a successful career which often involved her travelling abroad, but she was struggling to combine this with motherhood. Both lifestyles exposed them to the availability of drugs, social networks of drug users and ongoing temptation.

From the accounts of Siobhan and Margaret, it appears that women's use of substances can be strongly related to their position in society. Neither of these women had experienced abuse. However, a high percentage of women who are accommodated in bail hostels have suffered abusive experiences (nine out of the fifteen residents interviewed in this research). As indicated earlier in this chapter, many of the staff in all three hostels felt this to be one of the principal reasons behind women's use of drugs and alcohol. They noted how during the process of coming off these substances, emotions return to the fore. The impact of earlier experiences is thus presented to hostel staff as a crucial issue for which women require significant support. Access to counselling is limited and the process of change long and challenging. Hence, many of the women resort to alternative coping strategies, frequently the use of prescribed medication.

Prescribed medication

In common with many women in general, women awaiting trial used minor tranquillisers to enable them to cope. Whilst there has been a reported decrease in the consumption of minor tranquillisers since the 1980s, the number of people taking them remains high and women are over-represented among the recipients of minor tranquillisers (Doyal, 1995). Researchers have argued that such medication is used as a means of social control to keep women docile and passive. The widespread use of medication in penal establishments would seem to suggest that they have this potential (Sim, 1990). However, qualitative research has challenged the notion that women taking tranquillisers are passive victims (Gabe and Thorogood, 1986). Rather the research has illustrated how women use them as an active strategy to sustain themselves, weighing up the risks and benefits of this prescribed drug use. Many of the women interviewed had used tranquillisers in the past, or were using them while in the hostel, to cope with the anxiety of waiting for trial. All showed concern about taking them and preferred not to, but felt this was the only way in which they could deal with difficult periods in their lives. Often they had high expectations about what they felt the medication could do, as a hostel support worker described:

> People have such emotional baggage that they are often expecting doctors to work miracles, and go to the doctors and hope they will prescribe something to make them feel better, and that isn't going to happen.

Hence, at best, women's use of tranquillisers alleviates the pain in the short-term but the underlying damaging situation remains. For many women, minor tranquillisers could not help them to deal with the traumatic experiences they had experienced and often continued to experience.

> I'm not coping. I keep having anxiety attacks. I'm very low ... I don't like taking tablets ... I take them to level them out so I can cope but it's not working ... I like to control everything about myself, to be in control of my life and at the moment I don't have that control and it is hard to cope. (Kelly)

Kelly's experiences are similar to many others. Whilst prescribed medication, in common with illegal drugs and alcohol, may help to promote well-being, this is only a temporary solution. The problems behind women's use of substances remain unchanged, and possibly exacerbated. Similar arguments can be made about women's use of food

Women's use of food

Feminist theorists have challenged medical models which portray eating disorders as individual diseases. As Cline (1990) argues, women's use of food and eating disorders can be viewed as an extreme, but orderly, response to a disorderly world. In their struggle for control, women are unable to integrate the powerful and controlling part of the self, and therefore seek power and control in an indirect and self-destructive way with great implications for health. This keeps women's anger private. Moreover, the assertion of control over the body in this way can lead to others taking control over women's bodies. For example, women who experience eating disorders may then be subject to the control of health care professionals, counsellors and therapists. Drawing on her research on anorexia, Lawrence (1987) terms this the 'control paradox'.

Many women in the three hostels may have used food as an attempt to promote well-being and sometimes to seek power and control. Feminist research has demonstrated the symbolic value of food for women (Cline, 1990; Lupton, 1996). As Cline notes, food for women is 'more than mere nutrients. It has become a repository for a million meanings' (1990, p.2). For women, food is intricately connected with serving others, fulfilling emotional needs and their body image, yet it can also become a rhetoric of protest. A recent study of women's imprisonment (Smith, 1996) outlined the centrality of food as a strategy of rebellion and resistance. From the women's accounts of their lives and informal discussions, only one woman (Melanie) appeared to use food in this way. She could be described as 'anorexic', routinely denying herself of her daily sustenance 'as a technology of self-control and purification' (Lupton, 1996, p.133) in order to 'obliterate every human feeling of pain, fatigue, sexual desire, and hunger ... to be master of oneself' (Bell, 1985, p.20). However, as MacSween (1993, preface) argues, as a strategy of resistance, anorexia ultimately becomes its own prison because 'it seeks to do individually what can only be done collectively - to challenge the construction and control of women's bodies'.

Given the high numbers of women who experience eating disorders (Wolf, 1990), often without others knowing, many more women may have turned to food to manage their anger. Ideally, further data should have been collected on this emerging theme which only became apparent in the later stages of the fieldwork. This is a potential area for future research.

Women and substance use: recurring themes

This analysis of women's use of different substances (illegal drugs, alcohol, prescribed medication and food) has revealed a number of recurring themes, primarily the way in which the search for power and control articulated at the level of the body produces contradictory effects. Whilst important as strategies to deal with the difficulties women face in their daily lives, they fail to manage the underlying causes of the substance use. Consequently, the damaging situation may be perpetuated and additional problems introduced such as health problems or involvement in crime. Paradoxically, in their search for individual power and control through the body, women ultimately become subjected to even greater surveillance, regulation and control. These themes are also important to the analysis of women's use of self-harm techniques.

'Harming' women

The flexibility of semi-structured interviews, as used in this research, are that they allow issues such as self-harm to be discussed which were initially not the subject of explicit questions. Self-harm refers to acts of deliberate self-injury and includes behaviours such as cutting, scratching, hitting head or limbs against a wall or floor, and swallowing sharp or dangerous objects or substances. Within the literature on women's imprisonment, the use of self-harm techniques as a coping strategy has been well-documented (Casale, 1989; Coid et al, 1990; Liebling, 1992). In the first hostel studied (Victoria House), self-harm did not appear to be a significant issue. However, as the hostel manager explained, this reflected the population within the hostel at the time:

> When I first arrived in the hostel we had a number of women who were threatening suicide or who were self-harming. It actually hasn't happened for a while. It is something that there is always the potential for because a number of women in the past have self-harmed.

In contrast, the hostel manager at the next hostel studied, Carlton House, remarked:

> If you think about the number of times I've been to the hospital accident and emergency department. Hundred of times I've been there. It's amazing with accidents, or cutting up normally.

Two of the women interviewed described how they sometimes engaged in self-harm behaviour. Ruth stated 'I was in hospital the other week. You get aggravated quickly here. People just piss you off'. For Ruth, self-harm was primarily a way of responding to the tensions and frustrations of hostel life. Clare also used self-harm techniques as a coping strategy for the emotional consequences of a traumatic event she had experienced in the past. She commented, 'I can self-harm quite easily. I've done it for two years since I was attacked at work'. Both Ruth and Clare's explanations for harming themselves mesh with the available literature on self-harm. Coid et al (1992) suggest that self-harm may be a symbolic gesture, a symptom relief mechanism, or a response to external stresses. However, such explanations tend to downgrade women's agency and view self-harm as, at best, a maladaptive response to life's stresses, and at worst, attention-seeking behaviour. Moreover, through focusing on psychiatric explanations, the tendency to 'medicalize' women's problems and their criminality continues (Carlen, 1983; Dobash et al, 1986; Sim, 1990). Others have seen self-harm more explicitly as a coping strategy through which women seek power and control.

> The woman may cope with feelings of powerlessness by dissociating, or psychologically separating herself from her body, a tactic often used to survive the actual abuse during childhood. Self-harm may be a desire to reconnect with one's body - a desire to ensure that one can feel. In this sense it is a life-preserving measure.
> (Pollack, 1993, p.59, quoted in Faith, 1993).

In common with women's use of substances, women's search for power and control through self-harm of the body ultimately leads to increased control by others (e.g. medical professionals) over their lives. Whilst providing a means to obtain relief from distress in the short-term, the consequences for both physical and emotional health are severe. For example, there is a risk of death even if suicide was not the initial intention, and the reasons underpinning the decision to harm themselves remain in existence, unchallenged and unconfronted.

So far in this chapter, the empirical data collected on women's coping strategies and the body has been discussed. This data was collected using qualitative research techniques. The discussion now turns to an exploration of the use of qualitative methods for studying the gendered body.

Methodological reflections

There is not scope within this chapter for a detailed exploration of all the methodological issues which arise during a qualitative research project of this type (see Wincup, 1997). Instead, this reflexive discussion will explore the centrality of emotions in the research process. The role of emotions appears to be an important aspect of the debate about the use of qualitative methods. As others (e.g. Carter and Delamont, 1996) have noted, researching individuals who are experiencing distress, like the women in this chapter, raises interesting issues for both the interviewees who tell their stories and the researcher who listens. The discussion will initially focus on my experiences as an embodied researcher researching women's bodies and embodiment; in particular, my experiences of conflicting bodily emotions during the research.

Several qualitative researchers (e.g. Hammersley and Atkinson, 1995) have emphasised the need to adopt a reflexive approach when conducting research. In recent years this has resulted in the publication of edited collections on the practicalities of social science research written in a confessional style (Bell and Newby, 1977; Bell and Roberts, 1984; Roberts, 1981; Hobbs and May, 1993). The accounts of the researchers have included commentaries on their early days in the field, research roles, ethical dilemmas and experiences of leaving the research setting. However, a neglected dimension of these methodological reflections is the role of emotions.

The fieldwork proved to be a distressing experience for me. Through interviews, I heard stories of domestic violence, poverty, drug and alcohol dependency and abusive childhood experiences and learnt something of the difficulties of waiting for trial. Through observation, I saw first hand the impact of drugs and alcohol abuse, women returning with injuries caused by violence, and the depression, anxiety and anger which flow from waiting for trial. A particularly distressing experience for me was when a woman approached me and held in front of me her self-mutilated wrists. The goal of objectivity was not one I aspired to and certainly not one I could maintain. Coping with the emotional aspects of the research proved difficult. Like Cannon (1992) who studied the experiences of women living with and dying from breast cancer, fieldwork in stressful and emotionally charged situations impacted greatly on my life. I was not prepared for the emotional involvement it would entail or the lasting effect it would have on my life, exposing me to instances of abuse against women, the ways in which substance use can change an individual's life and stories of extreme poverty. Practitioners who confront these issues on a day-to-day basis receive, at least in theory, support in the form of supervision and staff meetings. This was an issue explored in interviews with hostel staff. However, as a researcher I did not have this support and used instead the safety valves suggested by Glesne and Peshkin (1992): taking a break, strong words in a fieldwork diary, and becoming involved in other research activities such as reading. Largely these could be described as 'sticky plaster' techniques, means of hiding rather than confronting the issues presented. They are no substitute for discussing feelings associated with fieldwork with other researchers. However, as May (1993) notes, feelings are equated with weakness and remain hidden and unarticulated in the qualitative research process.

Participating in the research was also an emotionally charged experience for the women residents who agreed to be interviewed. The women showed a diversity of emotions when telling their stories. Some became upset and began to cry, whilst others talked in an angry way about their experiences. Others appeared not to show any emotions at all. The interviews may have been empowering, an opportunity for the women to articulate their experiences in the hope that it might lead to change; or they may have been cathartic, providing an outlet for individuals to off-load. More simply, they may have provided women with an opportunity to talk about their experiences to another interested individual. I tried to convince myself of these benefits of the research. However, this had to be reconciled with a very real fear that in some ways I had caused harm, dredging up painful memories for women already experiencing a difficult period in their lives: was I contributing to the difficulties already experienced by vulnerable and marginalized women? It was certainly not my intention, but I could not rule this out as an unintended consequence of the research. This ethical dilemma led to much anxiety on my part.

At the design stages of the research, I had chosen methods which I felt to be compatible with the central agenda of feminist social science and scholarship. Feminist concerns with equality, reflexivity, establishing rapport and empathy informed the design of the research. Stacey's (1988) eagerness for a 'hands-on', 'face-to-face research experience' compatible with feminist principles' was shared by myself. However, like Stacey, I became increasingly concerned about this compatibility. I felt my presence amongst women, described by hostel staff as 'in crisis', to be intrusive and potentially exploitative. This feeling has been described by other researchers. As Glesne and Peshkin (1992, p.112) write

> Questions of exploitation ... tend to arise as you become immersed in research and begin to rejoice in the richness of what you are learning. You are thankful, but instead of simply appreciating the gift, you may feel guilty for how much you are receiving and how little you are giving in return.

Asking myself the question of who benefits, I felt that ultimately I was the one to benefit from the research, often resulting in feelings of guilt. Perhaps this feeling was heightened because I was very aware of how the research relationship with women residents was inevitably an unequal one. However, what has to be acknowledged is that the research participants did have choices about taking part in the research, and when answering questions had choices about how much detail to give. Researchers also have to request and negotiate access (Hammersley, 1992). This qualifies Stacey's (1988, p.23) view that 'elements of inequality, exploitation and even betrayal are endemic to ethnography', placing participants at greater risk of manipulation in order for the researcher to create a research product. Crucially, a reflexive approach is required to consider how to present findings which reflect and represent women's experiences.

Despite these dilemmas, I still feel that a qualitative approach which combined semi-structured interviews and ethnographic observation was an appropriate approach to the development of an understanding of the lives of women awaiting trial. Through adopting a grounded theory approach (Glaser and Strauss, 1967), emerging themes such as coping strategies used by the women, and the importance of the body and embodiment could be explored. Reflecting on the data gathered using these methods, I would strongly support Olesen's (1995, p.169) view that 'the complexities of women's lives ... are sufficiently great that multiple approaches via qualitative research are required'.

Concluding comments

Central to the theorising about power, control, regulation and resistance in this chapter is a focus on the importance of a gendered analysis of the body. Social theorists have argued that in conditions of high modernity, there is a tendency for the body to become increasingly central to the modern person's sense of identity (Giddens, 1991; Shilling, 1993). The body becomes a channel for expressing dissatisfaction and frustration and in a sense the body becomes a 'project' (Shilling, 1993) to be worked at as a means of self-expression, bound up with a struggle to maintain self-identify and control. Whilst the body has a material base, it is more than a simple physical organism. Social meanings are attached to the physical body, and it is shaped and regulated by social forces. The body is therefore centrally implicated in the construction of social relations of inequality and oppression (Shilling, 1993). However, as argued in feminist approaches to the body and embodiment (Davis, 1997) a gender analysis is essential for an understanding of women's lives, and indeed men's lives. This chapter has demonstrated that a sociological understanding of women's experiences of embodiment may be further enhanced by empirical qualitative research which exposes the relationship between women's bodies and society, incorporating recent developments within the sociology of the body and feminist thought.

One important contemporary debate within feminism is the need to recognize differences which divide women yet also to highlight common experiences. Whilst this chapter has focused on women awaiting trial, the findings are illustrative, not simply of the lives of women charged with a criminal offence, but of women's lives generally. By drawing parallels between the lives of women officially labelled 'criminal' and the lives of women in general, the tendency to portray female offenders as in some way pathological or 'other' is avoided. Detailed consideration of this issue is offered by Howe (1994) as part of her feminist project of mapping the differential impact of disciplinary power on female bodies. Rather than focusing on the aetiology of female offending or the conditions of women's imprisonment, she argues for the development of an understanding of the 'structural coercion' of women. This recognises the continuum from imprisonment to freedom, from social control in formal custodial institutions to informal sites of social control. The theme of regulation applies then to all women as Howe (1994, p.207) argues

> The challenge, then, is to continue the project of exposing and enlarging our vision of what constitutes discriminatory penal practices, while remaining cognisant of the theoretical and political significance of critical feminist analyses of the private prisons of docile yet rebellious bodies, drugged and tranquillised bodies, famished self-policing bodies in which many women live their lives, 'free' from penal control.

Specifically relating to women awaiting trial, the research described in this chapter reveals the diversity of life experiences amongst women who appear before the criminal courts, but also suggests that contained in their accounts are common themes; for example, experiences of multiple and complex problems. Close consideration of the social position of women in society suggests that women live with 'overburdened bodies' (Shilling 1993). This refers to the many demands which women experience at home and at work, the lack of time they have to meet all these demands, and consequently, their experiences of emotional and physical stress (Rosen, 1989). A further important theme which emerged relates to issues of power and control in women's lives. The development of individual coping strategies through the body can be seen as part of an attempt by the women to seek control, although such strategies are likely to ultimately increase the control of others over their lives. However, it is also suggested that there are important parallels here with the way in which women in general respond to stress in their daily lives. Many women may turn to substances such as food or prescribed medication to manage the realities of their lives. Fewer will use the coping strategies (e.g. illegal drug use and self-harm) used by women who appear before the courts. The similarities between the coping strategies used by women awaiting trial and women in general should not be glossed over. But while it is important to draw parallels between women, there is a need to remain cognisant of the structural divisions amongst women such as social class, age, ethnicity and sexuality. Consequently, a theoretical perspective is needed which recognizes these structural divisions, as well as gender. However, women should not be portrayed as passive victims, and as a result there is a need to strike a balance between individualistic, processual explanations and structural explanations. In this way, the required sensitivity can be shown towards individual agency and the structural divisions which permeate the lives of individual women. Perhaps women's use of substances and self-harm techniques can be viewed as an active strategy to achieve personal and social satisfaction which they are denied access to in other areas of their lives.

The aim of this chapter, and this edited collection as a whole, has been not only to discuss empirical research and add to theoretical debates about the body, but also to consider the appropriateness of qualitative methods for researching the body. Within this chapter, a reflexive account of the process of conducting qualitative research has been offered. Whilst advocating that ethnographic research can play a crucial role in exploring women's lives, an important aim of the account has been to destroy any misconception that ethnographic research is simple. It is a 'messy business' (Pearson, 1993, p.vii). The use of qualitative techniques, including ethnographic approaches, raises numerous questions at all stages in the research process which require reflection. Such reflections can only enhance qualitative research and demonstrate its strengths which include completeness, understanding and responsiveness to experience. Largely because of these strengths, qualitative approaches are particularly appropriate techniques for researching the gendered body.

References

Bell, C. and Newby, H. (1977), (eds) *Doing Sociological Research*, Allen and Unwin, London.

Bell, C. and Roberts, H. (1984), (eds) *Social Researching: Politics, Problems and Practice*, Routledge, London.

Bell, R. (1985), *Holy Anorexia*, University of Chicago Press, Chicago.

Binion, V. (1982), 'Sex differences in socialisation and family dynamics of female and male heroin users', *Journal of Social Issues*, vol. 38, no.2, 43-58.

Cannon, S. (1992), 'Reflections on Fieldwork in Stressful Situations' in Burgess, R. (ed.) *Studies in Qualitative Methodology 3: Learning About Fieldwork*, JAI Press, Greenwich, Co.

Carlen, P. (1983), *Women's Imprisonment*, Routledge, London.

Carter, K. and Delamont, S. (1996), (eds) *Qualitative Research: The Emotional Dimension*, Ashgate, Aldershot.

Casale, S. (1989), *Women Inside*, The Civil Liberties Trust, London.

Cline, S. (1990), *Just Desserts: Women and Food*, Deutsch, London.

Coid, J., Wilkins, B., Coid, B. and Everitt, B. (1992), 'Self-mutilation in female remanded prisoners II: a cluster analytic approach towards the identification of a behavioural syndrome', *Criminal Behaviour and Mental Health*, vol. 2, no. 1, 1-14.

Davis, K. (1997), 'Embody-ing Theory: Beyond Modernist and Postmodernist Readings of the Body' in Davis, K. (ed.) *Embodied Practices: Feminist Perspectives on the Body*, Sage, London.

Dobash, R., Dobash, R. and Gutteridge, S. (1986), *The Imprisonment of Women*, Basil Blackwell, Oxford.

Doyal, L. (1995), *What Makes Women Sick: Gender and the Political Economy of Health*, Macmillan, Basingstoke.

Ettorre, E. (1992), *Women and Substance Use*, Macmillan, Basingstoke.

Faith, K. (1993), *Unruly Women*, Press Gang Publishers, Vancouver.

Falk, P. (1994), *The Consuming Body*, Sage, London.

Featherstone, M., Hepworth, M. and Turner, B. (1991), (eds) *The Body, Social Process and Cultural Theory*, Sage, London.

Firestone, S. (1971), *The Dialectic of Sex*, Jonathon Cope, London.

Friedman, J. and Alicea, M. (1995), 'Women and heroin: the path of resistance and its consequences', *Gender and Society*, vol. 9, no. 4, 432-449.

Gabe, J. and Thorogood, N. (1986), 'Tranquillisers as a Resource' in Gabe, J. and Williams, P. (eds) *Tranquillisers: Social, Psychological and Clinical Perspectives*, Tavistock, London.

Giddens, A. (1991), *Modernity and Self-Identity*, Polity Press, Cambridge.

Glaser, B. and Strauss, A. (1967), *The Discovery of Grounded Theory: Strategies for Qualitative Research*, Aldine, Chicago.

Glesne, C. and Peshkin, A. (1992), *Becoming Qualitative Researchers*, Longman, White Plains, NY.

Hammersley, M. (1992), *What's Wrong with Ethnography*, Routledge, London.

Hobbs, D. and May, T. (1993), (eds) *Interpreting the Field: Accounts of Ethnography*, Oxford University Press, Oxford.

Howe, A. (1994), *Punish and Critique: Towards a Feminist Analysis of Penality*, Routledge, London.

Lawrence, M. (1987), *Fed Up and Hungry: Women, Oppression and Food*, The Women's Press, London.

Liebling, A. (1992), *Suicides in Prison*, Routledge, London.

Lupton, D. (1996), *Food, the Body and the Self*, Sage, London.

MacSween, M. (1993), *Anorexic Bodies*, Routledge, London.

Marsh, J. (1982), 'Public issues and private problems: women and drug use', *Journal of Social Issues*, vol. 38, no.2, 153-166.

May, T. (1993), 'Feelings Matter: Inverting the Hidden Equation' in Hobbs, D. and May, T (eds) *Interpreting the Field: Accounts of Ethnography*, Oxford University Press, Oxford.

Oakley, A. (1993), *Essays on Women, Medicine and Health*, Edinburgh University Press, Edinburgh.

Olesen, V. (1995), 'Feminisms and Models of Qualitative Research' in Denzin, N, and Lincoln, Y. (eds) *The Handbook of Qualitative Research*, Sage, Newbury Park, Ca.

Pearson, G. (1993), 'Taking a Good Fight: Authenticity and Distance in the Ethnographer's Craft' in Hobbs, D. and May, T (eds) *Interpreting the Field: Accounts of Ethnography*, Oxford University Press, Oxford.

Roberts, H. (1981), (ed.) *Doing Feminist Research*, Routledge, London.

Rosen , M. (1989), *Women, Work and Achievement*, Macmillan, London.

Rich, A. (1980), 'Compulsory heterosexuality and lesbian experience', *Signs*, vol. 5, no. 631-660.
Russell, D. (1993), (ed.) *Making Violence Sexy: Feminist Views on Pornography*, Open University Press, Buckingham.
Scott, S. and Morgan, D. (1993), (eds) *Body Matters*, Falmer Press, London.
Shilling, C. (1993), *The Body and Social Theory*, Sage, London.
Sim, J. (1990), *Medical Power in Prisons*, Open University Press, Buckingham.
Smart, C. (1992), (ed.) *Regulating Womanhood*, Routledge, London.
Smith, C. (1996), *The Imprisoned Body: Women, Health and Imprisonment*, Unpublished PhD thesis, University of Wales, Bangor.
Stacey, J. (1988), 'Can there be a feminist ethnography?', *Women's Studies International Quarterly*, vol. 11, no. 1, 21-27.
Taylor, A. (1993), *Women Drug Users: An Ethnography*, Clarendon Press, Oxford.
Turner, B. (1992), *Regulating Bodies*, Routledge, London.
Wincup, E. (1997), *Waiting for Trial: Living and Working in a Bail Hostel*, Unpublished PhD thesis, University of Wales, Cardiff.
Wolf, N. (1990), *The Beauty Myth*, Virago, London.

8. 'Sleeping on the sofa': preparation for ordained ministry and the 'curriculum of the body'

Trevor Welland

Introduction

Training in a residential setting over a two to three year period is a compulsory, if currently controversial, aspect of the professional preparatory of those offering themselves for ministry in the Anglican priesthood in England and Wales. This mode of preparation is seen as being essential to an inculcation of the 'attitudes and habits' (ACCM 1990, p.11) required of this occupational role and status for both the trainee and, where relevant, her/his partner and family. As such, therefore, the mode, as well as the content, of training are viewed as powerful facilitators of occupational socialization and identity. This chapter will describe how this residential training, through both the timetable, and the formal and informal 'gaze' of staff and other students, acts to inscribe and regulate the 'docile body' (Foucault, 1977) of the trainees in preparation for the critical transition to an ordained status; and the means by which students conform to, and contest, this 'curriculum of the body'. The data discussed in this chapter are drawn from the early stages of ethnographic research into the training of a cohort of students for the priesthood, based at a residential theological college in the UK during the 1990s. The first stage of this fieldwork was undertaken throughout the three terms of one academic year, and, using the methods of participant observation, in-depth ethnographic interviews, and documentary analysis, followed a group of mainly new entrants to the college as they negotiated the complex process of 'self presentation' and 'identity management' through various 'initial encounters' (Ball, 1980; Beynon, 1984) during this first year of training. Pseudonyms are used throughout this chapter for staff, students and place names, in order to ensure confidentiality (BSA 1992).

St David's : introducing the trainees and the course

The Theological Colleges in England and Wales provide a residential setting for the vocational training of candidates who have been centrally selected and sponsored by the various denominations of the Anglican Communion, and aim to equip these candidates for ordained ministry in the Church, through the various courses offered (ACCM 1990). St David's College, the setting for this piece of research, was founded early in the 1900s, and is situated in the fashionable area of Bishoptown, a 'leafy' suburb of Westcity. During the first year of fieldwork, the College was responsible for training twenty full-time residential students (four women, and sixteen men) in three year groups, with three full-time male members of staff, who were all priests. These staff also acted as leaders to tutorial groups of mixed composition, selected randomly from the student body. Academic courses were taught within the Department of Theology at the local University of Westcity, where the St. David's staff members also lectured. Different courses were designed to match the ability levels, previous educational experiences, and proposed length of study of the different students. New students were interviewed by college staff, and recommended for Certificate, Diploma or Degree courses in Theology or Ministry. In addition to these formal, academic aspects of training, St. David's arranged certain 'at home' courses with a more 'practical' focus. These included 'Pastoral Care in the Parish' which was designed to introduce students to particular pastoral skills in more of a role-play or 'hands on' manner e.g. marriages, funerals and baptisms; and Spirituality workshops exploring approaches to prayer and its role in parish life.

As with other ethnographic research in training settings and among groups of trainees (Atkinson, 1981; Salisbury, 1994a), these students were marked by their heterogeneity. Their ages ranged from twenty four to fifty five years, with married or engaged couples, and 'singles' living within the same community, or close to the College grounds in 'family houses' owned by the College. Some of the staff and students had children resident also, and there was evidence of this with children's artwork on college noticeboards and on staff study walls, as well as their presence at the main chapel services. In addition, the students had diverse occupational backgrounds - for example teaching, research science, financial, social, and police work. Others had entered St David's soon after graduating from university, or completing postgraduate research or degrees. Ethnographic research on experienced, but unqualified, Further Education teachers (Salisbury, 1994a), and midwives (Davies, 1988) has shown that these previous roles and statuses can be 'dramatically inverted' when students encounter the training setting for the first time. Similarly, my initial field experiences at St David's revealed that on entering the theological college, this inversion of status rendered the trainees 'vulnerable novices' (Salisbury, 1994b, p.78)as they adapted to becoming students and learners. This was clearly identified for the students when, on their first evening at St David's, the new students gathered to meet the Principal (Canon Johnson) in the Chapel to hear about 'The College Rule'. In talking about their previous experiences, and what they should expect from their training, Canon Johnson intoned solemnly from the front of the chapel:

> You must forget what you have experienced before. We do not want to hear 'in my parish we did this or that' from you. No, we are asking you to start afresh.

Witnessing this transparent desire that the trainees should 'start afresh', or become 'submissive *tabula rasa* ' (Merton et al., 1957), encouraged me to make problematic 'the body' within this setting, and consider its mechanisms of the 'insatiable management of social spaces, social practices and forms' (Scheurich, 1995, p.20). However, as Pillow (1997) describes in her research on pregnant teenagers in school settings, despite entering the field immersed in theory and existing empirical data, I felt completely unprepared for the 'utter physicality'(Pillow 1997, p.349)of the research process. Hence, just as the trainees' bodies became sites of both the reproduction of, and resistance to, occupational culture, I was physically engaged in the 'messy' and unpredictable business of using the 'self' as research tool 'par excellence'(Rock, 1979, p.78; Hammersley and Atkinson, 1995:19).

Training for ministry: training for 'total exposure'

> When you are training people for ministry, especially Anglican ministry, it is very much about community life - you've got to be available to people at all sorts of awful times of day and night ... there are services morning, noon and night ... there are the Barn Dances and the Festivals and whatever. You do get this feeling of total exposure of yourself and family. The vicarage is public property, and the parishioners see it as church property and they expect to be in and out of the living room, and they are (laughs). I think that it is that that has to be prepared for. (Donald Leavis- staff member)

> It is vital that in ministerial formation students live together for residential periods where they are vulnerable to one another's continued gaze and enquiry ... (ACCM 1990, p.7)

> The context is itself part of the learning process ... (ACCM 1990, p.1)

As the reflections of the 'Advisory Council for the Church's Ministry' (ACCM) and Donald Leavis, a senior member of staff at the college, indicate, this idea of being 'in the gaze', or 'total exposure', is seen as being an essential component of ministerial preparation, and served as a key principle in the structuring of the regime at St. David's. Thus, as with medical students (Becker et al., 1961; Atkinson, 1981), the students at St. David's were not only trained in skills appropriate to their future occupational roles, but they were also prepared for an imminent 'network of social expectation' in the parish (Towler and Coxon, 1979, p.168), which involved very public surveillance, not only of the student who would be ordained, but also members of their immediate family. Thus, the idea of a future 'being in the parish' and its implications for trainees and their families, legitimated officially, and at the local level, this intense, residential mode of preparation for full-time students. Exposure and surveillance are mediated via the timetable, which both structures and regulates the activity and location of the body, as well as the appropriate use of 'time', and the inevitable consequences of living in intimate and close proximity to staff and other trainees.

Student accounts of their first weeks of training revealed their positive expectations of some of the more routinized and regulated aspects of the programme, and expressed in many cases a keen desire to participate in what the college had to offer them as trainees. For some of the students this was explicitly and mainly linked to being 'open' to the demands of different elements of the residential training course, and what it could offer them.

> I came in all good faith, expecting to actually enjoy the course. And last term, the first term that I was here, I, you know, I did the business basically. I went to the lectures, I produced all the work I needed to produce, I handed in my essays. I joined in all the college things. I stayed in college from Monday to Friday. I joined in whatever was going on here. I only missed somewhere in the region of two or three chapel services the

whole of the term. I really gave it a go ... (Lucinda - first year student, aged 45)

TW: What did you expect to learn as a result of your time here?

Discipline, learning discipline, frequent prayer, immersing yourself in theology, and looking deeply into various theological matters. I suppose there is the naive view of coming out as an institutional superman. But in a way after you've gone through such a long process of testing the vocation, after you've gone through a horrible selection board, you kind of think, theological college is this great transforming period at the end of all this preparation and testing of vocation. You think it's the launch pad. So of course even in the most perfect of theological colleges there's going to be disappointment ... One of the things that attracted me to this college is the chapel. The very disciplined life of prayer, with the morning prayer and evening prayer each day, and Communion. And my first thought was I will really appreciate this structure. I'm not the most structured and disciplined of people ... (Gavin - second year student, aged 26)

Some students spoke about their expectations in more generalistic terms, revealing a more passive or compliant attitude.

I need to know what I hope to learn at theological college, to do the job that I feel that I've been called to do...I really feel that during the two years that I've got to spend here, I've got to observe and absorb as much possible ... (David - first year student, aged 50)

In cases such as this, the college and its regime was seen to be there to provide the students with the necessary knowledge and skills in order to be effective parish priests. Many of those students who had previous occupational experiences within highly regulated and hierarchical institutions, such as schools or the Police Force, tended to voice this language of conformity. However it did not go unnoticed by other students, who interpreted this as uncritically 'playing the system', as if given their occupational biography, more was expected from them in terms of critical engagement with the training environment.

thinking now particularly of the people who are doing, sort of, the course in three years, people like for example Roger, an ex-head of department of physics, or Simon, an ex-head of department of modern languages, that sort of thing, you know, they're playing the system and they're saying 'Right, I want to pass this course. I will put my head down and I will do what is required'. (Lucinda)

Learning the habits of 'clerical' time

> Social scientists from Weber to Foucault have argued that punctuated and sectioned time which provides strict guidelines for activity and rest periods was first developed in the monasteries of the West ... Through their analyses social scientists have established a link between the secular time discipline of contemporary life and the ascetic daily rounds of monastic existence ... In Western societies we have imposed the monastic schedule on ourselves ... (Adam 1995, pp.64-65)

> One of the things that you will notice here is the pattern and regulation of the day, this will set you up for life in the parish ... When you leave here you must be organized, so you must learn to manage your time sensibly. If you end up rushing around like some lunatic, and feeling as if you have had an awful day, it will be because you've been disorganized. In the parish, you must work at that balance between discipline and relaxation. (Canon Johnson, the Principal, introducing 'The College Rule')

As with other institutions, for example schools (Ball et al. 1984), and hospitals (Roth, 1963) time and timetables at St. David's were a significant organisational feature, and indicated that 'reified, abstracted time and its rationalized control' (Adam 1995, p.65) was a key educational strategy in regulating the body. In addition to this regulatory function, the timetable sought to make visible activity within the college. One of the senior students indicated on my first day of fieldwork that, since the college buildings all faced each other around a central lawn, student activity was apparent for anyone who wanted to inspect.

> After supper the previous Principal would sit at his French Windows, and check whose lights were on, and who was

working. It's like living in God's goldfish bowl here. (Oliver, second year student, aged 54)

That time was to be a phenomenological component of life at St. David's was introduced to students during the intensive 'induction period' during their first days of training. These 'initial encounters', then, during which the students became familiar with 'The College Rule', served to present them with the most explicit introduction to college values.

As with the temporal aspects of organisational structure in other examples of denominational educational institutions (Burgess 1983), secular time dominated the religious and liturgical calendar. The 'yearly cycle' at the College closely followed that of the university, in that there were three terms per year (30 weeks), with an additional 4-6 weeks in pastoral placements during vacations e.g. parishes, hospitals or schools. The daily temporal structuring of 'life in the gaze' at St. David's was outlined for students in the 'The College Rule', and the main elements consisted of : compulsory common worship in the college chapel; academic study at the university; 'in house' pastoral programmes; and the routine/schedule of communal life, such as shared meal times, tutor group meetings, domestic work (e.g. washing up and laying tables for meals), and times of silence. Hence the weekday 'College Timetable' would resemble a 'monastic day', and usually consisted of the following pattern of services and other activities:

Rising Bell	7.00am
Morning Prayer	7.30am
Silent Meditation in the Chapel	7.45am
Communion	8.00am
Breakfast	8.30am
University Lectures	(daytime)
Evening Prayer	6.00pm
Dinner	6.45pm

However, there would be some variation with a sung Communion Service on Tuesday and Thursday evenings, and a sung Evening Prayer at the nearby Bishoptown Cathedral on Wednesday evenings, when the students would dress formally in cassocks (long, coat-like black garments), and play a major public role in the service, mainly through leading the singing. As with schools, periods of change in activity were made publicly explicit through use of 'the bell'. At St. David's, as in monastic communities, the 'Rising Bell' would be rung at the beginning of the day, and signal 'the call' to communal morning worship. The bell would also be rung before other chapel services throughout the day.

The period of training and the regime of the Theological Colleges, then, are viewed as establishing 'regular routines, patterns and discipline' (ACCM 1990, p.13) for ministry . In relation to this function, time was observed to operate as a powerful 'coercive facticity' (Ball et al. 1984, p.45) at St David's, in regulating the student body, and the 'pressure of the schedule' was a fundamental means of testing competency in preparation for future occupational roles (Delamont and Galton, 1986). In general, the trainees respond to this form of regulation in the same way students have been observed to in other institutions. As Ball et al. (1984, p.43) have found from research in school settings:

> For the vast majority of school pupils ... school time is experienced passively and unquestioningly. Their personal timetables are subordinated to the standard period, school day, school week and term; and the synchronization and sequencing of the timetable ... Time is a boundary condition that imposes its own logical pattern upon social action.

Whilst students are seen to conform, 'time is something they want to claim for themselves' (Ball et al., 1984, p.42). Student opposition to 'institutional time' was most obvious when conflicts arose out of the tension between 'personal/individual' and 'official/collective' time (Adam, 1995, p.66).

The university and its time and demands were experienced as being dominant features in the students' lives, leaving them with the sense of the problems of living a 'straddled identity' or inhabiting 'multiple lifeworlds' (Schutz and Luckmann, 1973), through being both a university and clerical student, as well as experiencing the daily physical movements between Theological College and university. This living 'between two worlds' (Weis, 1985) created tensions for the students, especially in managing the demands of undergraduate academic pressures (attendance at lectures, essay writing etc.), in addition to the further expectations of occupational preparation within this residential setting.

> It's just very difficult coping with what's required of us in college, as well as all of the academic stuff in the university. It's like living in different worlds ... When things really get going it's going to be difficult to fit everything in. (William)

> Because we are so integrated with the university (all our lectures are in the university), and then there are a few 'add on'

> lectures, which give us ministerial additions in this college, I find that once that you have gone for a whole week of lectures on a degree course in a university and have things added on back here, you don't really want to do any more, like the daily chapel routine, and placement in a parish. This year I'm doing a placement with the 'Big Issue', working with them on Thursday afternoons. It does get very tiring with the amount that is asked of you. You're doing over and above what a normal degree student is expected to do. You're expected to do the same amount of academic work. (Gavin)

> The college really can't make up its mind what it wants to be. It is somewhere between being a college of higher education and a monastery ... Certainly for some here, they regard the academic side as keeping them away from work experience in the parish, from the practical side that really matters. (Nigel)

Even where students had adopted elements of the Principal's time management ideals, they signalled their rejection of aspects of the institutional sequencing of time and activities, indicating strategies for their own prioritization. This opposition was often justified through knowledge gained from their own pastoral placements, or previous students and, therefore, by reference to 'real experiences' in the 'real world' of the parish. In this way, narratives challenged the official justification for certain regulatory practices, and mirrored the 'contrastive rhetoric' (Hargreaves, 1984) and 'privileging of the practical' of trainees in other educational settings (Salisbury, 1994a).

> I cope very badly here at times. Much to my dismay, I have become a great list person. I'm so disorganised that I have had to adopt that system. There is always something for you to do here. But I've made relaxation as much a part of my list as anything else ... I have made a rule that I will never work here in the evenings. I certainly can't do the late shifts, as people call them, you know working until 2 or 3 in the morning. A friend who was ordained last year gave me a good piece of advice in that you should see the day as being divided into three segments. If you don't want to wear yourself out, only work two of these. Which is what I do now, and what I'll do when I get out. (Nigel)

> I have to apologise a lot for being disorganised. I keep on wondering how I'm going to cope when important things like funerals have to be attended. Otherwise the dead don't get buried. I just pray that I'll find some way. Just being very severe helps, like saying I don't think attending this lecture would be very important, in fact the time could be better spent doing some reading or writing an essay, or something else. I think that that is the only way to cope when your time is crammed in. (Gavin)

Other students located their opposition in experiences in previous professional occupational roles and identities, and expressed a desire for a degree of autonomy in terms of managing the demands of preparation within the training setting.

> I would call it panic management here, where you go from one potential disaster to the next, and you hope that you keep ahead all the way along the line. I think the important thing is to try and plan, you've got to keep ahead of the game and know what is going on. As far as the college is concerned ... there are a lot of pressures on time for a lot of people, and it does make life difficult. I think it would be far easier if we weren't fettered by the imposition of all of these activities at different times of the day ... I've worked in big organisations, and I think there are a lot of constraints that the college could do away with. Although I value the fact that I'm praying at certain times of the day, and I consider it a part of the discipline of the life that I've entered ... there just isn't going to be somebody standing over you saying 'You will go to morning prayer, you will go to evening prayer'. We could with a little less force feeding. (David)

'Looking out for each other': training in a state of visibility

The long and intense period of two or three years of training within an 'intimate and close-knit' residential setting (ACCM 1990, p. 50) was designed to 'reveal much of the student's personality and suitability for ordination' (ACCM 1990, p. 51). The 'enclosed' and 'bounded' nature of the training environment rendered them very visible, and vulnerable, to the appraisal of others living in the community. Surveillance of the ability of students to 'manage time' and cope with the pressure of the schedule and life 'in the gaze' of a community, was formally performed by staff, who were responsible for assessing student suitability for ordination and ministry (ACCM 1990, p.49):

> Not only are they (the staff) expected to teach, but also to assess students ... The assessing role of staff can at times be ambiguous and confusing to students. A College or Course prepares people for ordination, and there is a collective responsibility among the staff for recommending a student's suitability for ordination.

For the students, this was experienced especially in the case of monitoring their attendance in chapel for obligatory services and times of prayer. Each student on entering the college, was assigned a specific 'place' in chapel, and a 'floor-plan', attached to the noticeboard, indicated where each student should sit for worship. Whilst the student places were arranged in rows facing the altar at the front of the chapel, the staff sat in specially designated raised benches at the rear. From this 'vantage point' staff were able to identify which students were present or not. Students strongly rejected and criticized this aspect of assessment, and considered it to be one of the most negative experiences of their training. This was especially the case, since the surveillance was regarded as being extended, not just to physical presence in the chapel, but also to the way in which students led services, or performed other functions within worship.

> I think the atmosphere in the chapel can be quite oppressive. There is a sense that you have to conform to the way that the college recites prayers ... quite rigidly. And there's that terrible thing where all the staff sit on that great big throne at the back and look at the back of everyone, and they can see who has overslept, and can see who didn't realise there is another reading. And there's a real - especially when there is someone out the front to serve - there is always such a sense of nervousness of getting it right.
>
> TW: So you feel that you're being watched when you're doing those things?
>
> I know a lot of people feel that they are being watched. And I think just the physical nature of putting the staff back there isn't constructive. And spreading the students into their

designated slots isn't helpful. I do feel that there is an oppressive nature to the chapel - it's not conducive to worship. (Gavin)

Whilst it was the staff who formally performed this assessment and surveillance role, some students considered them to be ineffective, and indicated that it was the 'informal' gaze of other students, and their families, that noticed inappropriate behaviour away from 'institutional spaces' such as chapel or lectures.

> Even though the staff live in the community they will miss disputes, they probably miss the feelings that students have about other students. There will be students who are viewed in a certain way, and the tutors don't pick up on our views of x,y or z. We do assess each other, definitely. I don't know what others think of me, but I do know what is said about others. The staff miss out on that gossip side of things. It is difficult to pinpoint exactly, but I would say that we have more of an awareness of each other. (Michael)

This was also indicated by Donald Leavis, one of the members of staff, during an interview whilst negotiating 'access' to St. David's. He spoke of the role of students and their families in the 'assessment' of suitability for ministry, even though they had no formal role, and mentioned details of a recent 'weeding out of the insane' (in this case someone with a 'drink problem'), and that it was the other students in college who had raised the issue with staff.

Given the nature of surveillance, control and visibility at St. David's, the body, and physical practice, were seen to be effective domains or sites for the process of resistance to the incorporation of 'dominant identity'. Students could be very critical of the training regime, and indicated that they were not passive recipients of their 'official curriculum'. One of the main oppositional strategies for winning 'symbolic and physical space from the institution' (Weis, 1985, p.35) was absenteeism. As has already been mentioned, students would frequently prioritize activities for themselves, and often attend only what they considered to be most important. This strategy was certainly adopted in relation to university lectures, even though absence could be noticed by college staff, since they taught many of the Theology courses at Westcity University. For most students, this form of resistance to institutional practice and expectation, expressed their desire for more choice and autonomy within the training programme, even though they were being prepared for work within a hierarchical structure characterized by high levels of organizational control, and low levels of individual autonomy (Szafran, 1981). In the extreme, this resistance was intentionally very visible. Lucinda, one of the first year students, ceased attending her degree course lectures completely during the second term of her study, and saw this as a means of protest and achieving her goal of a course that she would actually benefit from.

> And I thought, what am I doing here which is in any way appropriate to what I'm going to do out there? ... I haven't been to any lectures this term, because if I did I feel that I wouldn't be taken seriously. (Lucinda)

In other situations, resistance through absence, or challenging acceptable notions of 'appropriate behaviour', could take on a more 'moral' and 'sexualized' dimension, given the nature and context of the training. One student, when speaking of his disappointment that he had not been sent to a more academically prestigious college, said:

> I warned them that because Prue (his partner) lives just down the road, I'd be at her place all the time ... this week I've slept here only twice. Unlike some of the students who have their girlfriends to stay, we would never sleep with each other here. If anyone ever asked I'd say: 'How dare you suggest that we are having sex before we are married, I'm training to be a priest. I sleep on the sofa'. There's nothing in the 'college rule' about where I sleep. (William)

Despite being aware of the pressures of their 'exposed condition' and the need for 'appropriate behaviour' whilst training for ministry, students could also identify some advantages to being 'in the gaze'.

> Everybody in the community looks out for each other ... if there's a problem with somebody then everyone is aware of it. I started here with someone I knew from university and naturally we bonded and became very close. But he was only here for two years, and then was ordained at the end of last year ... Last year I made very good friends with other members of the college, and that has followed through to this year. We do tend to form cliques, and the group that I am in this year (there are four of us) ... we are all in our third

> year, and we all had had good bonds with existing friends who since had left. It is very much a mutual support network. If you don't establish yourself in a clique ... it is very difficult to be alone here ... you very much need the support and care of other students because whilst pastoral support is available from staff, it is only available in crisis situations. You tend to look after your own in the group. (Nigel)

Surveillance within this intense community setting, therefore, was also related to support and friendship for students. Many of those interviewed, including Nigel, disclosed accounts of having been 'covered for' by friends or other members of the college, if they had infringed some element of 'The College Rule', such as being away without permission, especially if this was overnight, or if they had missed a compulsory event such as a chapel service. The highly visible nature of life in this residential training also meant that students could rely on each other to informally monitor and regulate behaviour, especially within their immediate groups of friends.

> When the stress was getting to me, and I was getting out of line ... when I was getting ratty and snappy, I would start to take it out on others. That was when I needed the others, and they were able to pull me up and say 'that's the line, and you have just crossed over it. We realize that you're under stress, but don't take it out on anybody else'. So in that way we keep each other in check. (Nigel)

Conclusion

Foucault (1977, pp.135-136) argues that bodies are compelled through disciplines, and that the 'docile' and 'inapt body' can be shaped and ordered towards identity.

> The classical age discovered the body as object and target of power. It is easy enough to find signs of the attention then paid to the body - to the body that is manipulated, shaped, trained, which obeys, responds, becomes skilful and increases its forces ... The body is docile that may be subjected, used, transformed and improved. (Foucault, 1977, p.136)

For Foucault, this discipline proceeds from 'enclosure', or 'the distribution of individuals in space' (Foucault 1977, p.141), and the control of activity/establishing of rhythms via the timetable, and visibility (Foucault, 1977, p. 201). Drawing on this perspective, this chapter has shown how the liturgical, pastoral and community aspects of training at St. David's were considered to be 'simulations', in relation to which students would develop appropriate modes of behaviour (Coxon 1965, p. 492) or 'life patterns' (ACCM 1990, p. 13) for the ordering of working lives, within which visibility, structure and routine for the body are regarded as playing an important part (ACCM 1990, p. 21). The emphasis of the training environment, therefore, was on the demands imposed by discipline, regulation and obligation (ACCM 1990, pp. 26-28), and these were mediated through the timetable, and the 'gaze' of staff, the other students, and their families. In this way, it can be argued that the 'emerging clerical identities' of the trainees, are written and inscribed on the body (Sutherland, 1977).

References

ACCM (Advisory Council for the Church's Ministry) (1990), *Residence: an education*. Occasional Paper No. 38.

Adam, B. (1995), *Timewatch : The social analysis of time* Polity Press, Cambridge.

Atkinson, P. (1981), *The Clinical Experience* Gower, Farnborough.

Ball, S. (1980), 'Initial Encounters in the Classroom and the process of establishment' in P. Woods (ed.) *Pupil Strategies,* Croom Helm, London, pp. 257 - 259.

Ball, S., Hull, R., Skelton, M. & Tudor, R (1984), 'The tyranny of the 'devil's mill': time and task in school' in S. Delamont (ed.) *Readings on Interaction in the Classroom,* Methuen, London and New York, pp. 41 - 57.

Becker, H. Geer, B Hughes, E. and Strauss, A (1961), *Boys in White : student culture in a medical school,* Chicago University Press, Chicago.

Beynon, J. (1984), *Initial Encounters in the Secondary School,* Falmer Press, Lewes.

BSA (British Sociological Association) (1992), *Statement of Ethical Practice,* BSA : Durham.

Burgess, R. (1983), *Experiencing Comprehensive Education,* Methuen, London.

Coxon, A. (1965), *A sociological study of the social recruitment, selection, and professional socialization of Anglican ordinands,* Unpublished Ph.D. Thesis University of Leeds.

Davies, R. (1988), *The Happy End Of Nursing : An Ethnographic Study Of Initial Encounters In A Midwifery School,* Unpublished MSc. Econ. Thesis. University of Wales, College of Cardiff.

Delamont, S and Galton, M (1986), *Inside the secondary classroom,* Routledge and Kegan Paul, London and New York.

Foucault, M. (1977), *Discipline and Punish : The Birth Of The Prison,* Penguin, London.

Hammersley, M. and Atkinson, P. (1995), *Ethnography: Principles in Practice,* (second edition), Routledge, London.

Hargreaves, A. (1984), 'Contrastive Rhetoric and Extremist Talk' in A. Hargreaves and P. Woods (eds) *Classrooms and Staffrooms,* Open University Press, Milton Keynes: pp.215 - 231.

Lortie, D. (1975), *School Teacher,* University of Chicago Press, Chicago.

Merton, R. K., Reader, K. and Kendall, P. L. (1957), *The Student Physician,* Harvard University Press, Cambridge Mass.

Pillow, W. (1997), 'Exposed methodology : the body as a deconstructive practice' *Interenational Journal of Qualitative Studies in Education* 10 (3), 349 - 363.

Rock, P. (1979), *The Making of Symbolic Interactionism,* Macmillan London.

Roth, J (1963), *Timetables,* Bobbs-Merrill, Indianapolis.

Salisbury, J. (1994a), *Becoming Qualified : An ethnography of a post-experience teacher training course,* Unpublished Ph.D. Thesis University of Wales, College of Cardiff.

Salisbury, J. (1994b), 'There is more than one way to kill a cat' : Making sense of post experience professional training, in A. Coffey and P. Atkinson (eds) *Issues in Occupational Socialization,* Avebury Press, Aldershot.

Salisbury, J. (1995), Untrained teachers' experiences in further education and their motives for training in J. Salisbury and S. Delamont (eds) *Qualitative Studies in Education,* Avebury Press, Aldershot.

Schutz, A. Luckmann, T. (1973), *The Structures of the Life-World,* Heinemann, London.

Scheurich, J. J. (1995), 'Policy Archaeology : A new Policy Studies Methodology' *Journal of Policy Studies*, 9 (4), 297 - 316.

Sutherland, A. (1977), 'The Body as a social symbol among the Rom', in J. Blacking (ed.) *The Anthropology of the Body,* Academic Press. London.

Szafran, R.F. (1981), 'Control Structures in Religious Organisations : Accounting for organizational patterns and individual perceptions', *Sociology of Work and Occupations,* 8(3) 327 - 352.

Towler, R and Coxon, A. (1979), *The Fate of the Anglican Clergy : A sociological study,* Macmillan, London.

Weber, M. (1904-5/1989), *The Protestant Ethic and the Spirit of Capitalism,* Unwin Hyman, London.

Weis, L. (1985), *Between Two Worlds : Black students in an urban community college,* Routledge and Kegan Paul, Boston.

Zeichner K. and Gore J. (1990), 'Teacher Socialization', in R. Houston (ed.) *Handbook of Research on teacher Education,* Macmillan, New York.

9. Wrinklies just wanna have fun!

John Richardson

Introduction

The capacity audience sighed in anticipation as Prince Charming reached out to place the slipper on Cinderella's foot. He wobbled a little as he bent down, and people seated in the front rows could see that his outstretched hand was lined and wrinkled. They may also have noticed the knotted tracks of varicose veins on Cinderella's legs. But no one seemed at all troubled by these physical imperfections, for this performance of the popular pantomime was being staged by an amateur cast of elderly people. Both the Prince and Cinderella were in their mid 70s and Buttons had just celebrated his 86th birthday. Now, the idea of *Cinderella* being performed by actors of this age probably seems rather odd or amusing. Elderly people are usually expected to move out of the spotlight, to wait in the wings, to take a comfortable seat in the stalls. It is as if their aged bodies condemn them forever to be passive spectators rather than active participants. But ageist stereotypes were not going to spoil this production of *Cinderella*. The entire cast may have been 'wrinklies', their bodies may have carried the tell-tale signs of advanced years, but they still knew how to have fun.

Cinderella was staged on this occasion by participants in Healthy, Wealthy and Wise (HWW), a community project for older people living in the Ely area of Cardiff. This chapter is based on a qualitative evaluation study of that project. Under the HWW initiative a small community team was given the task of mobilising the local elderly population to lead full and active lives. As the title of the project suggests, the intention was to promote the health, wealth and wisdom of participants in the scheme. But what linked the various HWW events was a common determination to challenge the fatalistic view that old age always imposes tight limits on people's physical and social activities. Even if our bodies are no longer quite so young, no longer quite so strong or healthy or supple, this does not necessarily prevent us from enjoying a wide range of pursuits and interests.

Thus the HWW project is an example of an imaginative and fun-oriented approach to old age.

HWW was evaluated using a combination of research methods, with special emphasis on qualitative techniques. This evaluation enables us, firstly, to draw optimistic conclusions about the potential of programmes such as HWW which adopt a positive approach towards old age. Secondly, it demonstrates the valuable role of qualitative methods in researching bodily matters. Thirdly, it provides important empirical evidence in an area, the sociology of the body, where theory has tended to outstrip research. In these various ways, then, the HWW study makes a contribution towards a fuller sociological understanding of the ageing body.

Representations, regulation and resistance

Before describing the methodology and findings of the HWW research, it is helpful first of all to recognise the extent to which the HWW project challenged many common assumptions about old age. According to the HWW philosophy, even 'wrinklies' can have fun. This is a relatively novel proposition in contemporary Britain where being old is seldom seen as something pleasurable and fulfilling. Old people tend to be represented in a negative light and their lives are tightly regulated. But HWW allied itself with those who are mounting a resistance to these ageist attitudes.

Representations

It is not surprising that many people approach old age with apprehension, since media representations typically portray elderly people as physically unattractive, sexually inactive and chronically incapacitated. The neurologist Oliver Sacks tells the story of one of his patients, an elderly man who suffered from the delusion that he was really a teenager. Every morning he would rush to the mirror and recoil in horror as he saw the wizened face of an old man staring back at him. It is easy to understand the revulsion he felt as he suddenly realised he had the physical appearance of a 'crumbly', a 'wrinkly', a 'geriatric'. Our culture teaches us to admire youthful strength and beauty and to dread the physical expressions of advanced years (Lasch, 1991). We shrink back from images of the aged body with its spidery lines and wrinkles, rheumy eyes, dry papery skin, thinning hair, sagging muscles and stiff-jointed movements. After all, these are the physical stigmata which mark off old age as the polar opposite of the youthful ideal. Furthermore, since our late modern society treats physical appearance as a mirror of the true self, we tend to regard older people as somehow less worthy than younger people (Shilling, 1993). They simply do not 'count' as much. On the contrary, they are resented as an alleged public burden on the rest of society and they are unfairly accused of making impossible demands on the resources of the welfare state (Hills, 1993). In the eyes of policy-makers, service providers and media commentators alike, older people often represent little more than a huge and growing social problem. Of course, representations of old people are neither uniform nor uncontested (Thompson et al, 1991). For example, the stock of cultural stereotypes includes the sweet, inoffensive and saintly (but highly idealised) grandmother as well as the ugly old crone. But it is difficult to avoid the conclusion that old age is typically represented as something to be pitied or feared rather than envied.

Regulation

In some respects elderly people seem remarkably free and independent. Released from paid work and childcare duties, they appear to have sufficient time and space to follow any lifestyle they choose. Yet their lives are regulated to varying degrees by such things as retirement rules, institutional policies, physical incapacities, cultural attitudes and levels of income and wealth. Indeed, their lives seem quite tightly circumscribed when we consider that old age is regularly associated with social, economic and political marginality. Their freedoms, such as they are, tend to be narrow and ghettoised, operating largely at the edge of society. Some gerontologists explain this marginality as a natural and inevitable result of the ticking away of the biological clock. Thus, Cumming and Henry (1961) maintain that the ageing process eventually leads to bodily decline (e.g. energy loss, physical deterioration) and psychological impairment (e.g. narrowing interests, diminishing concentration). As their biological and psychological powers fade, so elderly people start to withdraw from active social pursuits and responsible social roles. Cumming and Henry regard this 'disengagement' as perfectly appropriate since, in their view, old age is a time to prepare for death. Society assists aged people to concentrate on their impending death by reducing demands on them and releasing them from normal social obligations. In turn, society benefits when elderly people vacate social and occupational roles which can then be filled by younger and presumably more competent people.

In contrast, 'social constructionists' (e.g. Phillipson, 1982) reject the view that the marginality of elderly people in modern Britain is somehow 'natural' and biologically ordained. Social constructionists argue that marginality is the result of society choosing to impose dependency on elderly people and forcibly excluding them from mainstream institutions. According to this view, the problem of old age 'originates less in physical decline than in society's intolerance of old people, its refusal to make use of their accumulated wisdom, and its attempt to relegate them to the margins of social existence' (Lasch, 1991, p. 207). Therefore what old people suffer from is not the relentless ageing process *per se* but the discriminatory attitudes and practices of ageism. Ageism can be defined as 'the notion that people cease to be people, cease to be the same people or become people of a distinct and inferior kind, by virtue of having lived a specified number of years' (Comfort, 1977, p. 35). It is expressed in the negative stereotyping of 'wrinklies' and in a host of social practices which range from routine neglect right through to violent 'elder abuse'.

Resistance

We have been staring at a rather gloomy picture of an ageist society which represents elderly people in an unflattering light and confines them to the margins. But we get a different perspective when we turn to evidence which suggests that conventional assumptions about old age are currently being challenged, not least by elderly people themselves. This forces us to question whether there really is an automatic link between old age and the problems of poverty and social passivity. For example, in Britain there is a large group of retired people who have accumulated sufficient capital and pension entitlements to afford exotic foreign holidays and expensive consumer products. Moreover, some observers use the term 'grey power' to describe the ways in which pensioners are starting to use their voting and spending power to get a better deal for older people (Bunyan, 1988). It is not appropriate, therefore, to regard old people as perpetual victims. It seems that increasing numbers of elderly people are affirming and exploring the more pleasant experiences of later life. One survey of people aged 60-80 found that:

> Few if any of our interviewees actually fit the stereotypes of old people as being passive, inactive, helpless, dependent, rigid in their thoughts or behaviour, old-fashioned, or unproductive. Instead their lives are characterised by variety, vitality, diversity, activity, energy, interest; by youthfulness in attitude, outlook and activity...The people themselves are each unique and uniquely different from each other and from just about

every stereotyped image of old people that exists (Thompson et al, 1991, p. 121).

Some sociologists claim that this new mood of assertive individualism can be traced to the emergence of postmodern society. They argue that in a kaleidoscopic world it is no longer helpful to think in terms of fixed and stable life stages, since new lifestyles and identities are constantly being created. Even the body is not a fixed entity but a flexible project to be worked on and improved by means of exercise and dietary programmes or even cosmetic surgery (Shilling, 1993). In this rapidly changing and 'experimental' society, flexible biographical patterns and individually-designed life courses are becoming much more common. For example, Featherstone and Hepworth (1989) describe how the Sixties counterculture generation, now approaching late middle age, are apparently refusing to wear the 'mask of old age'. This mask fails to connect with their true aspirations, identities and feelings. So these 'baby-boomers' are now happily shedding ageist stereotypes in favour of more expressive, individualistic and 'youthful' lifestyles. This is precisely the new zestful spirit which the HWW project tried to capture and nurture. In order to measure the success of HWW in promoting resistance to ageism, the project was monitored using a variety of qualitative research tools. These tools are described in the next section.

Researching HWW

A great deal of research on the body has concentrated on its cultural representations. While this is an important avenue of research, it is not the whole story. After all, sociology 'is ultimately not an analysis of representational meanings, but a science or discipline of action and interaction. We need to understand the body in the processes of action and interaction at the level of everyday reciprocities and exchange' (Falk, 1994, pxiii). The HWW research contributes to such a sociological understanding by locating the body in social interactions in a particular time and place. The time was the early 1990s and the location was Ely, a long-established and sprawling housing estate on the edge of Cardiff. Ely has high levels of socio-economic deprivation and a poor social reputation, although older residents sometimes maintain that the decline of the area has not eradicated its community spirit. Ely has poor provisions for social and recreational activities, which was a key reason why it was selected as the base for HWW. The project was intended to reverse the downward spiral of the area, at least for older people, by introducing lively events and activities. These activities can be classified in terms of the three main types of intervention: spectaculars, tasters and clubs. Spectaculars were large-scale exhibitions or shows such as the *Cinderella* pantomime and the annual 50+ Eistedfodd. Tasters were sampler programmes designed to enlarge people's horizons by introducing them to new pursuits and interests (e.g. photography, music appreciation). HWW also created or revived a number of regular clubs (e.g. Watercolours, Gentle Exercise).

HWW lasted for just over three years during which it was jointly funded by the county council, the Welsh Office, the local health authority and Age Concern. Keenly aware that it was an innovative project in terms of aims and methods, the funding bodies insisted on an evaluation so that the lessons could be learned and shared. So the author was asked to monitor the project closely and to collect evidence on its impact. This evaluation relied on a range of research methods:

Observation

The researcher was able to observe all committee meetings and all spectaculars but only a sample of the many tasters and clubs. In all cases field notes were written up during the sessions or immediately afterwards. This method was most useful for recording interaction patterns and environmental details (e.g. layout of stalls and chairs).

Interviews

The interviewees consisted of project staff, liaison staff of allied agencies, and a sample of participants. Staff interviews were conducted with a semi-structured interview schedule but these sessions were usually followed by less structured discussions which were tape-recorded. Interviews with participants tended to be opportunistic and informal in nature, with notes taken contemporaneously. Older people sometimes have a reputation as prickly or rambling interviewees but the HWW participants were largely cooperative, coherent and informative.

Questionnaires

These were issued to participants at successive stages of the project. In the first year questionnaires were used to identify the needs and interests of participants. This feedback was used to plan the subsequent content and direction of the project. In the later stages questionnaires were used mainly to measure satisfaction levels within particular tasters and clubs. The response rates were encouragingly high (60-80 per cent), perhaps because questions were kept simple and short. All of the questionnaires contained open-ended questions which yielded valuable qualitative data.

Focus groups

Apart from a session centred on HWW's publicity material, these focus groups were based on particular clubs. The intention was to identify the motives and views of participants but this method had mixed success. Some of the discussions became rather chaotic with people getting more animated and talking simultaneously on different topics. Nevertheless, the sessions revealed a range of views and they served a useful role as an ice-breaker, as participants often approached the researcher afterwards to expand their ideas.

Documentary analysis

HWW produced three main types of document. First, the publicity material (e.g. flyers, posters, programmes) which was evaluated by means of a focus group. Second, routine administrative records such as minutes of meetings, membership lists and club files. These records were used to build a history of the project and to keep track of attendances across events and over time. Third, diaries were kept over a one year span by a volunteer sample of a dozen HWW participants. This device was used to reveal how HWW activities fitted into their daily life in Ely.

Each of these research tools played a useful role in the HWW evaluation. For example, quantitative data on attendance levels was gathered by means of observation and documentary analysis. But the main aim of the HWW research was to explore the motives, feelings and aspirations of the elderly participants. How did HWW connect with their lives? Did it make them feel better about themselves and their bodies? As Nettleton (1995) points out, we need to develop an understanding of how people interpret and experience the 'lived body'. In the HWW research it was the qualitative data, derived largely from interviews, questionnaires and focus groups, which provided the most interesting insights into peoples' experiences of living in an aged body.

The Impact of HWW

This section reports the main findings of the HWW investigation, starting with a profile of participants and moving on to identify some of the pleasures and problems of being a 'wrinkly'.

Bringing the wrinklies back in

The project managed to get about 1,000 names on its files, and attendance figures were generally impressive. The spectaculars pulled in large numbers (550 at the Second 50+ Eisteddfod). An average of about 100 attended each of the five taster series, some of which were extended beyond the scheduled dates because of the high level of enthusiasm. The clubs varied in size since they catered for minority pursuits (e.g. Trace Your Family Tree, 12 members) as well as popular interests (e.g. Travel Club, 330 members). Of course, attendance figures do not always reflect levels of interest: nobody turned up for the Improve Your Sex Life session but there were many inquiries afterwards about how that session went!

Clubs are not always popular, especially if they are places where 'others' organise activities on behalf of old people rather than allowing them to run their own lives (Jerrome, 1986). Aware of the dangers of 'doing things for old people', the HWW team decided to adopt a strategy of empowerment. People were treated as participants rather than 'clients' and their views and preferences were regularly canvassed. Replies to the open-ended items on the questionnaires show that they felt it was their project ('so different from a class where you just sit and listen and go home - with this project you participate'). But, perhaps inevitably, many local people stayed away. When members of the Meet for Lunch club were asked about non-joiners they speculated the reasons might be personal ('they're just too lazy, too stuck in a rut') or a result of misinformation ('they've got the wrong idea about this place - they think it's a day centre for people who need looking after').

So what sorts of people did HWW attract? The age range stretched from 50 to the mid-80s but the vast majority were over retirement age. As expected among this age group, women outnumbered men but the ratio varied from 1.1/1 in Watercolours to 5.6/1 in Sequence Dancing. The high proportion of people in council or private rented accommodation reflected the predominantly working class population of the area. Another feature was the high rate of cross-membership: people who attended one HWW club were likely to attend others. This supports the observation that 'people who go to the clubs at all tend to belong to several. Club-going is a way of life...' (Jerrome, 1986 p.350).

Stay young and beautiful

Some writers dismiss the 'amusements' of older people as mere escapism. For instance, Lasch (1991) argues that restoring zest to old peoples' lives is a vain attempt to avoid the terrors of ageing. According to Lasch the modern age has developed a culture of narcissism where people are unable to relate to each other in unselfish ways. Lacking inner resources, narcissists yearn to be admired for their beauty, charm, celebrity or power, but these are attributes that usually fade with age. That is why elderly people make desperate and futile attempts to 'stay young' and 'enjoy themselves'. Lasch's judgement seems rather harsh and it is certainly challenged by the findings of the HWW project. Admittedly, the task of making sense of life and death is not resolved simply by providing better leisure opportunities. Nevertheless, it could be argued that recreation and pleasure are essential for a rounded life. Moreover, fun pursuits are not always escapist or frivolous: they can unleash creative skills and lead to a sense of fulfilment. There were many instances of this in the HWW project. For example, the *Cinderella* cast not only acted, they also made the costumes, designed the scenery and wrote the script. One member of the cast recalled in interview how she had never been picked for school concerts since she was 'too plain and too fat'. But now, at last, she had been given the chance to act and it was the thrill of a lifetime. Another moving moment was the rapturous applause for the 84 year old harmonica player who rightly won the musical competition at the 50+ Eisteddfod. This Eisteddfod also allowed entrants to display their considerable talents in art, literature, cookery, needlecraft and handicraft.

HWW participants agreed that the project had enriched their lives in a number of ways. The coding and analysis of open-ended responses to the questionnaires disclosed that the main rewards of HWW were (in descending order of importance): companionship, stimulation and challenge, acquisition of skills and knowledge, improvements in fitness and health, and a renewed sense of dignity. (Note: these findings were supported by the data from interviews and focus groups, but in most cases the quotes that follow were culled from questionnaire replies).

Companionship Mixing with peers provides a supportive network, an opportunity for self-expression, and a chance to negotiate the ambiguities of ageing (Jerrome, 1989). The HWW respondents mentioned the loneliness of old age ('solitary meals', 'sitting alone in the house') and complained that most leisure venues are geared to younger people ('they don't want you there'). HWW, on the other hand, gave them the chance to mix with peers in a friendly environment ('you can talk to them'). This brought many benefits:

> 'As a widow living alone, it has transformed my life'
>
> 'you feel you belong'
>
> 'Ely has become more like a village'

Stimulation Older people are sometimes accused of having narrow interests and closed minds but the HWW participants appreciated the variety and novelty of taster events. They looked forward to 'something new' and felt invigorated and challenged by exposure to new hobbies and ideas:

> 'it prevents you becoming a cabbage'
>
> 'I never thought I'd be interested in classical music'
>
> 'it broadens your outlook'

Skills HWW encouraged participants to develop their skills within specialised clubs such as Watercolours and Gardening. The tasters also awakened dormant interests and inspired them to take things further:

> 'I was always a bit scared about painting but it's amazing what you pick up'
>
> 'I'm not really all that musical but I get a lot of enjoyment out of my keyboards'

Health HWW included sessions on health education and alternative medicine. Some clubs (e.g. Gentle Exercise) were directly concerned with physical wellbeing, while others (e.g. Travel Club, which arranged holidays and outings) made a more indirect contribution. Many respondents claimed that HWW had improved their mental and physical health:

'there would be far more people down at the doctor's if it wasn't for HWW'

'I would be rotting in the house if we didn't have this'

Dignity This was a recurrent theme in conversations with the Ely pensioners. For them, HWW was much more than a cluster of activities. It stood as a public recognition that older people have value and a valid claim to status, respect and hope:

'It feels like a new beginning, not the start of the end'

'It has made my retirement a more pleasant time rather than something I dreaded'

The body shop

HWW challenged many of our cultural assumptions about the elderly body and its capabilities. Even an aged body can take considerable pleasure in mental effort, physical activity and social stimulation. This can be illustrated by looking at the 'body' activities in HWW. Many of the HWW sessions were directly focussed on the care, maintenance and use of the body. The tasters included sessions on health education (e.g. hygiene, healthy eating), alternative medicine (e.g. aromatherapy) and exercise (e.g. yoga, Tai Chi). In addition, physical fitness and coordination were cultivated in the Gentle Exercise and Sequence Dancing clubs. Running through these sessions was the constant message that an elderly body is something to be enjoyed rather than endured. Participants were encouraged to explore, stretch and 'play' with their bodies rather than resign themselves stoically to a physically restricted old age. The project achieved a considerable amount of success in this mission. The Tai Chi workshops proved so popular that they were repeated on a number of occasions, but even their popularity was surpassed by the aromatherapy sessions (the only time on the HWW project when you could have heard a pin drop!).

The two 'body clubs' demonstrate the potential of imaginative approaches towards the elderly body. The Gentle Exercise club (membership 52, average attendance 34) met twice weekly for stretching and movement followed by a relaxing swim in the local leisure centre. Members felt that exercise had improved their health (e.g. it toned up the body, encouraged better movement and coordination, and improved back and neck problems). They were convinced that exercising to music and in pleasant company is far more effective than exercising alone at home, and they also believed the benefits ranged beyond the purely physical: the classes gave them a better outlook, adding a new zest to life. The other body club, Sequence Dancing, met on two afternoons a week. This club (membership 40, average attendance 29) had a warm, happy atmosphere with everyone enthusiastic and eager to participate. The growing confidence of the members was indicated by their stirring display at the second 50+ Eisteddfod. The two dance tutors, whose experience stretched over more than 40 years, said this was the liveliest club they had ever worked with. For their part, the club members reported great physical and mental benefits from dancing and they stressed the 'feelgood' effects of companionship.

A balanced life

Just as it would be foolish to represent old age as a period of unremitting despair, so it would be equally misleading to describe it as a Utopian fun palace. Old age involves a mixture of pleasures and pains, with each person struggling to make sense of it in his or her own way (Cole and Winkler, 1994). Having considered how the HWW project enabled participants to enjoy later life and their ageing bodies, we must also recognise that there are certain social and biological factors which make bodily pleasure more difficult for older people.

Social class There are 'two nations' of pensioners (Oppenheim, 1990). One is the retired but still prosperous middle class, and the other, to which most of the Ely pensioners in HWW belonged, consists of those with modest assets and a small income which keeps them in the margins of poverty. Of course, not all of the HWW members were poor (e.g. the 50+ Travel Club was able to arrange holidays as far afield as Paris, Austria and Tuscany). Nevertheless, many of them said they could not afford the high fees for commercial leisure clubs or adult education classes, and money was just too tight to be spent on designer sportswear or expensive leisure goods. Their lives were overshadowed by material deprivation which inevitably placed limits on their capacity for enjoyment. Consequently, it was much harder for them to join the postmodern game of 'trying on' different identities and lifestyles.

However, class is not just a matter of money but also of differences in values and preferences. This has relevance for the body since these class tastes may become embodied (Bourdieu, 1984), with classes developing different attitudes towards body size, shape and movement (e.g. ways of walking, talking, eating). Featherstone (1987) speculates that working class people tend to be more 'at home' with their bodies and therefore relatively indifferent to the advice of health educationalists and fitness gurus. They are more tolerant of middle age spread and they accept bodily decline rather than striving to maintain or improve their bodies. This attitude contrasts with that of middle class professionals who regard body maintenance 'as a means of combating ageing and eventually avoiding the repulsive properties associated with old age...' (Featherstone, 1987, p.127). But the HWW research suggests that class differences among older people are not clear cut. The Ely pensioners conformed to the 'working class' model insofar as they poured ridicule on aggressive, competitive approaches to body maintenance. The prospect of joyless jogging on hard pavements or grim hours on the treadmill held no appeal. They typically took a relaxed and irreverent attitude to their bodies, laughing at their shapelessness or lack of condition. Nevertheless, many of them took a keen ('middle class') interest in healthy eating and gentle exercise. Aware of their growing frailties, they responded positively to programmes which aimed to preserve and extend their physical powers. The only condition they laid down was that exercise also had to be fun.

Biological limits The problems of old age are not entirely due to class factors or to the way elderly people are labelled and treated by society. Biology sets limits to the degree to which old age can be made genuinely pleasant (Lasch, 1991). The body may be shaped by social influences but we still have to recognise the material limitations imposed by our physical embodiment. Few people escape the niggling aches and pains which come with old age. No matter how many Saga holidays we take, no matter how much ginseng, royal jelly and evening primrose oil we consume, our 'investments' in the body are ultimately doomed to failure: 'Bodies age and decay...what could signal to us more effectively the limitations of our concern with the young and fit, ideally feminine or masculine body than the brute facts of its thickening waistline, sagging flesh and inevitable death?' (Shilling, 1993, p.7).

The recognition that ageing takes its toll might seem to return us to the pessimistic messages of disengagement theory. But this pessimism needs to be qualified for a number of reasons. First, although it is true that rates of physical and mental impairment rise with age, the majority of older people do not describe themselves as sick or unhealthy. This is especially true of those aged 50-75, a group known as the young-old (Neugarten, 1974) or the Third Age (Laslett, 1989). Second, experts are revising their views on the deterioration associated with ageing. Thus, Buzan and Keene (1996) maintain that 'mind sports' and physical exercise can be highly effective in slowing down mental and physical decline. Third, even if older people suffer some physical impairment this does not necessarily destroy their zest for life. Indeed, Berger (1971) takes issue with the assumption that 'youthfulness' is a matter of chronological age. Berger argues that youthful qualities - being impulsive, spontaneous, energetic, exploratory, irreverent, playful and passionate - are found among older people too. Many elderly people do not feel old. Rather, they feel like young people who simply happen to inhabit old bodies, with all the physical problems that entails (Comfort, 1977).

The HWW participants ranged from the relatively fit and healthy through to the chronically infirm. But most of the participants interviewed admitted they were aware of their declining physical powers and they reported that over the years they had gradually re-defined the boundaries of their world ('you've got to slow down a bit'). But, like the respondents interviewed by Thompson et al (1991), they generally took a relaxed view ('it's just something you have to put up with'). Furthermore, they saw no reason why their aches and pains should disenfranchise them from leading active and enjoyable lives.

Conclusions

In this paper we have considered the findings of the HWW evaluation. But what relevance do these findings have for our attitudes towards ageing and the aged body? Do these findings reinforce or challenge conventional wisdom about later life?

It is commonly assumed that old age is a time for reflection, a time to take things easier, a time to mull over memories. It is the period when we have to deal with a sense of loss and waning physical powers. But it is more than that. It is also a time to smell the flowers, to treasure the remaining years of life and celebrate the joys of being alive. It may even be the case that celebration and lament feed each other: 'As we get older, we learn to grieve for what time inexorably devours while taking pleasure in moments of love or beauty or work or wonder' (Cole and Winkler, 1994, p.290). Yet the fun side of old age is often neglected. Policy makers, the caring professions and social scientists tend to highlight the problems of old age and ignore the opportunities it offers. This is not, of course, to deny that many older people suffer financial, social, emotional and physical problems which require support or reform. But the positive side of being old also deserves attention (we might even find that encouraging this side helps to reduce many of the serious problems).

Qualitative research methods offer a fruitful way of exploring these neglected aspects of the ageing body. The HWW research employed qualitative techniques such as observation, interviewing and focus groups as a means of gathering relevant data on the meanings and experiences of old age. By allowing elderly people to tell their own stories it illuminated how it feels to inhabit an aged body. The HWW project is basically a collective story of elderly people responding enthusiastically to opportunities to demonstrate their creativity, vitality and talent. The success of the project exposes the fallacies of ageist stereotypes which treat the elderly body as synonymous with mental passivity, physical dependency and social withdrawal. HWW therefore challenges the bleak view that the physical ageing process sharply restricts people's horizons and capabilities. It suggests that large numbers of elderly people want stimulation, excitement, novelty, risk-taking and a chance to reinvent themselves. If that is the case, then they are not so different from the rest of the population. Deep down they just wanna have fun.

References

Berger, B. (1971), *Looking for America,* Prentice-Hall, New Jersey.

Bourdieu, P. (1984), *Distinction*, Routledge, London.

Bunyan, N. (19.8.88), 'Time for the yuppies to move over', *Today.*

Buzan, T. & Keene, R. (1996), *The Age Heresy,* Ebury Press, London.

Cole, T. & Winkler, M. (1994), *The Oxford Book of Aging,* Oxford University Press, Oxford.

Comfort, A. (1977), *A Good Old Age*, Mitchell Beazley, London.

Cumming, E. & Henry, W. (1961), *Growing Old*, New York, Basic Books.

Falk, P. (1994), *The Consuming Body*, Sage, London.

Featherstone, M. (1987), 'Leisure, symbolic power and the life course' in J. Horne et al, *Sport, Leisure and Social Relations*, Routledge & Kegan Paul, London.

Featherstone, M. & Hepworth, M. (1989), 'Ageing and Old Age' in B. Bytheway et al (eds), *Becoming and Being Old*, Sage, London.

Hills, J. (1993), *The Future of Welfare*, Joseph Rowntree Foundation, York.

Jerrome, D. (1986), 'Me Darby, You Joan!' in C. Phillipson et al, *Dependency and Interdependency in Old Age*, Croom Helm, London.

Jerrome, D. (1989), 'Virtue and Vicissitude', in M. Jefferys (ed.), *Growing Old in the 20th.Century*, Routledge, London.

Lasch, C. (1991), *The Culture of Narcissism*, W. W. Norton & Co, New York.

Laslett, P. (1989), *A Fresh Map of Life*, Weidenfeld and Nicolson, London.

Nettleton, S. (1995), *Sociology of Health and Illness*, Polity, Cambridge.
Neugarten, B.L. (1975), 'The Future of the Young Old', *The Gerontologist*, vol. 15 no. 1., pp 4-9.
Phillipson, C. (1982), *Capitalism and the Construction of Old Age*, MacMillan, Basingstoke.
Shilling, C. (1993), *The Body and Social Theory*, Sage, London.
Thompson, P., Itzin, C. & Abendstern, M. (1991), *I Don't Feel Old*, Oxford University Press, Oxford.

10. Bodies on display: experiences from the fetish club field

Victoria Butler

(February 1994)

I watched as people sauntered into the club, some wearing restricting corsets with pierced nipples peeping over the top, and many tottering up the candle-lit stair case in cripplingly pointed four inch heeled shoes or boots. How will they dance in those I thought to myself? Without wanting to stare, I kept glancing at the vicious looking school Ma'am standing in front of me. I wondered what sex she was, not that it mattered, but she could be an amazingly well made-up transvestite. Her bun, make-up and general deportment added to her severity, but I tried not to focus on her because the way she tapped her cane across the palm of her hand seemed all too menacing. Perhaps she would punish people for anything, I thought, moving hastily towards the main room of the club. Amidst the smell of tobacco, rubber, leather and sweat I did a double take. That bloke is wearing a full red glossy rubber cat suit; and he's got a mask and thigh boots to match. But he's huge! I wonder where he finds clothes like that to fit him? How does he go to the toilet in that, or even, come to think of it, how does he drink with that mask on? He must get very hot.

(November 1995)

It's very tame here I thought to myself. Sure, there's a few whipping scenes going on here and there, but none of it is exactly major and there's no play and suspension room at all. I went to find T (one of my key informants) and her master. I eventually found them and asked permission from her master to chat to her. He happily obliged. T was bored as well. 'Excellent costumes' she said, 'but there's not much else

> happening'. 'No', I agreed. 'Did you see that woman in the rubber spider's costume, it was amazing! And the bloke with all those tubes'. 'Oh Yeah!' she agreed, and asked permission to go 'walk about' with me. As we left to wonder around the club she began talking about her dissatisfaction with her master and how she doesn't normally like red rubber but that the dress she was wearing was different. She was walking expertly in her high-heeled red shoes, and bondage restricting dress. 'You suit red', I said.

The above two extracts are from my first and last field notes respectively about my experiences and feelings during participant observation in fetish clubs. This research was conducted for part of an MPhil studying body piercing. They are included to exemplify the initiation process a researcher undergoes during the course of inquiry, as well as to orientate the reader to the social arena in question. This chapter is concerned with my experience of this learning process, which raised issues about the nature of participant observation and helped formulate theory about body practices. There have been developments in sociological theory about embodiment over recent years, but little of this theory is grounded in empirical evidence. My aim is to explore the nature of participant observation, ground a theory of embodiment experience in the data collected, whilst suggesting how participant observation can aid research about body practice and experience and contribute to the sociological literature on the body.

What is a fetish club?

Using Goffman's dramaturgical approach (1969) a fetish club can best be described as a semi-public performance arena. Although they are public spaces rather than private, they also have entry requirements (usually involving membership or invitation) and a strict dress code which severely restricts entry - similar to a private golf club but with different status attachments. They exist in large towns and cities throughout Britain, most having regular club nights, perhaps fortnightly or monthly. There are also fetish 'events' that occur annually, such as a fetish fashion ball, which differ slightly from a regular fetish club night by having a focal point of the evening, for example a fashion show. People meet regularly at clubs and events to display and discuss different types of body art, dress in fetishistic costumes, and to be involved in sado-masochistic scenes (i.e. pain pleasure experiences, referred to as S/M) and dominance-bondage scenes (i.e. power and humiliation scenes, referred to as D/B). Participants at these events may be involved in one or all of these practices. For some people these practices are interdependent, whilst for others they are exclusive activities. All of these practices are highly ritualistic involving adult play and consent to ensure that there is no coercion. For such activities to maintain their potency there is a high level of etiquette and the people who frequent these clubs function like Goffman's teams in order to continue the performance. That is, they share an interest in these activities like a hobby, but have little else in common. In the clubs it is rare for people to talk of their other identities in everyday life.

Although this describes a fetish club generally, they do vary. A few tend to revolve around costume and adornment, but most offer an arena for S/M and D/B scenes, often having an equipment area housing a whipping cross, suspension harness and stocks for people to use. Progressive clubs tend to attract a younger crowd and have an atmosphere of 'anything goes', celebrating diversity of sexuality, gender and sexual practices. Traditional clubs, on the other hand, attract an older crowd and centre on the more familiar patterns involved in 'master/mistress' and 'slave' relationships. However, these are generalisations. Some clubs specify a status for entry, such as being in a couple or of a certain sexual orientation. In addition to the fetish clubs and events there are a number of related activities, particularly in London, that can be marked in the fetishist's diary. These include fetish tea afternoons, paraphernalia markets where people meet each other and buy whips, cuffs etc., forums and workshops for the discussion and teaching of safe S/M practices, S/M support group meetings, and an annual S/M Pride march. This march is held in London and celebrates S/M as a valid sexuality as well as protesting about the verdict and implications of the Spanner case, which is discussed later in this chapter. The people who participate in these activities and accompanying sexual practices describe themselves as being 'on the scene'. 'The scene' and 'scene practices' refer to practices and events collectively. 'A scene' on the other hand, refers to the enactment of practices by individuals. This may appear confusing, but it is the terminology of the participants themselves. For detailed interviews about scene participation see Polhemus and Randall (1994). Since my research interest was in body piercing, I attended only key events - the stainless steel ball, the rubber ball, and S/M pride - and some club nights over a period of a year and a half, all of which were based in the South East of England.

Issues of participant observation

Text books (e.g. May, 1993; Burgess, 1984) offer guidance about conducting participant observation, including issues such as informed consent, overt research and different researcher roles. However, in the fetish club field, participant observation issues can be far muddier than textbooks suggest. The main problems that I faced and discuss below were ethical issues including covert research, informed consent, researcher role and anonymous reporting.

There have been many debates about covert research since the publication of Humphreys (1975). However, the arena within which I undertook observation made it difficult to conduct overt research causing a crossover into the grey boundary between overt and covert research. For example, informing 500 to 3,000 people in a club (and hence being overt) that I was present as a researcher would have been impractical. I could have gained permission from organisers, but this would not be equivalent to informing the participants themselves that I was observing them. I also think I would have been denied entry owing to the negative media and legal attention fetish clubs have gained over the last few years. I gained entry through personal knowledge of the scene, having been introduced to fetish clubs through work as a circus performer. I attended the S/M marches and met people there who became my key informants and told me about the other key events and club nights. Consequently, although I never resolved feeling on the boundaries of covert research, I told all club members that I spoke to of my research in body piercing and was open as to the extent of my involvement with the scene.

Getting participants to understand my research and thus gain informed consent from individuals at the outset of conversation proved problematic. Firstly, I had the dual problem of trying to accurately hear people over loud music, and sometimes finding myself in discussion with people who had taken stimulants. The effect of these drugs caused people to be overly willing to impart highly personal information about their piercings and sexual habits, which I had not asked for, and before informed consent had been established. In these few instances I have kept absolute confidentiality about what was said and who said it, as well as being cautious of using data gained under such circumstances. Secondly, getting people to understand my role as a researcher proved difficult. This second problem was related to my self-presentation and having a viable researcher role. My actions may have seemed at variance with my words when I informed participants at events that I was researching body piercing, because I was dressed entirely in fetish costume with no visible piercings.

(Nose piercing does not count as a proper piercing in such a setting). This did cause confusion. Some people on the scene talk of having a 'coming out' period, which involves being public and proud about one's own sexuality, and participants often thought that I was a shy person in this process. Consequently, I was seen as a part of their group regardless of what I said to the contrary, dismissing me as a researcher.

This problem arose because I wanted to avoid mimicking a role that could mislead people, and so I decided that in order to be viable I would have to maintain a personal position. I was neither an outsider nor insider, and tried to maintain the dubious position of being both simultaneously. I like subtle body piercings but do not have any myself; I love the spectacle and drama of fetishistic costume but do not want to try some of the practices. This position was tenuous because it confused people as to what I was and may have caused certain responses to me. For example, I felt emotionally and physically comfortable in my thigh boots, basque and knickers - a tamer variation of a classic dominatrix style - but this may have caused people to interact with me in certain ways. For example, dominants and submissives may have perceived me as a dominatrix and interacted with me according to the projection of my role and in a manner fitting their chosen role. There was no way of avoiding this, but being reflexive allowed for an awareness of intersubjectivity (Ellis and Flaherty, 1992). These issues are explored in the following section.

The last area of ethical concern involves the reporting of my data in the light of the Spanner verdict. Briefly, the Spanner case began in 1987 when the police in Bolton, England seized four home videos. These videos were made by S/M enthusiasts and contained scenes of extreme practices including laceration, branding and temporary genital piercing with pins and wires (Dyer, 1993; Polhemus and Randall, 1994). These videos were passed to the obscene publications squad who opened Operation Spanner, an investigation which lasted two years and involved interviewing over 100 gay people. At London's Old Bailey 26 people were cautioned and 11 received sentences for assault (Polhemus and Randall, 1994). These cases went to the Court of Appeal where the sentences were reduced but the convictions upheld. This means that it is an offence against the person to perform an act that is intended or likely to cause injury regardless of the willingness and consent of the other person involved (Law Commission Consultation Paper, no. 134). Hence a consenting couple or group who consent to share S/M activities can be prosecuted for assault upon the self and actual bodily harm. There are obvious issues here about prejudice, body ownership and the technicalities of law enforcement. However, since the creation of this law, fetish clubs have been raided by the police, shut down and arrests made for operating lewd houses. Consequently in my data I have a responsibility to anonymise places and people, and report events vaguely, to ensure the protection of concerned parties.

Reflexivity in researching embodiment

If a research topic is to be well documented, the research process and researcher's role and impact upon the data must be included, which involves a reflexive attitude and transparency from the researcher. We are all socialised with personal and cultural taboos surrounding body practices. In the course of this research there were practices that people talked of enjoying, such as giving enemas or having brandings, which I found disturbing. With an awareness of my preconceived feelings I could emotionally accept such activities, avoid moral judgement and gradually understand why other people enjoyed these things. Reflexivity is not about self-indulgence but self-awareness because:

> The self is used to study others. To argue that Anthropology is informed by the Anthropologist's self is not the same as any suggestion that the discipline should be about the Anthropologist's self (Okely, 1992, p. 20).

If we insert 'sociology' in place of 'anthropology' in this quote, the meaning is still clear. To avoid clouding data through an excess of personal information, I kept different observational notes for emotional, descriptive and analytical issues. The emotional notes contained data about things that occurred which had disturbed me and my responses to this; the descriptive notes described the venues and social relations of each event; whilst the analytical notes contained my initial theoretical links. I separated these issues so that my emotions would not inhibit my descriptions or theory, and used both mental and practical reflexivity to aid self-awareness.

Mental reflexivity involved suspending not only taboos, but pre-conceived ideas generally. For example, some feminists would find the sight of a woman wearing a dog collar and lead being led around a club by a man, or being whipped abhorrent, and initially I found this disturbing. However, through conversations with female 'slaves' my attitude altered, discovering that they felt dominant in everyday life and enjoyed the change of submissiveness. Generally, there was an awareness of gender politics from men and women of all sexual orientations, and all participants stressed the importance of the role of consent within a scene. Scene practices are about consented domination in the sexual sphere alone, regardless of sexual orientation and the gender of the submissive. This is why being female did not adversely effect my data and all participants were respectful and non-pressurising, avoiding the 'eyeing up' process that occurs in other night clubs. 'Sadism' is commonly thought to be the enjoyment of inflicting pain upon others, after the writings of De Sade (1964). However, this misses the crucial point that it is not so much inflicted as requested, via the submissive's consent. The form of the pain or humiliation is negotiated between the people involved, and everyone I spoke to had an 'opt-out' word. This means that if a scene goes too far physically or psychologically for any of the participants, then a word that has been previously agreed upon can be said, and that scene will immediately stop. Ultimately this is a lived world of psychological and physical fantasy, so there is no real coercion, but a stress on emotional, personal and physical safety. However, to know this information I had to suspend my perception of correct gender behaviour and retain an awareness of my own prejudices.

The essence of practical reflexivity is finding a position of comfortable involvement. This is linked to the point made in the previous section whereby a researcher role is maintainable but not misleading. I did consider having a body piercing in the name of research (like Danforth, 1989, who walked on fire for his research enquiry). However, an experience that is a mimicked action will lead to a phoney experience and not experiential knowledge. A researcher should not get involved with elements of the cohort's culture if it feels uncomfortable, even though such involvement may lead to acceptance or knowledge. Applying this to scene practices, any activities that I was unwilling to undergo could have led to emotional upheavals if I had undertaken them out of reluctant curiosity. For example, I was asked to join a couple for a spanking session. I also attended some S/M introduction and safety workshops, one of which was about temporary piercing. This involved getting into pairs and inserting small lines of needles under each other's skins, lacing them up and pulling on them. On both of these occasions I felt that involvement was beyond what I could comfortably do with my body, so I declined the couple and just observed the workshop. On the other hand, I did participate in activities that felt comfortable. This included a bondage for beginners workshop, which was light-hearted and involved tying people together and to objects such as chairs, learning basic knots and learning safety tips, such as symptoms of cut-off circulation. On another occasion, a foot and boot enthusiast fell prostrate in front of me and, whilst proclaiming me to be his goddess, proceeded to lick his way up the toe and ankle of my boot. I was not particularly offended and felt it would not have been appropriate to be angry, so I just tapped him away with my heel on his forehead and told him he was not worthy. Such involvement was comfortable, and gave me a small amount of experiential knowledge about fantasy power relationships and common D/B practices.

Practical reflexivity relates to choosing the appropriate role out of pure observer, participant observer and complete participant given the situational context. I used mental and practical reflexivity to gauge my involvement, assess my personal boundaries and to develop a personal code of ethics. This is particularly necessary and useful when researching embodiment. Through allowing my own body to undergo certain practices, via participant observation methods, I could gain experiential knowledge about the nature of embodiment. Participant observation also yielded secondary knowledge via conversations that I had with participants during the research process. Both forms of knowledge give data about embodiment experience, which forms the basis of formulating grounded theory.

A happy partnership - theory and data

There is an increasing amount of sociological theory about embodiment, but little of this work is based upon empirical evidence. In this research participant observation is used in an attempt to ground my theory in empirical data. When formulating theory about embodiment from my research, the first task was to bridge the dichotomy of mind-body, since this is too simplistic and does not allow for integrated, simultaneous experiences gained from these two aspects of the self. This dichotomy has historically pervaded Western philosophy and social theory, and implies that the body is somehow natural whilst the mind is cultural. It would be more accurate to claim that cultural norms subvert biological forms (Synott, 1993) and that a body practice defined as 'natural' is more a case of ascribed normality. Each society has its own cultural norms of what the body should look like and how it should be treated, so perceived natural practices are culturally relative (see Polhemus, 1978, for examples). Since body norms are culturally defined, it is possible to invert and transgress them, using clothing, adornments and deportment as tools. A discussion of norms of the body includes rather than ignores the body's physicality. It is these norms that a researcher may have to be reflexive towards if using qualitative methods for an investigation about embodiment.

Upon reading much of the sociological literature on embodiment two main issues become apparent. First is that many theorists categorise the body into 'types'. For example, Frank (1991) describes the disciplined, mirroring, dominating and communicative bodies as four dimensions of embodiment. Turner (1992) discusses the body as having four tasks – reproduction, restraint, representation and regulation - that are contextualized via social systems. Featherstone (1991) distinguishes between the inner and outer bodies. Leder (1990) analyses the differences between leib and korper before outlining the differences of varying bodies, including the ecstatic and dys-appearing bodies. Although the arguments that accompany these distinctions are important there is not space to engage with them here. However, many of these body categorisations are limited to particular areas of application. My own list of types, based on my research on embodiment, is intended to identify general categorisations which lie on a continuum of bodily experiences. It is hoped that they may be applicable to a wider range of body projects.

Before detailing my theoretical suggestions, the second issue that arises from the embodiment literature is that different theorists appear to be in disagreement with each other. This is most clearly outlined by Shilling (1993) and Turner (1991, 1996). Both describe different epistemological views surrounding the body. These include the social constructionist stance that views the body as a receptor rather than generator of social meanings (Douglas, 1970), and a naturalistic view of the body, which holds that our biological make-up determines the individual, as advocated by sociobiologists and some eco-feminists. Shilling also outlines a foundationalist view of the body which includes material, physical and biological phenomenon 'irreducible to immediate social processes and classifications' (Shilling, 1993, p.10). Although he does not propound such a view, he does suggest that it cannot be ignored in favour of social forces alone. Through close reading of different embodiment theorists it is clear that disagreements and fragmentation of theory stems as much from epistemology as from a confusion about which aspect of bodily experience is being researched. If these theorists are synthesised rather than pitched against each other, different aspects of the body can be seen in conjunction with each other. I will discuss this synthesis with reference to the scene practices mentioned in the first half of this chapter.

Rising to Shilling's (1993) call for a simultaneous biological and social analysis, and influenced by Turner's (1996) theoretical consolidation, I use Nietzsche's concept of herkunft as my starting point (Miller, 1994). Herkunft refers to a place where willing, feeling and thinking actions are rooted, and Foucault argued this place to be the body (Miller, 1994). However, these actions are more than just located in the body, since they are chosen by individuals to give different body experiences and interpreted according to social processes. This highlights the need to bridge the mind-body and social-physical dichotomies that were mentioned above, which I have attempted through synthesising theorists rather than advocating one over another. I have identified four bodily aspects, which are experienced simultaneously, and are like four points on a continuum of body experiences. Each of these aspects tends to correspond with a certain theorist or a particular epistemological stance. The four aspects are the lived, the ecstatic, the social and the political.

The lived aspect

This is physical and has huge importance for people on the scene. Inspired by Leder (1990) this aspect is labelled 'lived' because it refers to the immediate physical and emotional sensations that can be experienced through the body. It forms the basis of action in the scene, for example when a fetishist feels a favourite material, such as rubber next to their skin; or when an S/M enthusiast anticipates and feels the sensations of giving or receiving a pain-pleasure experience. More generally it refers to any physical sensation that is a direct result of embodiment - Nietzsche's place of feeling - and has been greatly overlooked historically by many sociologists (Turner, 1992). Although contextual in its importance, the lived body needs recognition because of the impact bodily sensations, such as wanting the toilet or feeling ill, have on everyday lived experience.

The ecstatic aspect

This is associated with being both object and subject to oneself, and involves presenting ourselves to others as we wish to be seen (Goffman 1968, 1969), having implications for self and group identity formation. This aspect of the body relates to how we interpret and negotiate in the social world to create viable selves and social networks - Nietzsche's place of thinking - which is much more than 'mind' in the traditional Cartesian outlook. For the scene, this is a complicated aspect because the fetish identity is often covert from the other social identities taken in everyday life, and consequently inhabits a world of secrecy. This gives some insight into how identities coexist and are not fixed, as well as how self uniqueness may be in conflict with group belonging. The ecstatic aspect is important in terms of team performance since it upholds the group ritualistic practices that are enjoyed in the clubs and informs the strict codes of etiquette.

The social aspect

This is the symbolic realm, which is omitted in herkunft. The social aspect is discussed by Douglas (1970) in relation to the body being symbolic of society. It is based in semiotics and relates to our choices of clothing and adornment that express our taste and cultural preferences. 'Symbols enable individuals to experience and express their attachment to a society or group without compromising their individuality' (Cohen, 1994, p. 19), and can be read by on-lookers as a non-verbal form of communication. This is present in the fetish world whereby all manner of symbolic clothing communicates if one is dominant ('top') or submissive ('bottom') and enhances the fantasy world and arena of the other. The instruments of the scene, such as collars and chastity belts, canes and shackles, are also used for their symbolic charge - when used or placed upon the body the symbolic image of pain and restraint adds to the creation of a disciplining arena. For example, compare the use of these instruments to beaded necklaces, a book and silk scarves for the same purposes - they would do the same job adequately but the symbolic effect would be lost!

The political aspect

This last aspect of embodiment involves Nietzsche's 'place of willing', which is political and Foucauldian in nature. There are two aspects to this. One is the way in which people use their body politically to express their opposition and resistance to societal control, which can be a reason for having facial piercings. The other way for the body to be political is when it comes in to conflict with the law, and a classic example of this is Operation Spanner. The S/M Pride marches are an example of people using their physical presence to express conflict. This is intensified by the fact that the marchers are dressed in fetish clothing, often leading each other, and usually following human carriages. (A human carriage involves having a master/mistress in a lightweight cart being pulled by human horses-harnessed slaves with blinkers.) This public display of pride in difference challenges what is culturally perceived to be natural deportments of the body.

Conclusion

Although these four aspects of bodily experience need more research and in-depth discussion, from this brief outline it is possible to acknowledge the importance of the sociology of embodiment to sociological theory generally. The body is intrinsically linked to other social arenas particularly identity, gender studies, semiotics, consumption, health and politics, all of which need empirical enquiry. However, this does raise the issue of whether embodiment should be its own area within a sociological context or researched within the aforementioned spheres as an inherent part of social experience and interaction.

The four aspects of bodily experience are important because they are not exclusive of each other, but occur and are experienced in social life simultaneously. Although they coexist, the importance of each varies according to social context. Following Nietzche, the body is a multiplicity of experiences, which can be integrated or unified (Haar, 1995). Within the scene, these aspects of embodiment complement each other via the same practices, but within the context of other body practices and experiences they could easily be in conflict with each other. The body is a site of unity and conflict, both within the individual, between people and in relation to the state. In sociological research, all physical and social aspects of embodiment need to be considered, grounded in social life and be discussed in relation to the unity or conflicts that are present within the particular experience of embodiment.

Participant observation can be an invaluable method since it allows for considered personal experience, observation and conversation of other people's embodiment experiences. Hence it allows for three types of knowledge - experiential, observational and secondary - that, when combined, can lead to a fuller sociological understanding. If research is about body issues then some experience of the sensations involved will be useful. I am not suggesting that a researcher has to experience in order to gain understanding, but rather that a taste of the physical aspect of their research can aid a comprehension of data. Final reporting of data will always be two or three experiences removed from the participants (Geertz, 1973) and when based upon information gained via participant observation there is always a tension of its validity. This is because a researcher has to gauge the extent of their involvement, so that their data is not too removed from participants owing to under involvement or too partial to one view point because of going native. Reflexivity, as outlined, allows the researcher to gauge the extent and usefulness of their involvement.

When investigating taboo areas, such as scene practices, reflexivity in participant observation also enables the consideration of the researcher's own emotions, so the initial infringement of personal values does not invoke negative responses to participants. Personal values are initially suspended by control of the emotions at the outset of research. However, as one is initiated into the life-world of the group, rules become understandable and hence less strange. During this process it is possible that the initial suspended values may change as experience and data gathering generates understanding, (although this will vary depending upon the researcher and the topic in question). In relation to research about the body, participant observation as a qualitative method is invaluable because it enables three types of complementary knowledge, including a gauged level of personal experience. This enhances a sociological understanding of the body by enabling the description of personal experience and observational data that can be used to formulate grounded theory about the integration of different bodily experiences.

References

Burgess, R.G. (1984), *In The Field*, George Allen and Unwin, London.

Cohen, A.P. (1994), *Self Consciousness,* Routledge, London.

Danforth, M. (1989), *Firewalking and Religious Healing*, Princetown University Press.

De Sade D.A.F. (1964) (ed.), *Justine*, Lancer books Inc., New York.

Douglas, M. (1970), *Natural Symbols*, The Cresset Press, London.

Dyer, C. The Guardian , March 12th 1993.

Ellis, C. and Flaherty, M.G. (1992), 'An Agenda for the Interpretation of Lived Experience' in Ellis, C. and Flaherty, M. G. (eds), *Investigating Subjectivity,* Sage, London.

Featherstone, M. (1991), 'The Body in Consumer Culture' in Featherstone, M. et al (eds), *The Body*, Sage, London.

Frank, A.W. (1991), 'For a Sociology of the Body', in Featherstone, M. et al. (eds), *The Body*, Sage, London.

Geertz, C. (1973), *The Interpretation of Cultures,* Basic Books, New York.

Goffman, E. (1968), *Stigma*, Penguin, Harmondsworth.

Goffman, E. (1969), *Presentation of the Self in Everyday Life*, 2nd ed. Penguin, London.

Haar, M. (1995), 'Nietzche and Metaphysical Language' in D. Allison (ed.), *The New Nietzche: Contemporary Styles of Interpretation*, 7th ed. MIT Press, Cambridge, Massachusetts.

Humphreys, L. (1975), *The Tea-Room Trade,* Aldine de Gruyter, New York.

Law Commission, Consultation Paper 134, 'Criminal Law: Consent and Offences Against the Person'.

Leder, D. (1990), *The Absent Body*, University of Chicago Press, Chicago.

May, T. (1993), *Social Research: Issues, Methods and Process*, Open University Press, Milton Keynes.
Miller, J. (1994), *The Passion of Michel Foucault*, Harper Collins Publishers.
Okely, J. (1992), 'Participatory Experience and Embodied Knowledge' in Okely, J. and Callaway, H. (eds), *Anthropology and Autobiography*, Routledge, London.
Polhemus, T. and Randall, H. (1994), *Rituals of Love: Sexual experiments, Erotic Possibilities*, Picador, London.
Polhemus, T. (ed.) (1978), *Social Aspects of the Human Body,* Penguin, Harmondsworth.
Shilling, C. (1993), *The Body and Social Theory*, Sage, London.
Synott, A. (1993), *The Body Social*, Routledge, London.
Turner, B.S. (1992), *Regulating Bodies,* Routledge, London.

11. Inter-corporeality and reflexivity: researching naturism

Odette Parry

Introduction

Recently researchers have become more visible in the research product, signifying the rejection of positivistic methodological paradigms which seek to cleanse the data from researcher contamination (Hammersley and Atkinson, 1983). In contrast, naturalistic research paradigms, which aim to understand data analysis as a reflexive process where meanings are made rather than found (Atkinson, 1992), celebrate the researcher in this process. From this perspective data are not fixed, but contingent, partial and dependent upon the conditions and contexts of their production. Hence it has been argued that, in order to understand both quantitative and qualitative data and the products of data analysis, they should be accompanied by detailed accounts of their production and the role of the researcher in that process (Coti, Foster and Thompson, 1995). This is a trend which has been particularly encouraged within feminist research, where the biography of the researcher, her theoretical, methodological, epistemological and political positionings are seen as an integral component of the research process and outcome (Roberts, 1981; Bowles and Klein, 1983; Wilkinson, 1986).

However, while there has been a growing interest in the role of the researcher in qualitative research, so far scant attention has been paid to issues of corporeality, or in other words the role of the physical body, in research processes. To date, interest in this topic has largely been restricted to consideration about how the researcher's physical presentation may affect the relationship with respondents. For example, Hammersley and Atkinson (1983) argue that respondents will cast the researcher into certain identities on the basis of ascribed characteristics as well as aspects of appearance and manner, and this must be monitored for its effects on the kinds of data collected. What is missing from this is a detailed consideration of the actual issue of inter-corporeality or inter-subjectivity;

namely the production of meanings through the actual physical interaction between researcher and respondent.

It is not surprising that this issue has been relatively neglected given that until recently the body as a subject of sociological theorising has been largely ignored and relegated to the biological domain (Scott and Morgan, 1993). There is, however, an increasing interest from sociologists both in the ways in which social situations make demands of the body and also in how social orders are concerned with the control and surveillance of bodies (Connell, 1987).

These are not ideas new to anthropology. In the early 1980s when I carried out fieldwork for an MSc study on social nudism (naturism) my theoretical interests at the time were informed by the tradition of French structural anthropology. Consequently my analysis was influenced by scholars like Mauss (1979) who, as far back as the 1930s, defined bodily techniques as ways in which we know how to use our bodies. Mauss argued that even the most mundane and routine of our everyday activities are based in corporeal-cultural techniques whose form varies both historically and cross-culturally. More recently from within the same tradition, Mary Douglas (1973a) focused upon the cultural manifestations of bodily expression, describing ways in which physical bodies reflect the social systems in which they reside. Douglas argues that the social categories which sustain a particular view of society modify the physical experience of the body. There is, she suggests, a continual interplay between the two types of body experience: physical and social, so that each reinforces the categories of the other. She further argues of the body:

> The forms it adopts in movement and response express social pressures in manifold ways. The care that is given to it in grooming, feeding and therapy, the theories about what it needs in the way of sleep and exercise, about the stages it should go through, the pain it can stand, its span of life; all the cultural categories in which it is perceived must correlate closely with the categories in which society is seen in so far as these also draw upon some culturally processed idea of the body (Douglas, 1973b, p.93).

Therefore by reaching some understanding of the individual's assumptions concerning his/her body we should achieve some understanding of his/her other 'body', namely society. Arguing that the scope of the body as a medium of expression is restricted by the demands of the social system concerned, Douglas suggests that societies characterised by weak social control tend to permit a wide range of physical expression. But societies with strong social control seek a high level of physical control; they strive to 'disembody' forms of physical expression. These ideas are further developed by Elias (1978) who argues that social control and physical control became inextricably linked in civilising processes which are characterised by the increasing domination of culture over nature.

This anthropological perspective was particularly suited to the study which I carried out for an MSc in the early 1980s, in which the physical body was the central focus of the research. Most of the fieldwork for the research was carried out inside a naturist club. Furthermore, the naturist club appeared to reflect a system which, in the interests of anaesthetising a perceived relationship between nudity and sexuality, demanded extremely high levels of control over bodily expression. To this extent the study reflected the interests of North American and Canadian scholars researching nudism in the late 1960s and early 1970s (Weinburg, 1967, 1970; Screaton Page, 1971). These researchers took as a starting point the nude/sexual appresentation (Schutz, 1962) and examined ways in which clubs constructed a 'situated morality' in which nudism was defined as a normal and moral pursuit. These studies, which relied upon postal questionnaire surveys, managed to highlight the strategies, organising principles and membership requirements of these naturist clubs, but they were unable to explore how the 'anaesthetising arrangements' were translated into actual behaviour by members inside the clubs. In contrast, my own study, which relied on data obtained from participant observation within naturist clubs, was able to focus on these processes. The following account of the history of a research project is based upon those experiences of carrying out research into naturism. It reflects upon how the corporeality of the researcher is an integral component of the research process.

History of a research project

When I embarked upon the study in 1982, I experienced some difficulty in locating naturists, who do not generally advertise their whereabouts or encourage interest from outsiders. The secrecy which pervades their activities affords some measure of protection from the unsympathetic and often hostile gaze of non-naturist others.

Shortly after the start of my study the Central Council for British Naturism, a national organisation representing the interests of British naturist clubs and their members, placed a series of advertisements in

Health and Efficiency in order to solicit interest from non-naturists. The journal issue which carried the advertisement drew attention to two major naturist organisations in Britain. The first, the Central Council for British Naturism (CCBN), was described as the older and more traditional organisation, whereas the other was described as having a more 'modern' approach to social nudity. While the first organisation called itself naturist and its practices naturism, the latter described itself as nudist and its practices nudism.

Having little information on which to base a comparison of the two groups, I wrote to both, expressing an interest in their respective organisations and naturism/nudism more generally. Whereas I received no immediate reply from the CCBN, the second organisation, which I call UNICORN, replied by return of post giving some, albeit limited, information about the organisation and about club membership. In the absence of any reply from the CCBN I decided to pursue my interest in UNICORN and as a result several letters passed between myself and the club proprietor. In the initial stages of this correspondence I merely expressed an interest in the club, but in a later letter I explained how my interest in UNICORN stemmed from the fact that I was carrying out a study on naturism for a postgraduate degree. There were two reasons for this disclosure. The first was ethical: I did not want to mislead respondents by misrepresenting my particular interest in naturism. Second, I used disclosure as a device to justify my own participation (Wax, 1980) and to put my relationship with the respondent and the intended research group on a different footing.

Despite having limited prior information about naturism, the little I did have suggested to me that UNICORN differed quite substantially from CCBN clubs. The more I found out about UNICORN the less inappropriate it seemed to me for the proprietor to describe himself (as he did in our early correspondence) as 'a naturist anarchist'. I was alerted to these differences by the sorts of activities and facilities which UNICORN advertised. For example, a special attraction of UNICORN was the weekly parties which it hosted. Whereas men were required to pay a membership and admittance fee to the parties, women were admitted free of charge. Furthermore, women attending the parties were not required to pay for any of the alcohol, provided by the club management, which they consumed. The parties started at 8pm on Saturday night and finished at 2am on Sunday morning. Ways in which UNICORN parties contradicted the ethos of CCBN naturism will be discussed in more detail later. At the time of my initial contact with UNICORN, although I was unaware of many of the CCBN club rules and regulations, naked partying did not seem to me to be compatible with the image of respectable nudity which the CCBN wished to portray. The 'common sense' association which I made between, on the one hand, night time, alcohol, parties and nudity and, on the other, sexuality, made me deeply suspicious about the naturist pretensions of UNICORN.

Despite this, and fuelled by a combination of intrigue and a pressing desire for data, I made one weekend fieldwork visit to UNICORN. During my stay at the club I talked to the proprietor, attended a party and spoke to some members. It appeared that membership of UNICORN was open to any applicant upon payment of the appropriate fee (waived in the case of women). The motto of the club was 'live and let live' and members were urged to treat others as they expected to be treated themselves. The proprietor insisted that under no circumstances should members be upset by the behaviour of others, or the law broken. In some respects the party at UNICORN was similar to a typical night club scene, in that it was characterised by subdued lighting, stuffy/smoky atmosphere, loud disco type music and alcohol consumption. But it also differed, in that participants were encouraged to remove all their clothing and the dance floor and surrounding seating areas were filled by bodies in various stages of undress.

Based upon that weekend experience I decided, for several reasons, to discontinue any association with UNICORN. First, I felt that the CCBN, as the traditional and long standing representative organisation of British naturism, was the more appropriate focus for the study. Second, given the probable differences between the two approaches to nudity, I suspected that association with one organisation might be tainted by an association with the other. It transpired that this suspicion was fully justified. The third and main reason why I discontinued association with UNICORN was that the experience of visiting, while not physically threatening, had been emotionally difficult. While I still find it difficult to describe my discomfort, I believe that it stemmed from an undercurrent of sexual innuendo which seemed to pervade the club. The expressed views of the proprietor, the activities of the club and the motivations of its members were far removed from my expectations of what constituted naturism. In subsequent discussions with friends and colleagues I played down the impact which the visit undoubtedly had, but I was troubled for some time afterwards. This led me to question whether or not to pursue the naturism study at all. In the immediate short term following my return from the visit I found myself taking many more baths and showers than usual, and recognised this as a symptom of feeling dirty and wanting to cleanse myself of an unpleasant experience.

It was shortly following this visit to UNICORN that I received a reply from the CCBN informing me that my details had been passed onto a local club (ELM), which would be contacting me in due course. I read with interest the naturist code which was included along with other information about the CCBN and its membership clubs. The code described naturism as a pursuit for individuals, families or social groups and it advocated outdoor recreation without clothes in daylight hours, in private grounds or in other suitable locations. Furthermore, the code disassociated naturism from any other forms of nudism which would be a departure from CCBN guidelines and which would be likely to bring naturism into public disrepute. One strategy employed by the CCBN for ensuring the reputation of naturism was the imposition of strict eligibility criteria for club membership.

The stark contrast between CCBN guide lines and the practices of UNICORN encouraged me to resume pursuit of CCBN membership, despite earlier experiences at UNICORN. When, following a protracted period of membership application, I did join a CCBN naturist club I was already keenly aware of some of the problems which members faced. However respectable naturist clubs purport to be, they celebrate an activity which is not socially acceptable. Furthermore, from my own experience I realised the difficulty in distancing naturist 'respectable' nudity from other forms of social nudity, such as that practised by UNICORN members. The CCBN club, ELM, which offered me the opportunity to join and carry out the research by participant observation was, as I had expected, very interested in my brief experiences at UNICORN. Had I continued the association with UNICORN, doubtless the application to ELM would not have been successful. However, the fact that I had visited and rejected the philosophy and practices of UNICORN certainly worked in my favour.

As a condition of membership, ELM insisted that I observed the rules and regulations which affected the other members. The two most important rules were that I did not reveal the site of the club or the identity of any member to outsiders, and that while at the club I took my clothes off. It is interesting that I felt the loss of my clothes signified the removal of a symbolic barrier between researcher and researched. I felt that, had I been allowed to remain dressed, my clothes would have afforded me a measure of protection from the vulnerability which participation seemed to evoke. At the same time I realised that the prospect of carrying out a study of naturists, while remaining dressed myself, would have been quite untenable.

The focus of my study became the ways in which CCBN naturists constructed and maintained a version of social nudity which is 'respectable'. Given my own prior involvement with UNICORN, and the doubts and concerns which dogged that experience, the construction of respectability in the naturist club assumed a particular personal importance. Hence the strategies employed by clubs and their members to sustain the club version of respectable naturism took on a personal significance for me as a participating member. These strategies, which I observed being routinely used by members and which I myself adopted, for what I feel to be similar reasons, have been discussed elsewhere in some depth (Parry, 1987, 1996) so they will be referred to only briefly in subsequent sections of this paper.

In their publication *Dare to Go Bare* (1978), the CCBN describe the initial experience of naturism as 'quite shocking'. However, they continue by comparing it to jumping into a swimming pool: shocking for the first thirty seconds but from then on soothing and enjoyable. Certainly on my first visit to ELM I was daunted by the prospect of disrobing in front of strangers and haunted by doubt about whether I should be doing it at all. But when I did take my clothes off during that first visit nobody appeared to pay any special attention to me and I was left alone to deal with, and conceal, any anxieties or embarrassment. I was reassured by the fact that, like me, everyone else at the club was naked and no-one seemed to be in the least bit perturbed. Nevertheless I did feel extremely self conscious about my body, which had never before been subjected to exposure in this type of social context. My immediate concern stemmed from insecurity about my physical appearance. These anxieties were expressed in the series of questions which I repeatedly asked myself. Would my body pass 'the test'? Was it an acceptable height and shape? Would people notice the irregularities? Did it look out of place?

These anxieties were of an immediate but temporary nature. Club members come in all sizes, shapes and ages and consequently I gradually realised I did not look out of place. However, whereas I slowly became less self conscious inside the club I was not so comfortable talking about my membership activities with people outside the club. In between visits to the club I was acutely aware that for most people, social nudity is neither respectable nor acceptable and therefore I was engaging in something the majority of non-naturists (including many of my friends, colleagues and family) would neither approve of nor understand.

I was not alone in having these concerns, since I learned from conversations that they were shared by many other members of the club. Members were well aware that their club activities fell outside definitions of what counted as respectable behaviour. Like me, they also feared discovery by friends, colleagues and family, and used a range of strategies to minimise disclosure. The ELM club was tucked away in the depths of the countryside and protected by tall walls and a solid gate, so there was little chance of accidental discovery. On top of this, members of the club exercised cautionary disclosure networks. The location of the club was a well kept secret. They also maintained strict barriers between the club and the outside. For example, inside the club they addressed each other by first name only and they refrained from discussing details about their non-naturist identities outside the club. Members were discouraged from meeting outside the club in non-naturist settings and, despite the fact that it was a long drive from the city where many members lived, they did not usually travel together to or from the club.

Much of my anxiety about participation stemmed from fear of discovery and disapproval from significant others. These anxieties reflected deep-seated gender expectations about what male and female bodies should and should not do. In modern British society there is a tendency to see women as being somehow more 'embodied', more essentially 'physical', than men. This attitude can be seen within popular culture, such as in the representation of female bodies as sexual objects in advertising and soft pornography (Morgan, 1993). Female bodies are culturally coded in complex ways within patriarchal society. In popular consciousness, however, the meanings with which male and female bodies are endowed are generally taken for granted and treated as a matter of commonsense. Yet these commonsense understandings of embodiment have all sorts of social consequences. For example, awareness of the meanings imposed on female nudity in our society makes it difficult for women to come to terms with naturism when they first join a club. In the words of one woman member, new to the club; 'nice women simply don't do that sort of thing'. Being a new member myself, I shared a commonality of experience with these women. After all, these women were voicing my own anxieties in talking openly about the difficulties of accepting the CCBN version of nudity as a 'respectable' activity.

All the men I talked to at the club said that their interest in naturism and the decision to join was either their own or a mutual decision made with their spouse, but none of the married women agreed it had been their decision to join. These married women said they had been persuaded, cajoled or bullied into joining by their spouses. Because married men were not allowed to join a club unless their wives also joined (and accompanied them to the club), it was necessary that their wives agreed to participate. Furthermore, while clubs get hundreds of applicants every year from single men, single women rarely apply. There were only two other single female members at ELM, apart from myself. Both these women had accompanied their parents to naturist clubs when they were children and were returning after a period of absence.

It is interesting that CCBN and its membership clubs insist that naturism is a non-sexual activity, yet they are preoccupied with limiting the number of male members. There are no restrictions on the numbers of women who can join, but restrictions are applied to single male members. As the secretary at ELM explained, this policy is necessary in order to ensure that single male members 'do not pose a threat to the married men and their wives'. This recruitment policy seems to reflect society's tendency to regard male sexuality as essential and instinctual rather than cultural. It endorses the widespread social assumption that men are unable to control their sexual needs. Women's sexuality is just not seen as problematic in the same way as men's. In contrast to men, women are seen as both instinctual *and* moral-rational. Indeed, it can be argued that women in naturist clubs are appointed to what Edwards (1993) describes as the role of 'moral gatekeeper'. But the adoption of this position presents women with a moral dilemma. This dilemma stems from the incompatibility between their perceived role as moral guardians and their participation in an 'immoral' activity.

Because wives were the least enthusiastic recruits to naturism it is not surprising they experienced the greatest difficulty in coming to terms with naturism. These women talked about the embarrassment they felt during their first visits, the self consciousness which they initially experienced about their bodies and nagging doubts about whether or not naturism was or was not a 'respectable' activity. All these concerns were very close to my own heart at that time of carrying out the fieldwork and as a result I was consumed with interest in how these women were able to rationalise their involvement in an activity so initially problematic for them. The focus of the research became the strategies which members employed to transform a potentially unrespectable activity into one which was moral, decent and respectable. As a result, the title of my thesis became 'Campaign for Respectability'.

Discussion

Naturism challenges societal expectations of what constitutes respectable behaviour. In particular it presents a dilemma for female participants because of cultural representations of female bodies as sexual objects. I have suggested that, despite the CCBN's construction of naturism as a non-sexual and respectable activity, female club members experience difficulties in coming to terms with their participation. However, this chapter has dealt not only with the substantive issues but has also explored my own relationship, as both a female participant and researcher, with naturism. Since the study specifically focused upon the body, it raised issues relating to reflexivity and corporeality in the research process. The provision of background information about my role in this process offers a contextual understanding of both the data which I collected and the subsequent thesis and articles which I have produced. Both the data and the analysis emanating from the study reflected my experiences of fieldwork participation. This was not in any sense a passive role. It was an active role in which data and meanings were constructed reflexively with the respondents through a process of inter-corporeality.

Acknowledging corporeality in the research process in this way raises a fundamental issue in sociology, relating to the Cartesian assumption that mind, or intersubjectivity, is a different and separate thing from the physical body. The Cartesian tradition, in which mind and body are separated, mirrors other dichotomies such as culture/ nature. It implies that the mind is located inside the body and is only accessible though the process of introspection. What is going on in other minds can therefore only be inferred. Crossley (1995) takes issue with this position, highlighting Merleau-Ponty's challenge (1962, 1965) to the assumption that the mind is an inner state. Merleau-Ponty views human beings as belonging to a common world and regards all distinctions between them as relational. Furthermore, he argues that mental predicates refer to visually verifiable aspects of behaviour (or embodied conduct), with the implication that the subjective or mental states of others are accessible to us through these behaviours. In this scheme of things, subjectivity is both worldly and available.

Crossley also provides a Merleau-Pontyan interpretation of the work of Goffman (1972). Crossley rejects the view of Shilling (1993) that, in subordinating body to mind, Goffman gives primacy to symbolism over corporeality. Against this, Crossley offers an interpretation of Goffman which denies the existence of an inner mental realm behind the body and argues that the inter-subjective meanings are necessarily embodied and are inseparable from their embodiment. He suggests that Goffman focuses on visible and tangible behaviour, not inner states, precisely because behaviour *is* embodied. Thus, in distancing Goffman from the Cartesian tradition, Crossley argues that bodies are active in the production and conveyance of inter-subjective meanings.

This has important implications not only for the sociology of the body but also for the role of the researcher in qualitative research and, in particular, for the construction of data. It implies, for example, that it is not sufficient simply to acknowledge that data are affected by the way in which personal presentation of the researcher is perceived by the respondent. This is inadequate because it treats the role of the body in this process as passive and denies it a sense of agency in the construction of meaning. Crossley (1995) has mentioned similar criticisms in relation to the anthropological accounts which were discussed earlier in this chapter. Where bodily presentation is interpreted only as the translation of social processes into material representations, the body is mistakenly seen a passive reflector of those processes and not an active agent in their production and reproduction.

In distancing itself from the Cartesian tradition in which there is a separation between inner and outer states, this chapter has attempted to bring issues of inter-corporeality into debates about the reflexive nature of research and the production of qualitative data.

References

Atkinson, P. (1992), 'The ethnography of a medical setting: reading, writing and rhetoric', *Qualitative Health Research,* vol. 2 no. 4, pp. 451-474.

Bowles, G. & Klein, R.D. (1983), *Theories of Women's Studies*, Routledge, London.

CCBN (1978), *Dare to go bare*, Central Council of British Naturism, Orpington.

Connell, R. (1987), *Gender and Power*, Polity, Oxford.

Coti, L., Foster, J. & Thompson, P. (1995), 'Archiving qualitative research data', *Social Research Update* vol. 10, pp.1-6

Crossley, N. (1995), 'Body techniques, agency and inter-corporeality', *Sociology*, vol. 29 no. 1, pp. 133-149

Douglas, M. (1973a), *Rules and Meanings*, Penguin Education, Harmondsworth.

Douglas, M. (1973b), *Natural Symbols; explorations in cosmology*, Redwood Press, UK.

Edwards, S.M. (1993), 'Selling the Body' in Scott, S. & Morgan, D. (eds), *Body Matters*, Falmer Press, London.

Elias, N. (1978), *The Civilising Process volume 1: the history of manners*, Urizen, New York.

Goffman, E. (1972), *Behaviour in Public Places*, Free Press, Glencoe.

Giddens, A. (1991), *Modernity and Self Identity*, Polity, Oxford.

Hammersley, M. & Atkinson, P. (1983), *Ethnography: Principles in Practice*, Tavistock, London.

Mauss, M. (1979), *Body Techniques in Sociology and Psychology*, Routledge, London.

Merleau-Ponty, M. (1962), *The Phenomenology of Perception*, Routledge, London.

Merleau-Ponty, M. (1965), *The Structure of Behaviour*, Methuen, London.

Morgan, D. (1993), 'You too can have a body like mine', in Scott, S. & Morgan, D. (eds), *Body Matters*, Falmer Press, London, pp. 69-88.

Parry, O. (1987), 'Uncovering the ethnographer' in McKeganey,N. & Cunningham-Burley,A.S. (eds), *Enter the Sociologist*, Avebury, Aldershot, pp. 82-96.

Parry, O. (1987), 'Uncovering the ethnographer in McKegnaney, N. and Cunningham-Burley, A. S. (eds), *Enter the Sociologist*, Avebury, Aldershot, pp.82-96.

Roberts, H. (ed.), (1981), *Doing Feminist Research,* Routledge, London.

Scott, S. & Morgan, D. (1993), 'Bodies in a social landscape' in Scott, S. & Morgan, D. (eds), *Body Matters*, Falmer Press, London, pp. 1-21.

Scott, S. & Morgan, D. (eds), (1993), *Body Matters*, Falmer Press, London.

Screaton-Page, G. (1971), 'Social nudism: the social organisation of Southern Ontario nudist Camps' in Mann,W.E. (ed.), *Social Deviance in Canada*, Copp Gek Publishing, Toronto, pp. 67-89.

Schutz, A. (1962), *Collected Papers,* Nijhoff, The Hague.

Shilling, C. (1993), *The Body and Social Theory*, Sage, London.

Weinburg, S.W. (1967), 'The nudist camp: Way of life and social structure', *Human Organisation,* vol. 26 no. 3, pp. 91-99.

Weinburg, S. W. (1970), 'The nudist management of respectability' in Douglas, J. (ed.), *Deviance and Respectability*, Basic Books, New York, pp. 375-405.

Wax, M.L. (1980), 'Paradoxes of consent to the practice of fieldwork', *Social Problems,* vol. 27, no. 3, pp. 272-283.

Wilkinson, S. (1986), *Feminist Social Psychology: developing theory and practice*, Open University Press, Milton Keynes.

12. 'Meat' in the machine: the centrality of the body in internet interactions

Kate Robson

Introduction

Recent years have seen a rapid expansion in the use of computer mediated communications in a wide range of work and leisure based activities. This chapter looks at the place the body has in these new forms of communication, and addresses notions that computerised communications are dehumanising, impersonal methods of interacting. From an identification of the factors that have contributed to computing and computer communications being perceived as impersonal and dehumanised environments, there is an examination of how physicality is both articulated and impacted upon within these environments. The latter part of the chapter illustrates how these issues of articulation and impact were evident in an email-based distribution list which was set up as a patient support discussion forum, and run as part of a wider project on the employment experiences of inflammatory bowel disease sufferers. This research exercise amounted to a computer mediated version of a qualitative focus group interview, and the qualitative nature of the project meant that participants were able to express the physical aspects of computer mediated communications.

The computer as impersonal machinery

In contrast to the increasing focus on the body as a central issue in sociological thought, the development of the internet has been popularly perceived as involving a rejection or sidelining of bodily, physical presence in human interactions. Technology is often perceived as an agent of separation, creating barriers between individuals (Argyle and Shields 1996). Computer networking developed from the U.S. Defense Department's Advanced Research Projects Agency, who pioneered the first

Wide Area Network (APRANET) as a tool for collaborative work in 1969 (Smith 1992). This origin, together with the scientific characteristics inherited from computing more widely, have contributed to the evolution of computing as a mechanical tool for logical, scientific, work based pursuits. A clear distinction has evolved between computer supported co-operative work and computer supported co-operative play (Stone 1995), and use of the medium for the maintenance of interpersonal relationships has been seen as more a frivolous and unimportant use of the technology than its use for commercial or academic work (Spender 1995). It is still the case that the computer is seen predominantly in terms of its technology rather than in terms of its practical uses, thus obscuring an image of anything other than 'machine'. Gray and Driscoll (in Escobar 1996) assert that the development of these new technologies may lead to a 'posthuman' order in which the body as a physical presence becomes obsolete. The apparent rejection of the body from these systems of communication by these new technologies is signalled by the use of words such as 'flesh' and 'meat' to refer to the body in a derogatory manner : 'The body, meat, is vulgar' (Argyle 1996, p. 139). However, this notion of an apparent absolute rejection or removal of the body from internet communications is far from accurate, either as a reflection of current practice or a desired goal for the medium by its users. Gradually, computer mediated communications have emerged from this chrysalis of 'the machine' to become a medium where humane, expressive individuality can flourish and be effectively articulated:

> A computer connected to the information superhighway is more like a telephone (with the added benefit of pictures and text) than it is like an adding machine. The computer viewed in this way will soon - like the telephone - cease to look like technology (Spender 1995, p. 192).

Conceptualisation of computer mediated communications as being external or dehumanising may also owe much to inherited notions regarding the written word. The written word has not traditionally been perceived as being as natural as the spoken word. Speech has living, organic qualities, in that it occurs and is gone: it lives and dies. The written word, in contrast, lacks this through its permanence, and, as Derrida (1988) contests, is thus seen as a betrayal of life. In email and internet based communications, there is a merging of the characteristics of writing and speech, retaining the organic quality of speech through its perception by users as producing transitory, impermanent messages (Langford 1995b; Young 1994).

The physicality of computer users in these communication networks can be broadly divided into two categories: action (the articulation of physical presence through the medium); and reaction (how use of the medium impacts the embodied self). These categories have a reciprocal relationship: what is articulated has an impact on others, and this impact is in turn articulated as a further response.

Action: the articulation of physical presence

Arguably, communication by typed, transmitted alphanumeric message is not explicitly side-stepping physical presence by choice, but rather by necessity, and indeed every effort is made to create as near a physical presence as is possible within the confines of the medium. The physical cues that convey emotion (body movement, facial expression, voice) can clearly not be used during computer mediated conversations, but communication researchers have noted that the medium has been adapted by users in order to convey these physical aspects of communication (Argyle and Shields 1996). Users have incorporated the body despite rather than because of the technology: the absence of the body in the medium, which the technology most readily offers has been rejected and overcome. This can be seen in the ways in which language and text characters are used in email and internet interactions to represent physical features of the body. The use of emoticons (or 'smiley faces') is familiar to almost all users of such communication. Using that which is available as best as possible, users convey a recognisable physical facial expression to convey their emotions regarding their message, or the conversation more broadly. So, :) denotes happiness, :(sadness, :o surprise, and :..(crying, to name just a few. Other movements or physical representations are signalled in email based communications by using <> around the description of the movement (e.g. <shudder>). Similarly there are also recognised conventions for expressing physicality in the real time interactions of, for example, MUDs (Multiple User Domains) and IRC (Internet Relay Chat). The use of action commands describes the movement of the writer as if the interaction was occuring in a 'real-life' face-to-face setting. In these real time interactions, a * is often used to denote the physical description, very much in the way <> is used in email, but often with more detail (e.g. * joe punches the air in triumph). The use of '.oO' before a comment indicates what the author is thinking about the conversation. The following example is taken from an IRC discussion between 2 Crohn's disease sufferers. Actions are signalled by *, and the names that the participants have chosen to be called for the discussion appear in <> at the start of each remark.

<Babyface> Don't forget the red *sigh*
<Wings> Yeah, and red
<Wings> And pink
<Wings> A nice birthday present
*Babyface nods
<Babyface> Is it your birthday then?

In environments such as MUDs and IRC, the language used to describe the activities of the medium is particularly resonant of physical presence. The use of terms such as 'rooms' for discussion areas, and command names like 'kicking' for the removal of unwanted participants from discussions hardly suggests that this is an environment where all that represents physical presence is rejected or unwanted. It is the technological confines of the medium that remove the body from these interactions, not the preference of participants to reject the body, or any notion of this being a move towards the obsolescence of human embodiment. Participants in group or private IRC discussions frequently exchange photographs of themselves, or audible greetings, sent as computer files through the IRC software program, in order to create a greater feeling of intimacy and friendship. Technological developments now allow spoken conversations and voice mail to be transmitted via computers, but this more usually represents users finding a cost effective alternative to traditional telephone communications rather than as an element of other computer mediated communications.

These new technologies allow a creative use of physicality in users' contacts with other participants within the medium, as people are enabled to side-step the limitations of the body. The self can be defined completely: gender, for example can be changed or left undefined in order to neutralise or counteract prejudice or preconception. Users are free to explore and examine their identities with regard to such issues as physical characteristics, extreme opinions, or more open or more experimental sexuality (Young 1994). Personal identities can be constructed solely by use of text, allowing users to reinvent themselves freely without the stigma of social identities (Smith 1992). Here, in Goffman's (1968) terms, the management of undisclosed, discrediting information ('passing') is achievable without the unpredictability and danger that face-to-face contacts pose. Everyone has to represent themselves using the same tools, and consequently it becomes all but impossible to distinguish those who recreate their 'real' selves from those who alter their characteristics. In the Internet's real time, multiple user social environments of MUDs, such manipulation is commonplace. The development of similar programs using animated graphics rather than text to create these environments and representations of participants is beginning to improve on the limited options for creating physical presence that text based communication can offer. Users create an image of themselves by selecting from a menu of physical parts, allowing unprecedented control over their appearance to others in a social setting. Chosen representations are absolute: there is no possible way of distinguishing how accurate a reflection of the 'real' person the moving, reacting, human form on the screen is. The character is accepted as given. In environments such as these, it has been reported (Stone 1995) that the ratio of male to female users signing on to the program is 4:1, but the ratio of male to female characters is 3:1. This discrepancy reflects not only an indication of users experiments with their own gender identities, but also an acknowledgement that, because of the predominance of men in the environment, a 'female' presence will attract attention to the user, and give the participant greater prominence in the activities of the domain (Stone 1995).

Reaction: impact on the embodied self

Computer mediated communications have had a clear effect on the physical being of those who use the technology in a number of ways. The technological advancements of recent decades have led to a situation whereby the production of bodies and organisms increasingly involves production in conjunction with machines and computers (Escobar 1996). According to Turkle (in Escobar 1996), increased use of and familiarity with these technologies has impacted the way people conceptualise their own capacities: people have begun to think of themselves in computer terms, using them as a model for the human mind.

Most clearly however, participation in the social activities that email and internet communications facilitate has direct physical implications for participants: the body becomes as involved as the mind. This is illustrated by Argyle's (1996) account of the reaction of a 'Usenet' community to the death of one of its key participants. Argyle quotes from the message of one contributor in reaction to the death: '"this is visceral. words words words words meat"' (p. 139) and comments:

> what is felt in the words is also felt in bodies…His physical death has been transformed from that of an individual dying, to a representation of this in text, and finally to a feeling in the body of other human beings (Argyle 1996, p. 139).

In turn, such felt, visceral reactions are fed back through the strategies of articulating physical presence as outlined above.

A great focus of criticism of the new 'cybercommunities' in the mainstream media has been the area of sex on the internet. Although much of this concern has focussed on the accessibility of pornography, there has been also been concern about internet interactions of an explicit sexual nature. In real-time social environments such as MUDs, sexual encounters take the form of 'high-speed two-way erotica typing, which sometimes involves masturbation' (Young 1994:20). Stone (1995) draws close parallels between 'netsex' and the phone sex industry: the range of senses that sexual encounters involve (sight, touch, smell, taste, hearing) are translated by one participant into audible (and therefore transcribable) form and transmitted down telephone lines where they are reconstituted by the recipient.

> What's being sent back and forth over the wires isn't merely information, its bodies - not physical objects, but the information necessary to reconstruct the meaning of body to almost any desired depth and complexity (Stone 1995, p. 244).

While recognising the similarities between netsex and the phone sex industry, Young (1994) identifies an important distinction between the two. The phone sex industry is motivated by commercial gain, has no purpose of social activity other than the sexual encounter, and usually involves one participant who is satisfying (through pretence) the other. Sexual encounters in cyberspace do not involve any financial transaction, and arise from non sexual social encounters and relationships. Much the same as 'real' sexual relationships, netsex can be seen as a way individuals articulate particular kinds of intimate, personal relationships with others. Shields (Argyle and Shields 1996) relates her own experiences of these encounters:

> You might feel as if you are having sex, in your body, forgetting that there is a computer mediating the encounter. Hotchats, as I have experienced them, have left me with all the emotions and physical arousal of a sexual act, but when its

> over, my sense aloneness is heightened. To break the connection seems more painful than fulfilling (Argyle and Shields 1996, p.64).

As well as being used to stimulate and communicate physically felt sensations, computers and computer mediated communications can be used to reconstruct identities by providing access to information about other cultures and 'the outside world'. By use of these networks, such information can be explored and experimented with, and in turn may be adopted as changes made to the 'real life' of the user. It is here that the development of patient support networks brings the body centre stage in the realm of computerised communication. The development of the internet for logical, scientific and practical work applications has gradually melted into the development of more social aspects of collaborative work. The development of networks of individuals sharing discussions on topics of common interest has in turn spawned the development of patient support networks. In the early 1990's, having recently been diagnosed with Inflammatory Bowel Disease, one sufferer started posting messages on IBM Prodigy's computer dial-up Bulletin Board Service as a way to address the feelings of isolation and confusion that arise from the onset and diagnosis of a chronic illness. Attendance at a traditional ('real') patient support group was not possible because of the severity of her condition, the tiredness that is a common symptom of IBD, and the inconvenience of the timing and location of meetings. At the time there were no patient support groups on Prodigy's Bulletin Board Service, and no dedicated areas for the discussion of illness: her initial messages were posted under the 'Food' section. Soon, a thriving 'Medical' section of the Bulletin Board Service evolved as sufferers of IBD and other conditions began to communicate with fellow sufferers. Such groups offer both support and information exchange on both medical treatments and self-help regimes: the IBD group on Prodigy, for example, now has its own on-line gastroenterologist to answer general questions about the condition (Sveilich 1995). Thus the development of and participation in such networks has direct implications for the physical status of participating sufferers, in addition to the social and psychological implications of increased support and decreased isolation.

Example: the IBD project

As has been discussed, the importance of the body has been an area neglected in the study of communication technologies. Until relatively recently, the discipline of medical sociology has neglected to focus on the physical aspects of accounts of chronic illness. As Kelly and Field (1996) argue, in most sociological narratives of chronic illness, the body retains an 'ethereal' presence. Medical sociology has, until recently, had little to say directly about the body (Morgan and Scott 1993). Accounts of chronic illness have tended to focus on the disruption to routine, and on coping behaviours. Such accounts must, argue Kelly and Field (1996), be underpinned by addressing the physical body. The research project reported here, therefore, combines two areas where issues of the body have been largely neglected, but where the body has an important and active role.

As part of a wider research project on the employment experiences of Inflammatory Bowel Disease (the collective term for ulcerative colitis and Crohn's disease) sufferers, computer mediated patient support networks were used as a tool to collect qualitative research data. In the project, a 'virtual focus group' was conducted, using an email based distribution list discussion to gather data in a manner not unlike a traditional focus group interview: data was generated from the interaction of participants discussing the topic of the research, guided where necessary by a moderator.

Distribution lists (sometimes also known as listservs) are email based discussion forums. Each list has its own central email address to which contributions are sent and then automatically forwarded to all those who subscribe to the list. Distribution lists have a number of features that make them particularly suitable for use as a social research tool, as they can safeguard the privacy and confidentiality of participants in the way that other discussion media such as newsgroups and IRC can not. In this project, the distribution list had a closed subscription policy, meaning that only selected participants were privy to the discussion. The list was moderated, so that the email 'headers' that identify the origin of email messages could be removed before the messages were distributed to subscribers, and messages were not distributed individually as they were submitted, but were sent in batches ('digests') on a weekly or twice weekly basis. The distribution list in this project had 57 active participants, and ran for a total of 12 weeks, during which time there were 15 digests containing a total of 98 messages. The length of individual messages ranged from 43 words to 1478 words.

This approach was borne of the well established and very active patient support networks that exist on the internet for IBD sufferers. IBD is characterised by symptoms that often include chronic and unpredictable diarrhoea, rectal bleeding, emaciation and fatigue. Mobility disorders such as arthritis, sacroiliitis, ankylosing spondylitis and osteporosis often develop alongside the conditions (Bouchier 1982). IBD is most frequently experienced in alternating and unpredictable periods of exacerbation and remission, with only 10 per cent of ulcerative colitis and 20 per cent of Crohns disease sufferers experiencing unremitting disease (Binder 1988). Consequently, for many sufferers, the presentation of normality is under continuous threat from the unpredictability of intrusive, visible symptoms, which in the case of loss of bowel control particularly, are at odds with normal adult identity and suggest flawed moral character (Kelly 1992). As Eddie observed in Digest 4 of the distribution list discussion:

> I knew that society as a whole would accept only the healthy ... so I faked health the best I could. I had a young body that would give me renewed strength each day, if only for brief daily moments, and I played those moments like the young man I wanted to be. Could some of us be compared to Oscar nominees, acting as if nothing was out of place, even though it was a bad performance and you didn't have a chance in Hades to win?

The reciprocal nature of the words-meat relationship of social interaction on the internet was apparent in the distribution list discussion in all the ways that have been outlined. The physical presence of participants was articulated by the use of language to describe the discussion group. Contributors were referred to as if they were physically present to other contributors : 'It's so wonderful, like Paul from Italy said, to run into familiar faces' (Katie, Digest 3). The use of text characters to convey non-verbal prompts was also common through the use of smiley faces and action words:

> As a matter of fact, this will be the first year in all the years I've worked that I will actually have vacation time that hasn't been used for sick time! :) (Pauline Digest 3).

> I've found that I have a tendency to string myself along as far as possible in all three areas until I reach total collapse (or near total anyway..<<grin>>) (Georgina Digest 14).

The physical impact of participation in the discussion was also referred to by participants. One of the group in particular, Natalie, made frequent reference to the felt consequences of the discussion: 'I almost cried in the last issue when I read [it]' (Digest 4), and 'When I read the letters from this newsletter group, I find myself sitting at the computer and nodding my head all during the issue ... this is somehow reaffirming and comforting' (Digest 8). Physical consequences of participation were also directly linked to the particular nature of the conditions being studied. The impact of the symptom of fatigue had been a contributory factor in one of the earliest developments in the establishment of an on-line support community for Crohn's disease and ulcerative colitis sufferers, and for one of the participants in this discussion, whose first language was not English, participation in this support group environment also affected and was affected by this symptom: 'I have answered you only one time, but then unfortunately, I was [sic] always very busy, and for me, write a letter in English means to do a beautiful fatigue always' (Paul Digest 2). Finally, the discussion often covered topics and raised questions that would impact how participants managed their condition and thus their physical experience of IBD. There were frequent exchanges on issues such as advice on combating fatigue at work, what medication people were finding effective, and how to reduce the noise that stoma bags make. In Digest 9, Nicola had a very important issue she put to the group:

> My husband and I want to have a baby and I mean right now I don't even have the energy to feed myself a lot of the time…I want to have kids in a big way. So I guess I would appreciate any info from people with IBD who have jobs and children…Is it possible???

A number of participants responded with accounts of their own experiences of parenthood, and their advice relative to Nicola's own situation. The final message posted to the final digest the distribution list also sought information to help manage the condition:

> I have found out (yesterday) that my husband has gotten a big promotion…but the job is in London…Yikes! I am totally stressing over this one…Any advice from any of the folks over in the UK???? re: employment, work environment, good GI doctors?? I sure could use it (Molly Digest 15).

Although the initial and primary purpose of the distribution list had been to discuss the ways in which sufferers manage their work routines, participants used the opportunity to seek out information that would help them alter their physical experience as IBD sufferers.

Conclusion

As social science begins to embrace computer mediated communications as both a topic of study and as a tool for collecting research data, the importance of the body in these environments must not be overlooked. In the study of chronic illness within medical sociology, the body was slow to be recognised as an important focus of attention, and where the discipline meets the realm of computer mediated communications and cybercommunities, issues of embodiment take on important and enlightening new dimensions. In an environment where the chronically ill and disabled can potentially free themselves of the characteristics that stigmatise them in the 'real world', there is a (perhaps surprising) keenness to focus on and articulate these features. The invisibility and malleability of identity that cyberspace so freely facilitates allows the chronically ill to make use of participation in patient support networks in order to benefit from support and information, but to also effectively and effortlessly disguise or alter these stigmatising characteristics in other social settings on the internet.

The internet and email communications are not bodiless, dehumanising environments where physicality is either obsolete or rejected. Computer mediated communications provide environments where individuals can escape the confines of their body, but this is done by individuals exercising greater control over what they desire their body to be, in order to convey the preferred message in a given situation. Bodies are moulded and exchanged, not rejected.

Although computer mediated communications are now commonly used for the collection of quantitative data, by the administration of questionnaires, using the medium to collect qualitative data has not been forthcoming. Consequently the place of the body in these new social environments has not been apparent. The qualitative research reported in this paper has indicated that only by using the medium in a way that allows respondents to articulate themselves freely can the physical aspects of computerised communications be seen.

Wherever people communicate by computer, they use the tools available in the various applications to give some kind of physical presence to their exchange. This ranges from the simplest forms of smiley faces and stark descriptions of actions, to photographs transmitted between users, to animated graphical representations of human forms. That computer usage has evolved in ways that enable users to make these representations is testament to how fundamentally we are drawn to the importance of the presence of our bodies in our social interactions with others.

References

Argyle, K (1996), 'Life After Death', in Shields, R (ed.) *Cultures of Internet*, Sage, London.

Argyle, K and Shields, R (1996), 'Is there a Body in the Net?', in Shields, R (ed.) *Cultures of Internet,* Sage, London.

Binder, V. (1988), 'Prognosis and Quality of Life in Patients with Ulcerative Colitis and Crohn's Disease'. *Int. Disabil. Studies*, Vol. 10, no.4, pp. 172-174.

Bouchier, I. (1982), *Gastroenterology* (3rd ed.), Bailiere Tindall, London.

Derrida, J (1988), *The Ear of the Other*, University of Nabraska, Lincoln.

Escobar, A (1996), 'Welcome to Cyberia: Notes on the Anthropology of Cyberculture', in Sardar, Z and Ravetz, J.R. (eds) *Cyberfutures*, Pluto, London.

Goffman, E. (1968), *Stigma. Notes on the Management of Spoiled Identity,* Penguin, Harmondsworth.

Kelly, M. P., & Field, D. (1996), 'Medical Sociology, Chronic Illness and the Body'. *Sociology of Health and Illness*, Vol. 18, no. 2, pp. 241-257.

Langford, D. (1995), *Practical Computer Ethics*, McGraw Hill, Maidenhead.

Morgan, D. J. H., & Scott, S. (1993), 'Bodies in a Social Landscape', in Scott, S. & Morgan, D. J. H. (eds), *Body Matters*, Falmer Press, London.

Smith, M.A. (1992), *Voices From the WELL: The Logic of the Virtual Commons,* [http://www.sscnet.ucla.edu/soc/csoc/papers/voices].

Spender, D (1995), *Nattering on the Net: Women, Power and Cyberspace*, Spinifex Press, Melbourne.

Stone, A. R. (1995), 'Sex and Death Among the Disembodied: VR, cyberspace and the nature of academic discourse', in Star, S.L. (ed.), *The Cultures of Computing*, Blackwell, Oxford.

Sveilich, C. (1995), 'Support on the Information Highway'. *I.B.Details*, Vol. 3, no. 2, pp. 2-3.

Young, J. R. (1994), *Textuality in Cyberspace: MUDs and Written Experience,* [http://www.ludd.luth.se/mud/aber/articles/writtenexperience.thesis.html].